SCHOLA

C000252490

GCSE 9-1

COMBINED

SCIENCE

EXAM PRACTICE

FOR ALL EXAM BOARDS

Sarah Carter, Darren Grover, Sam Jordan and Kayan Parker

Authors Sarah Carter (Chemistry), Darren Grover (Chemistry), Sam Jordan (Physics) and Kayan Parker (Biology)
Editorial team Haremi Ltd
Series designers emc design ltd
Typesetting York Publishing Solutions Pvt. Ltd.,INDIA
Illustrations York Publishing Solutions Pvt. Ltd.,INDIA
App development Hannah Barnett, Phil Crothers and Haremi Ltd

Designed using Adobe InDesign
Published by Scholastic Education, an imprint of Scholastic Ltd, Book End, Range Road, Witney, Oxfordshire, OX29 0YD
Registered office: Westfield Road, Southam, Warwickshire CV47 0RA
www.scholastic.co.uk

Printed by Bell & Bain Ltd, Glasgow
© 2017 Scholastic Ltd
1 2 3 4 5 6 7 8 9   7 8 9 0 1 2 3 4 5 6

British Library Cataloguing-in-Publication Data
A catalogue record for this book is available from the British Library.
ISBN 978-1407-17696-3

Due to the nature of the web, we cannot guarantee the content or links of any site mentioned.

Note from the publisher:

Please use this product in conjunction with the official specification that you are following and sample assessment materials for the exam board that will be setting your examinations. Ask your teacher if you are unsure where to find them. Mapping grids showing you which content you need to know for the main specifications are found online at www.scholastic.co.uk/gcse.

The marks and star ratings have been suggested by our subject experts, but they are to be used as a guide only.

Answer space has been provided, but you may need to use additional paper for your workings.

Acknowledgements

The publishers gratefully acknowledge permission to reproduce the following copyright material:

Photos: p10 Heiti Paves/Shutterstock; p13 Dlumen/Shutterstock; p14 and 15 Jose Luis Calvo/Shutterstock; p65 grass-lifeisgood/Shutterstock

p29: Source: Australian Institute of Health and Welfare, reproduced under a Creative Commons (CC) BY 3.0 licence; p30: Contains public sector information licensed under the Open Government Licence v3.0; p33: Source: 'Comprehensive care with antiretroviral therapy for injecting-drug users associates to low community viral load and restriction of HIV outbreak' © 2012 Kivelä, P et al; licensee International AIDS Society, Creative Commons (CC) BY 3.0 licence; p37: Source: https://sites.google.com/site/livingithealthy/jointpain; p50: Source: https://sofi avenanzetti. wordpress.com/2014/03/23/stiffness-and-hormones/; p64, online content, top: adapted from worksheet 'Toxic chemicals and food chains 2', http://www.sciwebhop.net, © Pearson Education Limited 2002; p64 adapted from Odum, Fundamentals of Ecology, Saunders, 1953; p206: Source: Quandl. IMF data published by the ODA under an open data licence.

Every effort has been made to trace copyright holders for the works reproduced in this book, and the publishers apologise for any inadvertent omissions.

How to use this book

This Exam Practice Book has been produced to help you revise for your 9–1 GCSE in combined science. Written by experts and packed full of exam-style questions for each subtopic, along with full practice papers, it will get you exam ready!

The best way to retain information is to take an active approach to revision. Don't just read the information you need to remember – do something with it! Transforming information from one form into another and applying your knowledge will ensure that it really sinks in. Throughout this book you'll find lots of features that will make your revision practice an active, successful process.

EXAM-STYLE QUESTIONS

Exam-style questions for each subtopic ramped in difficulty.

For mapping grids to show you exactly what you need to know for your specification and tier, go to www.scholastic. co.uk/gcse

DO IT!

Tasks that support your understanding and analysis of a question.

WORK IT!

Worked examples with model solutions to help you see how to answer a tricky question.

 This icon means there is more content online to help with your revision.

Callouts Step-by-step guidance to build understanding.

NAIL IT!

Tips to help you perform in the exam.

★ STAR RATING ★

A quick visual guide to indicate the difficulty of the question, with 1 star representing the least demanding and 5 stars signposting the most challenging questions.

MARKS (5 marks)

Each question has the number of marks available to help you target your response.

STRETCH IT!

Questions or concepts that stretch you further and challenge you with the most difficult content.

PRACTICE PAPERS

Full mock-exam papers to enable you to have a go at a complete paper before you sit the real thing!

For an additional practice paper, visit: www.scholastic.co.uk/gcse

Use the Combined Science Revision Guide for All Boards alongside the Exam Practice Book for a complete revision and practice solution. Written by subject experts to match the new specifications, the Revision Guide uses an active approach to revise all the content you need to know!

Contents

Biology

Chemistry

Topic 7 Biology

Topic 1 Chemistry

Topic 2 Chemistry

Topic 3 Chemistry

Topic 4 Chemistry

Contents

Topic 3 Physics

Topic 4 Physics

Topic 5 Physics

Topic 6 Physics

Topic 7 Physics

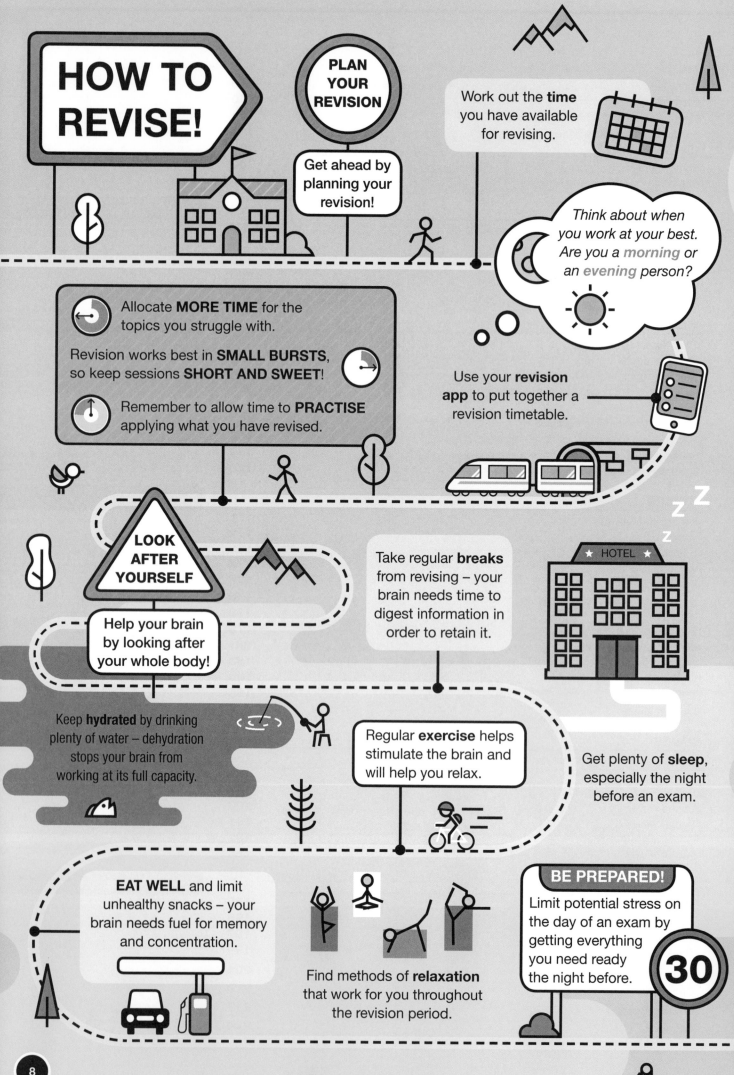

HOW TO REVISE!

PLAN YOUR REVISION

Get ahead by planning your revision!

Work out the **time** you have available for revising.

Think about when you work at your best. Are you a morning or an evening person?

Allocate **MORE TIME** for the topics you struggle with.

Revision works best in **SMALL BURSTS**, so keep sessions **SHORT AND SWEET!**

Remember to allow time to **PRACTISE** applying what you have revised.

Use your **revision app** to put together a revision timetable.

LOOK AFTER YOURSELF

Help your brain by looking after your whole body!

Take regular **breaks** from revising – your brain needs time to digest information in order to retain it.

HOTEL

Keep **hydrated** by drinking plenty of water – dehydration stops your brain from working at its full capacity.

Regular **exercise** helps stimulate the brain and will help you relax.

Get plenty of **sleep**, especially the night before an exam.

EAT WELL and limit unhealthy snacks – your brain needs fuel for memory and concentration.

Find methods of **relaxation** that work for you throughout the revision period.

BE PREPARED!

Limit potential stress on the day of an exam by getting everything you need ready the night before.

30

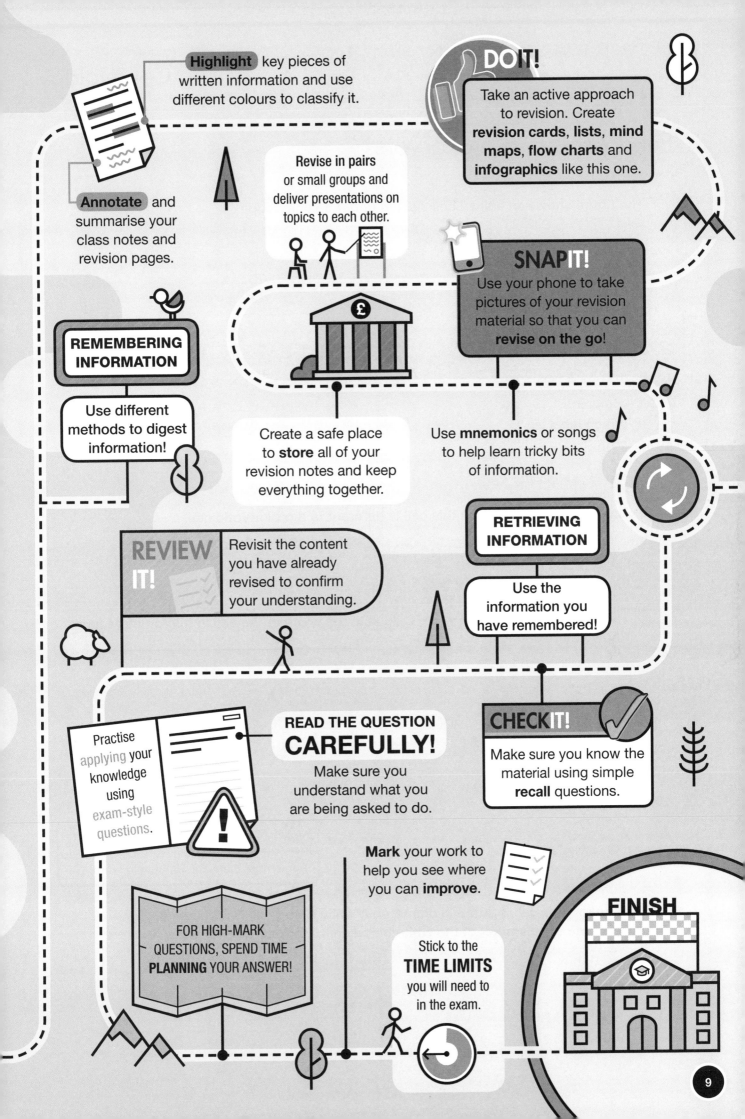

Highlight key pieces of written information and use different colours to classify it.

DO IT!
Take an active approach to revision. Create **revision cards**, **lists**, **mind maps**, **flow charts** and **infographics** like this one.

Annotate and summarise your class notes and revision pages.

Revise in pairs or small groups and deliver presentations on topics to each other.

SNAP IT!
Use your phone to take pictures of your revision material so that you can **revise on the go!**

REMEMBERING INFORMATION

Use different methods to digest information!

Create a safe place to **store** all of your revision notes and keep everything together.

Use **mnemonics** or songs to help learn tricky bits of information.

RETRIEVING INFORMATION

Use the information you have remembered!

REVIEW IT!
Revisit the content you have already revised to confirm your understanding.

Practise applying your knowledge using exam-style questions.

READ THE QUESTION CAREFULLY!
Make sure you understand what you are being asked to do.

CHECK IT!
Make sure you know the material using simple **recall** questions.

Mark your work to help you see where you can **improve**.

FOR HIGH-MARK QUESTIONS, SPEND TIME **PLANNING** YOUR ANSWER!

Stick to the **TIME LIMITS** you will need to in the exam.

FINISH

Eukaryotes and prokaryotes

① **The figure shows an animal cell viewed under a microscope.**

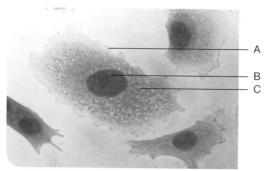

A
B
C

a **Which label is:**

• the nucleus? ....

• the cytoplasm? .... (2 marks, ★)

b **Name two ways in which this cell is different to a prokaryotic cell.** (2 marks, ★★)

i ....

ii ....

c **The central cell is 0.1 mm wide. Calculate the width of the cell in micrometres (μm). Show your working.** (2 marks, ★★★)

.... μm

NAILIT!

Remember there are 1000 μm in 1 mm.

d **A prokaryotic cell is 10 μm in diameter. A white blood cell is 60 times bigger. Calculate the diameter of the white blood cell. Tick one box.** (1 mark, ★★★)

60 000 nm	
6000 μm	
60 mm	
0.6 mm	

Animal and plant cells

1 Match each function to the correct sub-cellular structure. One has been done for you.
(3 marks, ★)

Absorbs sunlight for photosynthesis

Contains the genetic material of the cell

Provides strength to the cell

Filled with cell sap to keep the plant turgid

Cytoplasm

Nucleus

Permanent vacuole

Cell membrane

Chloroplasts

Cellulose cell wall

DO IT!

Mark the student's answer below using the mark scheme, and suggest how to improve the answer.

What are the differences between animal and plant cells? (3 marks, ★★)

Plant cells have a cell wall, chloroplasts and vacuoles, and animal cells do not.

MARK SCHEME
Plant cells have a cellulose cell wall (1), chloroplasts (1) and a permanent vacuole (1), and animal cells do not.

Number of marks for student's answer:

....

How to improve the answer:

....
....

2 The image shows a plant cell.

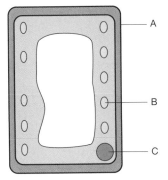

a Label the structures A, B and C. (3 marks, ★★)

A ....

B ....

C ....

b Explain why cells near the surface of a leaf contain more of structure B. (2 marks, ★★)

....
....

NAILIT!
If a question is worth two marks, then you must make two separate points.

Cell specialisation and differentiation

(1) **a** **Which of these is a feature of sperm cells? Tick one box.**

(1 mark, ★)

Long axon	
Many mitochondria	
Large surface area	
Hollow tube	

b **Name two types of cell that work as a tissue.** (2 marks, ★★)

i ....

ii ....

c **Ciliated epithelial cells have cilia on their top surface. Explain why this is important for their function.**

(2 marks, ★★★)

....

....

(2) **a** **What is a stem cell?** (1 mark, ★)

....

b **Where would you expect to find a large number of stem cells? Tick one box.** (1 mark, ★)

Embryo	
Mature animal	
Mature plant	

c **Using your knowledge of cell differentiation, suggest how stem cells could be used to make new organs for transplant.** (4 marks, ★★★)

....

....

....

....

....

DOIT!

Mark the student's answer below using the mark scheme, and suggest how to improve the answer.

What is the definition of a tissue? (2 marks, ★★)

A group of cells working together to perform a particular function.

MARK SCHEME
A group of similar cells working together (1) to perform a particular function. (1)

Number of marks for student's answer:

....

How to improve the answer:

....

....

NAILIT!

Remember that phloem cells transport sugars around the plant.

NAILIT!

This question asks you to apply your knowledge and understanding of cell differentiation and stem cells to a situation that you may not have studied before. Remember to use scientific terminology.

Microscopy

1 **This image shows some cells seen through an electron microscope.**

a **A student thinks the cells are plant cells. Use features in the image to explain whether the student is right.** (2 marks, ★★)

....

....

....

b **In another image, a cell is 0.5 μm wide but appears to be 5 cm wide. Calculate the magnification of the electron microscope.** (3 marks, ★★★)

> **NAILIT!**
>
> Electron microscopes have a high magnification. Your answer should be in the range of × 50 000 – 500 000. Remember to convert the size of the image into micrometres (μm). 1 cm = 10 mm and 1 mm = 1000 μm

Magnification = ...

2 **What are the advantages of using an electron microscope rather than a light microscope?** (2 marks, ★★★)

....

....

....

....

3 **One early microscope had a magnification of × 200. How large would a 10 μm cell have appeared to be? Show your working.** (3 marks, ★★)

Size of image = ...

Using a light microscope

1. The image shows some blood cells as seen through a light microscope.

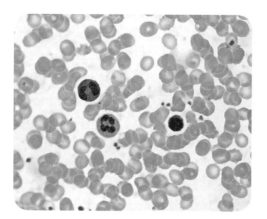

a **Describe how to focus the microscope so that the nuclei of the cells are clearly visible.** (3 marks, ★★)

....

....

....

....

b **Explain why microscope slides are often stained.** (2 marks, ★★)

....

....

c **The eyepiece lens of the light microscope has a magnification of × 10. The objective lens has a magnification of × 40. What is the magnification of the microscope?** (1 mark, ★★)

Magnification = ...

2. An investigation looked at the effect of mitotic inhibitors on cell division. Cells were grown for 12 hours in one of two conditions: with or without mitotic inhibitor. The cells were then counted. The table shows the results.

	Number of cells after 12 hours			
	1	2	3	Mean
With mitotic inhibitor	12	10		11
Without mitotic inhibitor	108	110	106	

MATHS SKILLS

To work out the mean, add the three numbers in the row together and divide by three.

a **Complete the missing data in the table.** (2 marks, ★★)

b **Name two variables that must be kept constant during the investigation.** (2 marks, ★★★)

i ....

ii ....

c **Suggest one improvement to the investigation.** (1 mark, ★)

....

Mitosis and the cell cycle

1 **a** **Match each stage of the cell cycle with what happens in that stage.** (3 marks, ★★)

G2 phase

The cell divides into two daughter cells.

S phase

Chromosomes are replicated.

Physical process of cell division.

M phase

Sub-cellular structures are replicated.

Cytokinesis

Chromosomes are checked.

b **Why do the sub-cellular structures need to double?** (2 marks, ★★)

....

....

....

NAILIT!

Think about what will happen to the cell at the end of mitosis.

2 **This image shows onion cells going through mitosis, as seen with a light microscope.**

a **i** **Draw and label the cell marked A.** (2 marks, ★★★)

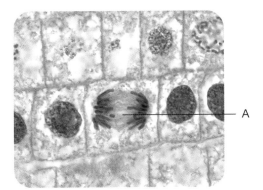 — A

NAILIT!

Draw the cell with a pencil. Label as many features as you can see.

ii **Describe what is happening inside the cell.** (2 marks, ★★★)

....

....

3 **This graph shows the percentile growth curve for baby girls aged 0–36 months.**

What is the mass in pounds of a baby girl on the 75th percentile line at 18 months? (1 mark, ★★★)

....

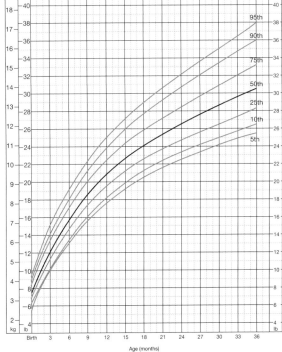

Weight-for-age percentiles: Girls, birth to 36 months
CDC Growth Charts: United States

Stem cells

(1) **Which of the following statements about stem cells is/are true? Tick one box.** (1 mark, ★)

1 **Stem cells are undifferentiated cells.**

2 **Stem cells can become any type of cell.**

3 **Stem cells can only divide a certain number of times.**

A Statement 1 only	
B Statements 1 and 2 only	
C Statements 2 and 3 only	
D All of the statements	

(2) **Name two uses of stem cells.** (2 marks, ★★)

i ....

ii ....

(3) **Some areas of plants contain tissue that has the same properties as stem cells. Name this tissue and state where it is found in the plant.** (2 marks, ★★)

....

(4) **Describe two advantages and two disadvantages of using stem cells in medicine.** (4 marks, ★★★)

NAILIT!

Advantages and disadvantages can be practical, social and/or ethical.

....

....

....

....

....

WORKIT!

What are the advantages in using embryonic stems cells (as opposed to adult stem cells) in the growth of tissue/therapeutic cloning? (2 marks, ★★★)

Embryonic stem cells can develop into any type of cell in the body. (1)

Embryonic stem cells can be used to grow organs that will not be rejected by a patient's body/immune system. (1)

Diffusion

(1) a **What is diffusion?** (2 marks, ★★)

....

....

b **Give an example of diffusion in the human body.** (1 mark, ★)

....

> **NAILIT!**
>
> Think about an exchange surface in the body.

(2) a **Organism A has a surface area of 24 cm² and a volume of 8 cm³. Organism B has a surface area of 96 cm² and a volume of 64 cm³. Which has the smallest surface area to volume ratio?** (3 marks, ★★★)

....

....

....

> **MATHS SKILLS**
>
> Simplify the surface area to volume ratio to the lowest figure, e.g. 12:2 can be written as 6:1.
>
> The organism with the smallest difference between the surface area and the volume has the smaller surface area to volume ratio.

b **Why do organisms with a small surface area to volume ratio need specialised exchange surfaces?** (3 marks, ★★)

....

....

....

(3) **A piece of Visking tubing is being used as a model cell. Plan an experiment to show that glucose solution inside the model cell diffuses into the surrounding pure water. Explain what factors you would need to know to calculate the rate of diffusion (refer to Fick's law).** (5 marks, ★★★★)

....

....

....

....

....

Osmosis

(1) **Define osmosis.** (2 marks, ★★)

....

....

(2) **An animal cell is placed in a concentrated solution. In which direction will water move?**
(1 mark, ★)

....

(3) **A disc of plant tissue has a mass of 10 g. It is placed in a dilute solution for 6 hours. The mass is measured again and found to be 14 g. What is the percentage increase in mass? Show your working.** (3 marks, ★★★)

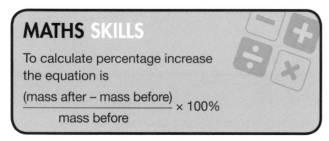

MATHS SKILLS

To calculate percentage increase the equation is

$$\frac{(\text{mass after} - \text{mass before})}{\text{mass before}} \times 100\%$$

Percentage increase in mass = ... %

(4) **The graph below shows the percentage change in mass of potato cubes placed in sugar solutions of different concentrations.**

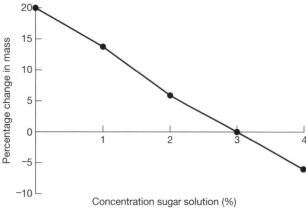

a **Using the graph, identify the sugar concentration at which the sugar concentration inside the potato cells is the same as in the sugar solution. Justify your answer.** (2 marks, ★★★)

....

....

....

....

....

....

b **At the concentration you gave in (a), why is the sugar concentration inside the potato cells the same as in the sugar solution?** (1 mark, ★★)

....

....

Investigating the effect of a range of concentrations of salt or sugar solutions on the mass of plant tissue

(1) The table below shows data collected after slices of cucumber were placed in salt solutions of different concentration for 12 hours.

a Complete the table to show the percentage change in mass to **one decimal place**.
(4 marks, ★★)

> Carefully check the column headings and numbers in the table. Is anything missing? Has all the data been recorded to the same number of decimal places?

Salt solution concentration (%)	Mass of cucumber slice at start (g)	Mass of cucumber slice after 12 hours	Percentage change in mass (%)
0	4.0	5.4	35.0
1	4.2	4.9	
2	4.1	4.1	
4	4	3.0	
5	4.1	2.7	

b **Correct any mistakes in the table.** (2 marks, ★★★)

Mistake 1: ....   Correction 1: ....

Mistake 2: ....   Correction 1: ....

c **On a separate piece of graph paper, draw a graph showing the percentage change in mass at different salt concentrations.** (4 marks, ★★★)

d **Using the graph, what is the percentage change in mass of the cucumber slice at 3% salt concentration?** (1 mark, ★★)

....

....

....

> **NAILIT!**
>
> Depending on your exam board you may need to refer to water potential in your answer. Make sure you check your mapping grid.

e **The cucumber slice at 5% salt solution was examined under a light microscope. Describe how you would expect the cells to look and explain why.**
(3 marks, ★★)

....

....

....

....

....

Active transport

(1) **What is active transport?** (2 marks, ★★)

....

....

(2) **Give one example of active transport in plants.** (1 mark, ★)

....

(3) **Complete the table to show the features of diffusion, osmosis and active transport. For each type of movement, tick the statement(s) that are true. The first row has been done for you.** (3 marks, ★★)

Type of movement	Involves the movement of water	Involves the movement of particles	The movement is from dilute solution to concentrated solution	The movement is from concentrated solution to dilute solution
Diffusion		✓		✓
Osmosis				
Active transport				

(4) **Suggest why cells in the wall of the small intestine contain many mitochondria.** (3 marks, ★★★)

....

....

NAILIT!

Remember that respiration is carried out in mitochondria.

(5) **Carrot seedlings were grown in aerobic and anaerobic conditions. The amount of potassium ions absorbed by the seedlings was measured every 30 minutes. The results are shown in the table below.**

Time (minutes)	Total amount of potassium ions absorbed (arbitrary units)	
	With oxygen (aerobic)	Without oxygen (anaerobic)
0	0	0
30	210	120
60	280	170
90	340	185
120	380	210
150	420	230

a **Compare the amount of potassium ions taken up by seedlings grown in each condition.** (1 mark, ★★)

....

b **Explain the pattern of potassium uptake in each condition.** (3 marks, ★★★)

....

....

c **How could this investigation be made more valid and reliable?** (2 marks, ★★)

....

....

Tissues, organs and organ systems

The human digestive system and enzymes

1   a **Name two organs in the human digestive system.** (2 marks, ★)

   i ....   ii ....

   b **Describe what happens to food as it moves through the human digestive system.** (5 marks, ★★★)

   ....

   ....

   ....

   ....

   ....

NAILIT!

Include any substances that are added to the food as it passes through the digestive system.

2   a **The table below shows types of enzyme used in digestion. Fill in the missing information.** (3 marks, ★★)

Enzymes	Substrate	Products
	carbohydrates	sugars
proteases		amino acids
lipases	lipids	

   b **Explain the role of bile in digestion.** (2 marks, ★★★★)

   ....

   ....

   ....

WORKIT!

Where in the body are proteases made? (1 mark, ★)

Proteases are made in the stomach/pancreas. (1)

3   **Describe how the amount of energy in food can be measured.** (2 marks, ★★)

   ....

   ....

④ a **What does the term biological catalyst mean?** (1 mark, ★★)

....

b **The enzyme amylase breaks down starch. Explain why amylase would not break down lipids.** (2 marks, ★★★★)

....

....

c **Amylase has an optimum pH of 7. Describe and explain what would happen to amylase at a pH of 2.** (3 marks, ★★★★)

....

....

....

⑤ **Catalase is an enzyme that breaks down hydrogen peroxide into water and oxygen. If hydrogen peroxide is converted into 24 cm³ of oxygen in three minutes, what is the rate of reaction? Show your working.** (2 marks, ★★★)

....

....

MATHS SKILLS

To calculate the rate of reaction per minute, divide the volume of oxygen produced by the time (number of minutes).

NAILIT!

Topic link: Enzymes are proteins so you may also be asked about protein synthesis in exam questions about digestion or enzymes.

⑥ **Sketch the shape of the rate-of-reaction graph you would expect to see for a reaction with a fixed concentration of enzymes, but limitless substrate. Explain the shape of your graph.** (3 marks, ★★★★)

....

....

....

....

....

....

Food tests

(1) Match each food type to its test.
(3 marks, ★★)

Starch

Protein

Lipid

Biuret test

Benedict's test

Iodine test

Emulsion test

(2) A food sample turns lilac after testing. Identify which test was used, and explain what the result shows. (2 marks, ★★★★)

Name of test:

....

What the result shows:

....

....

....

(3) A student wants to test a sample for the presence of glucose. Describe the procedure that the student should use. (4 marks, ★★★)

....

....

....

....

NAILIT!

Describe the steps that the student should follow to carry out the test, and what the results would show.

(4) Two students use iodine solution to test a solution at two different times. After one minute, the solution turns blue-black. After five minutes, the solution has turned orange.

Student A says that the solution must have contained starch and amylase, and the amylase must have digested the starch into maltose.

Student B says that the iodine solution might not be working properly and that one of the results must not be correct.

Explain how you could work out who is correct. (4 marks, ★★★★★)

....

....

....

....

The effect of pH on amylase

(1) **Describe the role of amylase in humans.** (2 marks, ★★★)

....

....

(2) **Some students investigated the effect of pH on amylase. The graph shows their results.**

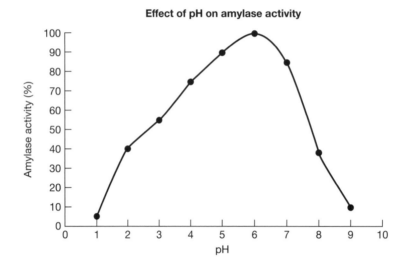

Effect of pH on amylase activity

a **Describe the pattern of the graph.** (2 marks, ★★★)

....

....

b **What is the optimum pH of this amylase?** (1 mark, ★)

....

NAILIT!

The **optimum pH** is the pH at which the enzyme has the fastest rate of reaction.

c **In the investigation, 10 cm³ of starch was used in 120 seconds at pH6. What was the rate of reaction?** (2 marks, ★★★)

Rate of reaction = ...

MATHS SKILLS

Use the formula:

$$\text{Rate of reaction} = \frac{\text{amount of reactant used}}{\text{time}}$$

The heart

(1) **Fill in the missing words below.** (4 marks, ★★)

Blood enters the right side of the heart through the .... and leaves the

right side of the heart through the ....

Blood enters the left side of heart through the .... and leaves the left

side of the heart through the ....

(2) a **Describe how blood is moved through the right side of the heart.** (3 marks, ★★★)

....

....

....

....

NAILIT!

Include the names of the chambers of the heart, the relevant blood vessels and the names of the valves.

DOIT!

What does the pacemaker in the right atrium control and what happens if it stops working?

b **What is the role of valves in the heart?** (2 marks, ★★)

....

....

(3) **Explain what an artificial pacemaker is and why a person might have one fitted.**
(3 marks, ★★★)

....

....

....

....

The lungs

(1) **Describe how air travels from outside the body to the alveoli.** (3 marks, ★★★)

NAILIT!

Include the names of the airways in the lungs: trachea, bronchi and alveoli.

....

....

....

....

(2) **Match each adaptation of the lung to its purpose.** (3 marks, ★★)

Adaptation of the lung

Many alveoli

Alveolar wall is one cell thick

Good supply of blood capillaries

Purpose

Gives short diffusion pathway for gases.

Keeps the concentration gradient of gases high.

Increase the surface area of the lungs.

DOIT!

Mark the student's answer below using the mark scheme, and suggest how to improve the answer.

Explain why oxygen moves out of the alveoli and into the blood capillary. (3 marks, ★★★★)

There is more oxygen in the alveoli than in the blood capillary. Oxygen moves from the alveoli to the blood capillary. The blood moves the oxygen away from the alveoli, keeping the concentration of oxygen in the blood capillary lower than the concentration of oxygen in the alveoli.

MARK SCHEME

The concentration of oxygen in the alveoli is higher than the concentration of oxygen in the blood capillary. (1)

The blood moves the oxygen away from the alveoli, keeping the concentration of oxygen in the blood capillary lower than the concentration of oxygen in the alveoli. (1)

Oxygen diffuses from the alveoli to the blood capillary. (1)

Number of marks for student's answer: ....

How to improve the answer: ....

....

Blood vessels and blood

① **Which of the following statements are true? Tick one box.** (1 mark, ★★)

A   Arteries have a thin muscular wall.

B   Veins contain valves.

C   Capillary walls are one cell thick.

A and B only
B and C only
A, B and C

② **Blood flows through a 2mm capillary in four seconds. What is the rate of blood flow?** (3 marks, ★★★)

....

....

> **MATHS SKILLS**
>
> Use the formula:
>
> $$\text{Rate} = \frac{\text{distance}}{\text{time}}$$

③ **Two students are examining the walls of some blood vessels. Student A says that the blood vessel with thick walls must be an artery. Student B says that the blood vessel with the widest lumen must be the artery. State who is correct and explain why arteries have their particular features.** (3 marks, ★★★★)

....

....

④ **Name two components of blood that are not cells.** (2 marks, ★)

i ....   ii ....

⑤ **Identify the type of blood cells labelled A and B in the image below.** (2 marks, ★★★)

A   ....

B   ....

⑥ **What is the function of the following blood cells?**

a **Red blood cells** (1 mark, ★★★)

....

....

b **White blood cells** (1 mark, ★★★)

....

⑦ **Describe how white blood cells are adapted for their function.** (3 marks, ★★★★)

....

....

....

> **NAILIT!**
>
> Include one adaptation of phagocytes, neutrophils and lymphocytes in your answer.

Coronary heart disease

(1) What type of disease is coronary heart disease (CHD)? (1 mark, ★)

....

(2) Describe how CHD develops. (2 marks, ★★★)

....

....

(3) Match each symptom of CHD to the correct description. (3 marks, ★★)

Symptom	Description
Angina	Muscle weakness in the heart or a faulty valve.
Heart failure	Chest pains due to restricted blood flow to heart muscle.
Heart attack	The blood supply to the heart muscle is suddenly blocked.

(4) Name two treatments for CHD. For each, state one advantage and one disadvantage. (4 marks, ★★★★)

1   Treatment: ....

Advantage: ....

Disadvantage: ....

2   Treatment: ....

Advantage: ....

Disadvantage: ....

DO IT!

In this topic you may be asked to evaluate different methods of treatment, considering the advantages and disadvantages of each.

Here are six treatments for CHD. What are the advantages and disadvantages for each?

stents, statins, mechanical valve replacement, biological valve replacement, heart

transplant, artificial heart (temporary)

Health issues and effect of lifestyle

(1) **What is a communicable disease?** (1 mark, ★)

....

(2) **Name two communicable diseases.** (2 marks, ★)

i .... ii ....

(3) **Describe two health conditions that can interact.** (2 marks, ★★★)

....

....

(4) **The graph below shows the number of deaths per 100 000 population from cardiovascular disease (CVD) in Australia in 2012.**

Deaths per 100 000 population

Describe the pattern in the graph.

(2 marks, ★★★)

....

....

> **NAILIT!**
>
> When asked to **describe** a graph, you are not being asked to **explain** the reasons for a pattern/correlation, just what the pattern/correlation is.

(5) **What is a non-communicable disease?** (1 mark, ★)

....

(6) **A doctor sees a patient for a check-up and asks about the person's lifestyle. The patient smokes, drinks some alcohol each week, and does little exercise. What advice could the doctor give about possible health risks of this lifestyle?** (3 marks, ★★★)

....

....

....

(7) **Describe the human and financial costs of non-communicable diseases.** (3 marks, ★★★★)

....

....

....

....

> **NAILIT!**
>
> Think about the changes that people would have to make and the cost of things they might have to do because of their illness.

Cancer

(1) **Name some of the risk factors associated with cancer.** (2 marks, ★)

....

....

(2) **Describe how normal cells can become cancerous.** (3 marks, ★★★)

> **NAILIT!**
>
> Include the word **mutation** in your answer.

....

....

....

....

(3) **Name and compare the two types of tumour.** (3 marks, ★★★★)

....

....

....

....

....

> **NAILIT!**
>
> Compare similarities and differences between the two types of tumour.

(4) **The graph shows the number of cases of breast cancer in women and the number of deaths per 100 000 population in the UK, before and after screening was introduced in 1987.**

Describe patterns on the graph and suggest reasons for them. (4 marks, ★★★★★)

....

....

....

....

....

....

....

....

Plant tissues

(1) **Match each plant tissue to its function.** (4 marks, ★★)

Plant tissue	Function
Spongy mesophyll	The main site of photosynthesis in a leaf.
Palisade tissue	Transport of sugar sap around the plant.
Xylem	Site of gas exchange in the leaf.
Phloem	Transport of water to the leaf.

(2) **Describe how palisade cells are adapted to their function.** (2 marks, ★★★)

....

....

(3) **The drawing below shows a transverse section through a leaf.**

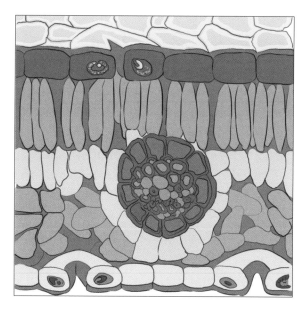

Label the following:

- a spongy mesophyll cell (1 mark, ★★)
- a palisade cell (1 mark, ★★)
- the xylem. (1 mark, ★★)

NAILIT!

Palisade cells are found at the top of the leaf where there is more sunlight.

Transpiration and translocation

(1) a **Name the apparatus used to measure the rate of transpiration.** (1 mark, ★)

....

b **In a transpiration experiment, 20 cm³ of water was lost in five hours.**

Calculate the rate of transpiration. Show your working. (2 marks, ★★★)

> **NAILIT!**
>
> Use the formula:
>
> $$\text{Rate} = \frac{\text{volume of water}}{\text{time}}$$

Rate of transpiration = ...

(2) **Describe and explain how guard cells control the loss of water from the leaf.** (3 marks, ★★★★)

> **NAILIT!**
>
> Include how the guard cells change shape in your answer.

....

....

....

....

(3) **What is the difference between transpiration and translocation?** (4 marks, ★★★★)

....

....

....

....

(4) **Xerophytes are specialised plants that can live in habitats with very little water. Describe two adaptations of xerophytes and explain how they help the plant to survive.** (4 marks, ★★★★)

....

....

....

....

....

Infection and response

Communicable (infectious) diseases

(1) **What is a pathogen?** (1 mark, ★)

....

(2) **Match each disease to the pathogen that causes it.** (3 marks, ★★)

Disease	Pathogen
Tuberculosis	Bacterium
	Virus
Malaria	Fungus
Athlete's foot	Protist

(3) **Compare the lytic and lysogenic lifecycles of viruses.** (3 marks, ★★★)

....

....

....

(4) **The number of cases of HIV among intravenous drug users (IDUs) in Finland is shown in the graph below. A needle exchange programme was introduced in 1999.**

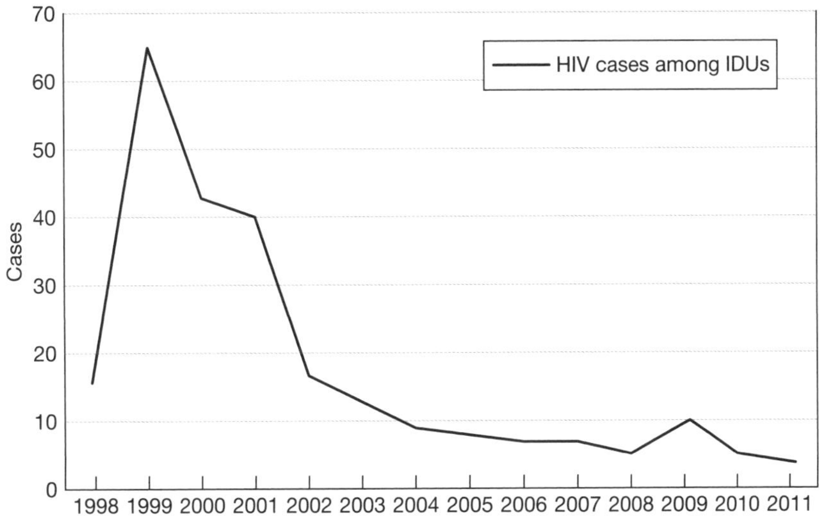

Graph: y-axis labelled "Cases" from 0 to 70; x-axis years 1998 to 2011. Legend: HIV cases among IDUs.

> **NAILIT!**
>
> Make sure that you describe each stage of the graph and use numbers (from the graph) to justify your explanation.

Use evidence from the graph to describe and explain the pattern of HIV cases among intravenous drug users from 1999. (3 marks, ★★★★)

....

....

....

....

Viral and bacterial diseases

(1) **Describe the symptoms of measles.** (2 marks, ★★★)

....

(2) a **What is tobacco mosaic virus (TMV)?** (2 marks, ★)

....

....

b **Explain why plants with TMV carry out less photosynthesis than plants that do not have TMV.** (2 marks, ★★★)

....

....

(3) **During the First World War, many soldiers living in trenches caught influenza. At the end of the war, a global influenza pandemic killed more than 20 million people worldwide. Describe and explain how this virus could have infected so many people.** (4 marks, ★★★★)

....

....

| **NAILIT!**
.... | Recall how viruses are transmitted from person to person.

....

(4) a **What are the symptoms of salmonella poisoning?** (2 marks, ★)

....

b **Describe how severe cases of salmonella poisoning are treated.** (2 marks, ★★)

....

....

(5) a **Antibiotics are often used to treat gonorrhoea infections. Recently, some strains of bacteria that cause gonorrhoea have become resistant to antibiotics. Explain what this means.** (2 marks, ★★★★)

....

| **NAILIT!**
.... | A strain is a sub-group of a species of bacterium.

b **The number of cases of gonorrhoea infection in the UK increased by 11 % from 2014 to 2015. Suggest what may have caused this increase.** (1 mark, ★★★★)

....

Fungal and protist diseases

(1) a **Fill in the missing words.** (3 marks, ★★)

Rose black spot is a .... disease that affects roses. The leaves

of the rose are covered with .... This reduces the rate of

.... in the leaves.

b **Describe how rose black spot is treated.** (2 marks, ★★)

....

....

(2) a **Malaria is spread by mosquitoes. List some ways of preventing malaria infection in areas where there are mosquitoes.** (3 marks, ★★)

....

....

....

b **A group of scientists studying malaria found that there were more cases of malaria in areas with shallow pools of water. Describe and explain how they could use this knowledge to reduce the spread of malaria.** (2 marks, ★★★★)

....

....

....

NAILIT!

Topic link: Mosquitoes are part of a food chain. The food chain will be disrupted if the mosquitoes are removed.

STRETCHIT!

Can you find out which species populations would be affected by mass mosquito removal?

(3) **Ash dieback is a fungal disease that could cause the extinction of ash trees in the UK. Suggest two ways that this could be prevented.** (2 marks, ★★★)

i ....

ii ....

Human defence systems and vaccination

1. **Match each body part to the non-specific defence.** (4 marks, ★★)

Body part	Defence
Skin	Cilia move mucus up to the throat.
Nose	Contain lysozymes which kill bacteria.
Trachea	Hydrochloric acid and proteases kill pathogens.
Stomach	Physical barrier against pathogens.
Tears	Small hairs and mucus trap airborne particles.

2. a **Name two types of white blood cell that kill pathogens.** (2 marks, ★)

   i ....

   ii ....

   b **Describe how white blood cells attack a specific pathogen.** (5 marks, ★★★)

   ....

   ....

   ....

   NAILIT!
   Discuss the action of antibodies in your answer.

   ....

   ....

3. **Fill in the missing words.** (3 marks, ★★)

   Vaccines contain a dead or an .... form of a ....

   Vaccines are injected into the body where they stimulate the ....

4. **Describe and explain how a vaccine works.** (4 marks, ★★★★)

   ....

   ....

   ....

   NAILIT!
   Remember to include antibodies in your answer.

   ....

   ....

5. **Give one advantage and one disadvantage of vaccination programs.** (2 marks, ★★★)

   ....

   ....

   ....

Antibiotics, painkillers and new drugs

(1) **Give an example of an antibiotic and an example of a painkiller.** (2 marks, ★)

Antibiotic .... Painkiller ....

(2) **Describe how antibiotics work.** (2 marks, ★★★)

....

....

(3) **Antiviral drugs are used to treat viral infections. Explain why antiviral drugs are not always effective.** (2 marks, ★★★★)

....

....

(4) **The graph below shows the effectiveness of two painkillers. What is the advantage of using each painkiller?** (2 marks, ★★★★★)

[Graph: Pain score (y-axis, 0.5 to 3.0) vs Time (weeks) (x-axis, 0, 1, 2, 4, 8). Two lines: Glucosamine sulfate and Ibuprofen.]

....

....

....

....

....

....

....

(5) **Some strains of bacteria are becoming resistant to some antibiotics. Suggest how antibiotic resistance could be reduced.** (3 marks, ★★★★)

....

....

....

(6) **Match each drug to the plant or microorganism that it was discovered in.** (3 marks, ★★)

Drug　　　　　**Plant or microorganism**

Aspirin　　　　　*Penicillium*

Digitalis　　　　　Willow bark

Penicillin　　　　　Foxgloves

(7) **A new painkiller is being developed. Describe how the new painkiller is tested to make sure it is safe for patients to take. On a separate piece of paper, explain the purpose of each step.** (4 marks, ★★★★)

NAILIT!

Make sure you describe preclinical and clinical trials.

Photosynthesis and the rate of photosynthesis

(1) a Write the word equation for photosynthesis. (2 marks, ★)

....

b What type of reaction is photosynthesis? (1 mark, ★)

....

NAILIT!

It is the type of reaction that takes in more heat than it gives off.

c Explain the use of carbon dioxide in photosynthesis. (2 marks, ★★★★)

....

....

d A student wants to measure the rate of photosynthesis in a plant at different temperatures. On a separate piece of paper, plan an investigation to do this.
(4 marks, ★★★★)

(2) Name a factor that increases the rate of photosynthesis. (1 mark, ★)

....

(3) a What is a limiting factor? (2 marks, ★)

....

....

b Which of these graphs shows the rate of photosynthesis at increasing light intensity? Tick one box. (1 mark, ★★★)

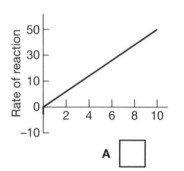

A ☐

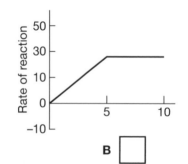

B ☐

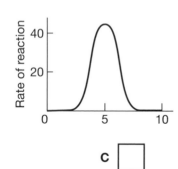

C ☐

(4) **The rate of photosynthesis is calculated by measuring the volume of oxygen that a plant gives off in a given time.**

A plant gives off 24 cm³ of oxygen in four minutes. Calculate the rate of photosynthesis. Show your working. (3 marks, ★★★)

> **NAILIT!**
>
> Use the formula:
>
> $$\text{Rate} = \frac{\text{volume of product released}}{\text{time}}$$

Rate of photosynthesis = ...

Investigating the effect of light intensity on the rate of photosynthesis

(1) **Some students investigate the rate of photosynthesis in pondweed at different intensities of light. The students placed a lamp at different distances from the pondweed and measured the volume of oxygen given off after five minutes.**

a **Name the independent and dependent variables in this investigation.** (2 marks, ★★)

Independent variable ....

Dependent variable ....

b **Describe what the students could have done to make sure that this investigation is valid.** (3 marks, ★★★)

....

....

....

NAILIT!

Think about the variables that need to be kept the same – these are called the **control variables**.

MATHS SKILLS

$$\text{Rate} = \frac{\text{volume of product released}}{\text{time}}$$

c **Students recorded the volume of oxygen released in five minutes. The table shows their results.**

Distance of lamp from plant (cm)	Volume of oxygen released (cm^3)	Time (min)	Rate of photosynthesis (cm^3/min)
0	200	5	40
25	195	5	
50	85	5	
75	40	5	
100	10	5	

Calculate the rate of photosynthesis of the plants for each distance from the lamp and complete the table. (4 marks, ★★★)

d **Explain why the rate of photosynthesis decreases as the light is moved further from the pondweed.** (1 mark, ★★★)

....

....

Uses of glucose

(1) **Name two uses of glucose in plants.** (2 marks, ★)

i ....

ii ....

> **NAILIT!**
>
> Glucose is used in plants to make substances.

(2) **Which statement is true? Tick one box.** (1 mark, ★★)

Glucose is a lipid.	
Glucose has the chemical formula $C_6H_{12}O_6$.	
Animals need glucose to make starch.	

(3) **How do plants make glucose?** (1 mark, ★★★)

....

....

....

> **NAILIT!**
>
> Glucose is the product of a reaction.

DOIT!

Mark the student's answer below using the mark scheme, and suggest how to improve the answer.

Explain why glucose is important in animals. (3 marks, ★★★)

Glucose is needed for respiration to release energy, and is converted into glycogen for storage.

MARK SCHEME

Needed for respiration to release energy. (1)

Converted into glycogen for storage. (1)

Used to produce fat for storage. (1)

Number of marks for student's answer: ....

How to improve the answer: ....

....

....

Respiration and metabolism

(1) a What is the word equation for aerobic respiration? (1 mark, ★)

....

b What type of reaction is respiration? (1 mark, ★)

....

> **NAILIT!**
> Does respiration release more heat than it takes in?

(2) a Where in the cell does aerobic respiration take place? (1 mark, ★)

....

b What is the chemical equation for aerobic respiration? (2 marks, ★★★)

....

(3) Describe what happens in muscle cells during anaerobic respiration. (3 marks, ★★★)

....

....

....

(4) A group of students wanted to measure the rate of respiration in yeast. Describe a method that they could use. (3 marks, ★★★)

....

....

....

....

(5) Describe some metabolic reactions that happen in the body. (2 marks, ★★★)

....

....

(6) Explain why metabolic reactions need energy. (2 marks, ★★★★)

....

....

> **NAILIT!**
> The amount of energy stored in food can be calculated using calorimetry, this measures the energy transferred when food is burned and heats up water.

Response to exercise

(1) a **Describe how to measure a person's pulse rate after exercise.** (3 marks, ★★★)

....

....

....

....

....

NAILIT!

The pulse is found in the **arteries** of the body.

b **If a person's pulse is measured as 18 pulses in 15 seconds, what is the pulse rate in beats per minute?** (1 mark, ★★★)

....

....

MATHS SKILLS

To calculate the beats per minute from the number of pulses in 15 seconds, multiply the number by four.

(2) a **Describe and explain two effects of exercise on the human body.** (4 marks, ★★★★)

....

....

....

b **An athlete's stroke volume is 80 cm³ and heart rate is 60 beats per minute. Calculate the cardiac output.** (2 marks, ★★★)

....

....

....

NAILIT!

Cardiac output = stroke volume × heart rate
Check if your exam board requires you to know this calculation.

(3) **Marley runs a 100 m race in 12.8 seconds but his breathing rate remains high for several minutes after he has finished, even though he has sat down to rest. Explain why his breathing rate does not return to normal straight away at the end of the race.**
(4 marks, ★★★★)

....

....

....

Homeostasis

(1) **Complete the following sentence about homeostasis.** (3 marks, ★)

Homeostasis keeps all the .... conditions of the body

.... whatever the .... conditions might be.

(2) **a** **Controlling the levels of blood sugar is one example of homeostasis. Name two other examples of homeostasis.** (2 marks, ★)

....

....

b **Describe how homeostasis controls the blood sugar levels in the body.** (5 marks, ★★★★)

....

....

....

....

....

....

....

> ## NAILIT!
>
> You need to include what happens when blood sugar levels are high and when they are low, so make sure you mention insulin *and* glucagon in your answer. Thinking about how diabetics treat 'hypos' and 'hypers' might help you to remember.

(3) **What is the role of the brain in homeostasis?** (3 marks, ★★★)

....

....

....

WORKIT!

Explain why it is important to maintain an internal body temperature of 37°C. (4 marks, ★★★)

Enzymes are needed to carry out reactions in the body. (1)

Enzymes have an optimum temperature of 37°C. (1)

If the temperature is too low, the enzymes will not react quickly enough to maintain life. (1)

If the temperature is too high, the enzymes will denature, and no longer be able to carry out their function. (1)

The human nervous system and reflexes

(1) **Which one of the following statements is true? Tick one box.** (1 mark, ★★)

A The peripheral nervous system is made of the brain and the spinal cord.	
B Sensory neurones detect stimuli and send nerve impulses to the brain.	
C Motor neurones receive nerve impulses from the brain.	
D The brain is an effector and responds to the stimuli.	

(2) a **Put the terms receptor, response, coordinator and stimulus into the correct order.**
(4 marks, ★★)

.... ⟶ .... ⟶ .... ⟶ effector ⟶ ....

b **Describe the role of the coordinator.** (2 marks, ★★)

....

(3) **A person is testing their reaction time by pressing a button when a light appears on a screen. Describe and explain the action of the nervous system when the light appears on the screen.** (4 marks, ★★★)

....

....

....

(4) **Name two neurones involved in a reflex arc.** (2 marks, ★)

i .... ii ....

(5) **Compare the structure and function of the three different neurones found in a reflex arc.** (3 marks, ★★)

....

....

....

....

NAILIT!

You may be asked to compare the different types of neurons in the exam. You need to know:

- the physical differences
- the functions of each type
- the order they perform in a reflex arc.

(6) a **Compare reflexes and voluntary reactions.** (2 marks, ★★)

....

....

b **Explain why reflex actions are important.** (2 marks, ★★)

....

....

Investigating the effect of a factor on human reaction time

(1) **A student decided to measure their reaction time before and after drinking caffeine. Here is their method.**

Measure reaction time by timing how long it takes them to press a button when they see a light on a screen.

Drink a cup of coffee.

Measure reaction time again.

a **Describe how you could alter the method to make it more valid and reliable.** (4 marks, ★★★)

....

....

....

....

NAILIT!

- The **independent variable** is the one which you deliberately change (in order to observe its effects on the dependent variable).

- The **dependent variable** is the one which may change as a result of changes to the independent variable.

- All other variables must be controlled to make the experiment a 'fair test'. These are called the **control variables**.

- The **independent** variable always goes in the left-hand column of a results table and on the horizontal axis (*x*-axis) of a results graph.

b **The student found the reaction times before drinking coffee were 0.55, 0.45 and 0.50 seconds; and 0.40, 0.35 and 0.3 seconds after drinking coffee. Record this data in a table.** (3 marks, ★★★)

c **Calculate the means and add them to the table.** (2 marks, ★★)

Human endocrine system

(1) Match the glands of the endocrine system with their hormones. (4 marks, ★★)

Gland	Hormones
Pituitary gland	Insulin and glucagon
	Growth hormone, FSH and LH
Pancreas	Testosterone
Thyroid	Thyroxine
Ovary	Progesterone and oestrogen

(2) How is the endocrine system controlled? (2 marks, ★★★)

....

....

....

(3) Compare the properties of the endocrine system and the nervous system. (4 marks, ★★★)

....

....

....

....

....

NAILIT!

Think about the speed and lasting effects of each system.

Control of blood glucose concentration

(1) **Where in the body are insulin and glucagon produced?** (1 mark, ★)

....

(2) **Describe the effects of insulin on the body.** (3 marks, ★★)

....

....

....

(3) **Glucagon is released when the blood sugar levels are low. Explain how glucagon returns the blood glucose level back to normal.** (3 marks, ★★★)

....

....

....

....

(4) **Suggest what could happen in the body if insulin is not released.** (2 marks, ★★)

....

....

....

 DO IT!

Each of the following are part of every control system. Make sure you can write a definition for each:

- receptor
- coordination centre
- effector.

What are the receptors, coordination centre and effectors involved in the control of blood glucose?

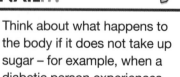 **NAILIT!**

Think about what happens to the body if it does not take up sugar – for example, when a diabetic person experiences hyperglycaemia.

Diabetes

(1) **What is diabetes?** (2 marks, ★★)

....

....

(2) **What is hyperglycaemia?** (1 mark, ★)

....

(3) **Compare and contrast type 1 and type 2 diabetes.** (4 marks, ★★★)

....

....

....

....

....

NAILIT!

Compare what is happening inside the body, the causes and the treatment.

(4) **Describe what happens to the blood sugar levels of people with diabetes after a meal.**
(2 marks, ★★★)

....

....

....

DOIT!

Mark the student's answer below using the mark scheme, and suggest how to improve the answer.

Student A says that all people with diabetes inject insulin. Student B says that only people with type 1 diabetes inject insulin. Who is correct and why? (3 marks, ★★★)

Student B is correct. People with type 1 diabetes need to inject insulin because they don't have any.

MARK SCHEME
Student B is correct. (1) People with type 1 diabetes do not produce any/enough insulin. (1) They need to inject insulin so that cells and the liver can take up glucose after a meal. (1)

Number of marks for student's answer: ....

How to improve the answer: ....

....

Hormones in human reproduction

(1) **Match the hormone to the endocrine gland where it is made.** (3 marks, ★)

Hormone	Endocrine gland
Testosterone	Ovaries
Oestrogen	Pituitary gland
Follicle-stimulating hormone	Testes

(2) **a What is the role of follicle-stimulating hormone (FSH)?** (1 mark, ★)

....

b Which hormone stimulates the release of LH? (1 mark, ★)

....

(3) **The graph below shows hormone levels during the menstrual cycle.**

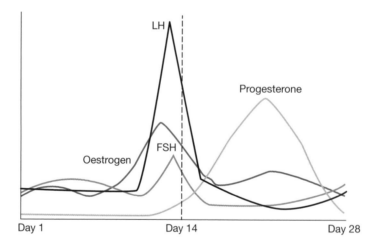

a What happens when luteinising hormone (LH) peaks just before day 14? (1 mark, ★★)

....

b What effect does progesterone have on the uterus after day 14? Explain why this is important if the egg is fertilised. (2 marks, ★★)

....

....

....

Contraception

(1) **Match the non-hormonal methods of contraception to how they work.** (3 marks, ★)

| Condoms | Kill sperm |

| Intrauterine device (IUD) | Prevents implantation of an embryo |

| Spermicidal agents | Trap sperm |

(2) a **Name two examples of hormonal contraception.** (2 marks, ★)

i ....

ii ....

b **Explain how hormonal contraceptives work.** (3 marks, ★★★)

....

....

....

NAILIT!

Think about the hormones that are in different types of hormonal contraceptives. Don't forget to include the effects of progesterone in your answer.

(3) **Compare the effectiveness of hormonal and non-hormonal methods of contraception.**
(4 marks, ★★★★)

....

....

....

....

....

....

Using hormones to treat infertility

(1) Which of the following statements are true? Tick one box. (1 mark, ★)

A   IVF is a type of fertilisation that happens outside of the body.

B   FSH and oestrogen are given to the woman before IVF.

C   Several eggs are usually fertilised by IVF at the same time.

i	A and B only
ii	B and C only
iii	A and C only

(2) Describe the IVF procedure. (3 marks, ★★)

....

....

....

(3) Explain the advantages and disadvantages of using IVF. (4 marks, ★★★)

....

....

....

....

....

DO IT!

Mark the student's answer below using the mark scheme, and suggest how to improve the answer.

Describe how hormones are used in infertility treatment. (2 marks, ★★★)

Follicle-stimulating hormone and luteinising hormone are given to increase the number of eggs.

MARK SCHEME
Follicle-stimulating hormone is used to increase the number of eggs (1) and luteinising hormone is given to release the eggs/stimulate ovulation. (1)

Number of marks for student's answer: ....

How to improve the answer: ....

....

Negative feedback

(1) **What is negative feedback?** (2 marks, ★)

....

....

(2) a **Where in the body is adrenaline produced?** (1 mark, ★)

....

b **Which of the following is an effect of adrenaline? Tick one box.** (1 mark, ★)

A, B and C only	
B, C and D only	
A, B and D only	
A, C and D only	

    A Heart rate increases.

    B Breathing rate increases.

    C More blood flows to the skin and intestines.

    D Stimulates the liver to release glucose from glycogen.

(3) **The diagram shows how the level of thyroxine in the body is maintained by thyroid releasing hormone (TRH) and thyroid stimulating hormone (TSH).**

Use information from the diagram to explain how thyroxine levels are maintained.

(3 marks, ★★★★)

Hypothalamus
→ Stimulates
--→ Inhibits
TRH
Anterior pituitary
TSH
Thyroid gland
Thyroxine
Target cells

....

....

....

....

....

....

....

 **NAILIT!**

Don't forget that thyroxine is a hormone controlled by a **negative feedback** cycle. When answering questions about the action of the hormones which regulate thyroxine, remember to mention it is the **levels of thyroxine** (high or low) which stimulate the hypothalamus actions.

Sexual and asexual reproduction

1 **a** **Name the male and female gametes in animals.** (2 marks, ★)

Female ....

Male ....

b **What is the process that produces gametes?** (1 mark, ★)

....

2 **Match the organism with the type of asexual reproduction they use.** (4 marks, ★★)

Organism	Asexual reproduction
Bacteria	Runners
Yeast	Budding
Strawberry plants	Binary fission
Potatoes	Tubers

3 **Malarial parasites reproduce sexually in mosquito hosts and asexually in human hosts. Explain the advantages of this to the malarial parasites.** (4 marks, ★★★)

....

....

....

....

....

NAILIT!

Include ideas about genetic variation and natural selection.

Meiosis

① **Complete the table below.** (3 marks, ★★)

	Mitosis	Meiosis
Number of daughter cells	2	
Number of chromosomes	Full	
Genetically identical		No

NAILIT!

At GCSE, you will not be asked to name or describe the separate stages of meiosis, but you need to be able to say what happens in general terms. Make sure you know the difference between **haploid** and **diploid** cells.

② **Describe what happens during meiosis.** (3 marks, ★★★)

....

....

....

....

③ **What happens during fertilisation?** (3 marks, ★★★)

....

....

....

....

DOIT!

Mark the student's answer below using the mark scheme, and suggest how to improve the answer.

Explain why meiosis is important in variation. (3 marks, ★★★★)

Meiosis makes sex cells that are genetically different. This means that when male and female sex cells

fuse, there is a wide possibility of different alleles.

MARK SCHEME
Meiosis makes genetically different sex cells. (1) During fertilisation, there are many different possible combinations of alleles, (1) resulting in a wide variation of genotypes in a population. (1)

Number of marks for student's answer: ....

How to improve the answer: ....

....

DNA and the genome

① **Which of the following statements are true? Tick one box.** (1 mark, ★★)

A   DNA is found in the nucleus of the cell.

B   Each gene contains a code to make a specific protein.

C   Many genes are folded into large structures called chromatin.

D   DNA is made of two stands that form a double helix.

i	A, C and D only.
ii	A, B, and C only.
iii	A, B, and D only.
iv	B, C, and D only.

② a **How many chromosomes are there in human body cells?** (1 mark, ★)

....

b **If an organism has 38 chromosomes in the body cells, how many chromosomes will there be in the gametes?** (1 mark, ★)

....

③ **Explain why studying the human genome is useful in medicine and science.** (3 marks, ★★★)

....

....

....

....

NAILIT!

Consider why this might be important for the study of diseases, treatments and human migration.

④ **Two students extracted DNA from a banana using the following method.**

1.   Crushed the banana in a beaker containing soap and water.

2.   Filtered the crushed banana into a test tube.

3.   Added ice-cold ethanol to the test tube.

4.   The DNA was carefully removed from the ethanol using a glass rod.

Explain the purpose of steps 1 and 3. (3 marks, ★★★★)

....

....

....

....

Genetic inheritance

(1) **Match the genetics keywords to their meaning.** (4 marks, ★)

Homozygous	The alleles that are present in the genome.
	When two different alleles are present.
Heterozygous	
	An allele that is always expressed.
Genotype	
	When two copies of the same allele are present.
Phenotype	The characteristics that are expressed by those alleles.

(2) **A mouse with black fur and a mouse with brown fur had offspring. The black mouse has the genotype, Bb. Mice with brown fur always have the genotype, bb.**

a **Draw a Punnett square to show the genotypes.** (2 marks, ★★★)

b **What are the possible phenotypes of the offspring?** (1 mark, ★★★)

....

c **What is the ratio of the phenotypes?** (1 mark, ★★)

....

(3) **This pedigree chart shows the inheritance of colour blindness; circles represent females and squares represent males. Colour blindness is caused by a recessive sex-linked allele.**

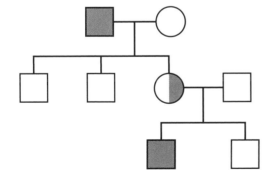

Explain why the daughter of the man with colour blindness is a carrier for colour blindness, but the sons are not. (2 marks, ★★★)

....

....

....

....

....

....

Inherited disorders

(1) **Cystic fibrosis is a disorder that affects the cell membranes of the lungs and pancreas. It is caused by having two copies of a recessive allele.**

a **Two parents both have one recessive allele for cystic fibrosis. Draw a Punnett square to show the genotypes of their children.** (2 marks, ★★★)

b **What is the probability that one of the children will have cystic fibrosis?** (1 mark, ★★★★)

....

NAILIT!

Remember: probability is represented as a number between 0 and 1, not as a percentage. You can also show probability as a fraction.

NAILIT!

You need to be able to draw a Punnett square accurately and interpret the results as a ratio.

You should also be able to make predictions about the results of a genetic cross.

c **People who know that they are a carrier for cystic fibrosis may have genetic counselling. What does this mean?** (2 marks, ★★)

....

....

....

....

(2) **Use the example of blood groups to explain the following terms:**

a **Multiple alleles** (2 marks, ★★)

....

....

b **Codominance** (2 marks, ★★★)

....

....

Variation

(1) **What are the two types of variation?** (2 marks, ★)

....

....

(2) a **What is a mutation?** (2 marks, ★★)

....

....

b **Explain how mutations give rise to new variations.** (3 marks, ★★★)

....

....

....

....

c **Explain the role of new variations in natural selection.** (3 marks, ★★★★)

....

....

....

....

....

NAILIT!

Explain how advantageous and disadvantageous changes in the phenotype spread or do not spread through a population.

DOIT!

Look back at the beginning of this topic. Which type of reproduction leads to genetic mixing and therefore genetic variation in the offspring?

(3) **What is the Human Genome Project and why is it important?** (3 marks, ★★★)

....

....

....

Evolution

(1) **Put the process of natural selection into the correct order.** (4 marks, ★)

    A   These individuals are more likely to have offspring.

    B   Some individuals have characteristics that are better suited to the environment.

    C   Individuals in a population have variation.

    D   The offspring will have characteristics that are better suited to the environment.

    E   These individuals are more likely to survive.

    ....B....   ....

(2) **What is evolution?** (2 marks, ★★)

....

....

....

....

(3) **a** **Half of a population of snails living on a rocky island have brown shells and half have yellow shells. The rocks on the island are brown. New predators come to the island and begin to prey on the snails. Describe how the number of snails with each colour shell could change due to natural selection.** (4 marks, ★★★)

....

....

....

....

....

    b **A scientist studying the snails wants to know if they are from the same species as the snails on a nearby island. How can they work this out?** (2 marks, ★★)

....

....

....

....

Selective breeding and genetic engineering

(1) Which of the following statements are true? Tick one box. (1 mark, ★★)

A   Selective breeding selects males and females with desired characteristics and breeds them together.

B   In selective breeding, all of the offspring will have the desired characteristics.

C   Selective breeding takes a small number of generations.

D   Selective breeding is also called artificial selection.

i	A and B only	
ii	A and D only	
iii	C and D only	
iv	B and C only	

(2) a A cat breeder wanted to create a breed of cats that did not cause allergies. On a separate piece of paper, explain how this could be done. (4 marks, ★★★)

b Suggest two other reasons that people might selectively breed cats. (2 marks, ★★)

i   ....

ii   ....

c Why is it important not to breed cats that are closely related to each other? (2 marks, ★★)

....

....

(3) a What is genetic engineering? (2 marks, ★★)

....

b Give an example of genetic engineering. (1 mark, ★)

....

(4) Golden Rice is a type of rice that has been genetically engineered to contain the genes that control beta carotene production.

a Suggest why genetic engineering was used instead of selective breeding. (2 marks, ★★★)

....

....

b Give one advantage and one disadvantage of producing Golden Rice. (2 marks, ★★)

....

....

Classification

(1) **Complete the table below.** (4 marks, ★★)

Group	Example
Kingdom	Animal
	Vertebrate
Class	
Order	Carnivore
Family	Felidae
	Panthera
	tigris

(2) **What features are used to group organisms into different classifications of species?**
(3 marks, ★★★)

....

....

....

(3) **Carl Linnaeus proposed a system for naming organisms in the 18th century.**

a **What did he call his system of naming organisms?** (1 mark, ★)

....

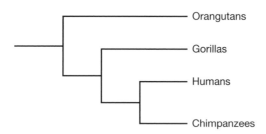

Orangutans

Gorillas

Humans

Chimpanzees

NAILIT!

You may be asked to interpret an evolutionary tree diagram like this which shows how organisms are related.

b **Using the evolutionary tree above, explain which two species are the most closely related?** (2 marks, ★★★★)

....

....

Ecology

(1) Match the communities keywords with their meaning. (4 marks, ★)

Keyword	Meaning
Population	The environment in which a species normally lives.
Habitat	A group of populations living and interacting with each other in the same area.
Community	A community and its abiotic environment.
Ecosystem	A group of organisms of the same species living in the same area at the same time.

(2) Organisms of different species compete with each other for resources.

a Give **two** examples of resources that species compete for. (2 marks, ★)

i ....

ii ....

b What is this type of competition called? (1 mark, ★)

....

(3) a What is interdependence? (3 marks, ★★)

....

....

....

b Ladybirds eat aphids in an apple tree. The apple tree begins to wither and several branches die. Describe and explain what will happen to the number of ladybirds and aphids. (2 marks, ★★★)

....

....

....

Abiotic and biotic factors

(1) **Which of the following are biotic factors? Tick one box.** (1 mark, ★)

A	Temperature
B	Competition between species
C	Light intensity
D	Predators

i	A and C only
ii	B and D only
iii	A and B only
iv	C and D only

(2) **A researcher measured the number of sea campion plants growing on a coastal cliff edge, and the number growing 10 m inland. The results are shown in the table below.**

	Number of sea campion plants			Mean number of sea campion plants
	1	2	3	
On cliff edge	8	12	10	
10 m inland	21	22	20	

a **Complete the table above by calculating the mean number of sea campion plants in each location.** (2 marks, ★★)

b **Suggest why there are more sea campion plants 10 m inland than on the cliff edge.** (2 marks, ★★)

....

....

(3) **The graph below shows the population sizes of snowshoe hares and lynx in different years. Describe and explain the pattern of the graph.** (4 marks, ★★★★)

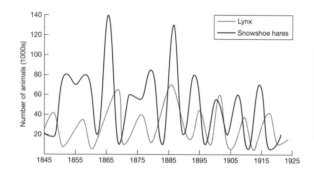

NAILIT!

You need to be able to read and interpret information from charts, graphs and tables for this topic.

....

....

....

....

....

....

Adaptations

(1) **Adaptations enable species to survive in the condition in which they normally live. What are the different types of adaptation?** (6 marks, ★★★★)

....

....

....

....

....

....

(2) **The photo below shows a cactus plant.**

NAILIT!

Give the name of the type of adaption and include a description for each.

Describe and explain two adaptations visible in the photo which allow the cactus to live in a desert. (4 marks, ★★★)

....

....

....

....

DOIT!

Name the type of organism that lives in extreme environments.

Food chains

1 **The diagram below shows a food chain.**

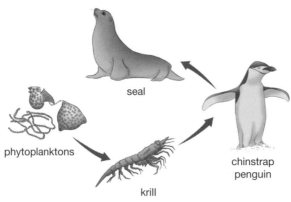

seal

phytoplanktons

krill

chinstrap
penguin

a **Which organism is the producer?** (1 mark, ★)

....

b **Which organism is the tertiary consumer?** (1 mark, ★)

....

c **Where do the phytoplankton get their energy from?** (2 marks, ★)

....

....

d **Explain what would happen to the other organisms in the food chain if the numbers of krill decreased.** (3 marks, ★★★)

....

....

....

DO IT!

Mark the student's answer below using the mark scheme, and suggest how to improve the answer.

Explain why there are usually only a maximum of five or six trophic levels in a food chain. (3 marks, ★★★)

Energy is lost from each stage of the food chain. There is not enough energy at the top of the food chain.

MARK SCHEME
Energy is lost from every trophic level (1) as heat from respiration. (1) There is not enough energy at the top of the food chain for another trophic level. (1)

Number of marks for student's answer: ....

How to improve the answer: ....

....

Measuring species

(1) **A group of students were estimating the number of buttercups in a 50 m by 20 m field. They used 1 m by 1 m quadrats.**

  a **What is the best method of using the quadrats?** (1 mark, ★)

      A   Put several quadrats down where there are a lot of buttercups.

      B   Put several quadrats down randomly on the field.

      C   Place the quadrats in a line from one end of the field to the other.

      Method = ...

  b **Explain why you have chosen this method.** (2 marks, ★★★)

      ....

      ....

  c **The students used 10 quadrats. The number of buttercups in each quadrat are shown in the table below.**

Quadrat number	1	2	3	4	5	6	7	8	9	10	Mean
Number of buttercups	3	4	0	1	2	4	1	1	3	5	

      i **Calculate the mean number of buttercups and add it to the table.** (1 mark, ★★)

      ii **Use the mean to estimate the number of buttercups in the whole field.** (3 marks, ★★★)

        ....

        ....

(2) **A group of researchers wanted to estimate the population of snails in a woodland area.**

  a **Describe and explain a good method of capturing the snails.** (2 marks, ★★)

      ....

  b **The number of snails can be estimated using the 'capture, release, recapture' method. Suggest a good way of marking the snails.** (1 mark, ★)

      ....

  c **Explain why the method of marking should not harm the snails in any way.** (2 marks, ★★)

      ....

  d **The number of snails caught the first time was 10. The number of snails caught the second time was 16, and two of them were marked. Estimate the number of snails in the population.** (2 marks, ★★★)

      ....

> **NAILIT!**
>
> To estimate the number of snails, multiply the number of snails caught each time and divide by the number that were marked.

  e **What assumptions about the population must be made in order to estimate the size of the population?** (3 marks, ★★★)

      ....

      ....

The carbon cycle, nitrogen cycle and water cycle

(1) Describe how water moves through the water cycle. (4 marks, ★★)

....

....

....

....

(2) a What is the process by which carbon dioxide is absorbed by plants? (1 mark, ★)

....

b Name two processes that release carbon dioxide into the atmosphere. (2 marks, ★)

....

....

c Describe how the carbon in dead and decaying organisms is released back into the atmosphere. (2 marks, ★★)

....

....

(3) Explain why the amount of carbon dioxide in the atmosphere is greater now than it was 200 years ago. (4 marks, ★★★)

NAILIT!
Think about human activities that increase the amount or prevent the uptake of carbon dioxide from the atmosphere.

....

....

....

....

(4) A farmer wanted to add more nitrogen to the soil in a field.

a Describe two ways in which the farmer could do this. (2 marks, ★★★)

....

....

b Explain how the nitrogen is lost from the field. (3 marks, ★★★★)

....

....

....

Biodiversity

1) **What is biodiversity?** (1 mark, ★★)

....

2) **Pollution affects biodiversity in several different ways. Match the types of pollution to their source.** (3 marks, ★)

Type of pollution	Source of the pollution
Land pollution	Smoke, acidic gases from vehicle exhausts or power stations.
Air pollution	Decomposition of rubbish and from chemicals.
Water pollution	Sewage, fertiliser leeching off the fields, chemicals.

3) **On a separate piece of paper, describe and explain how human activity leads to decreased biodiversity.**
(5 marks, ★★★★)

4) **Suggest how biodiversity can be increased.**
(3 marks, ★★★)

> **NAILIT!**
>
> All human activities affect biodiversity (whether in a positive or negative way). You need to know how land use, waste management, global warming and our use of resources affects biodiversity.

....

....

....

5) **Name two positive human interactions that impact biodiversity.** (2 marks, ★★)

....

....

> **NAILIT!**
>
> Include protecting the habitat as well as protecting the animals.

6) **Conservation areas are one way of reducing the negative effects of humans on ecosystems. Explain how they increase the biodiversity of the area.** (4 marks, ★★★★)

....

....

....

....

....

Global warming

(1) **What is global warming?** (2 marks, ★★)

....

....

(2) **Describe how greenhouses gases in the atmosphere cause global warming.** (3 marks, ★★★)

....

....

....

(3) **Describe and explain the biological consequences of global warming.** (5 marks, ★★★★)

....

....

....

....

....

....

....

....

STRETCH IT!

Global environmental policies can help to reduce the human impact on the environment. For example, the hole in the ozone layer is getting smaller because CFC gases have been banned since 1996.

What environmental policies could reduce the effect of global warming? Find out about the Paris Climate Agreement. Which aspects of this agreement relate to global warming?

NAILIT!

Think about how climate change and rising sea levels will affect animals.

Atomic structure and the periodic table

Atoms, elements and compounds

1 **This question is about atoms, elements and compounds.**

  a **Draw one line from each word to its correct description.** (4 marks, ★★)

Atom	A substance that contains two or more elements chemically combined.
Element	A substance that contains two or more elements not chemically combined.
Compound	A substance made of only one type of atom.
Mixture	The smallest part of an element that can exist.

  b **Which of the following substances are elements? Tick two boxes.** (2 marks, ★★)

Br_2	☐
Na_2CO_3	☐
Ar	☐
H_2O	☐

DO IT!

Look through your Revision Guide for different formulae, and then work out the numbers of each type of element present. This will also help to familiarise you with the different substances you need to know.

  c **Which of the following represents a compound? Tick one box.** (1 mark, ★★)

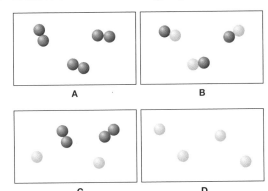

A

B

C

D

A	☐
B	☐
C	☐
D	☐

  d **How many atoms are there in a molecule of magnesium nitrate, $Mg(NO_3)_2$?** (1 mark, ★★★)

    ....

  e **How many different elements are there in a molecule of sulfuric acid, H_2SO_4?**
  (1 mark, ★★★)

    ....

2 **Use your periodic table to help you to answer the following questions.**

  a **Name two elements that are found in group 7.** (2 marks, ★)

    ....

  b **Give the symbols of two elements that are found in group 1.** (2 marks, ★) ....

Mixtures and compounds

1. **Place each substance under the correct heading in the table below.** (3 marks, ★)

| air | salty water | oxygen |
| hydrogen | water | sodium hydroxide |

Element	Compound	Mixture

2. **A student prepares a soluble salt by reacting copper(II) oxide with hydrochloric acid. He ends up with a solution of copper(II) chloride. Describe how a dry sample of copper(II) chloride could be obtained from this mixture.** (2 marks, ★★)

....

....

3. **A mixture of salt and water can be separated by simple distillation.**

   a **Name the piece of apparatus labelled A.**
   (1 mark, ★)

   ....

   b **Explain how a sample of pure water can be collected using this apparatus.**
   (3 marks, ★★★)

   ....

   ....

   ....

   ....

   ....

   ....

4. **Rock salt is a naturally occurring mineral that consists of a mixture of sodium chloride and sand. Sodium chloride is soluble in water and sand is insoluble in water. Describe how both the sodium chloride and sand could be separately extracted from the rock salt.**
   (4 marks, ★★★)

   ....

   ....

   ....

   ....

   ....

   ....

Pure substances and formulations

(1) **Explain what is meant by the term pure.**
(1 mark, ★)

....

....

(2) **Milk is sometimes described as pure.**

> **MATHS SKILLS**
>
> The formulae you will need for formulation calculations are:
>
> $$\text{Percentage} = \frac{\text{mass of component}}{\text{total mass}} \times 100\%$$
>
> $$\text{Number of moles} = \frac{\text{mass}}{M_r}$$

  a **Explain why milk is not scientifically pure.** (2 marks, ★★)

....

  b **Outline how you could show this in an experiment.** (3 marks, ★★★)

....

....

(3) **Pure aspirin melts at 136°C. A sample of an aspirin tablet starts to melt at 125°C. What does this tell you about the aspirin tablet?** (1 mark, ★★★)

....

(4) **A paracetamol tablet has a mass of 2g. It contains 500mg of paracetamol ($C_8H_9NO_2$), 1.25g of starch ($C_6H_{10}O_5$) a bulking agent, and 0.25g of magnesium stearate ($Mg(C_{18}H_{35}O_2)_2$) a lubricant to prevent the tablet sticking to the packaging.**

  a **Explain why the paracetamol tablet is an example of a formulation.** (1 mark, ★)

....

  b **Calculate the percentage composition of paracetamol in the tablet, in terms of mass.**
(2 marks, ★★★)

....

  c **Calculate the number of moles of each compound in the tablet.** (6 marks, ★★★★)

    i **Paracetamol**

....

    ii **Starch**

....

    iii **Magnesium stearate**

....

  d **On a separate piece of paper, calculate the percentage composition of paracetamol in the tablet, in terms of moles.** (2 marks, ★★★★)

Chromatography

① **Tick two statements that are correct.** (2 marks, ★)

Chromatography is a technique that can be used to separate mixtures into their components.	
Chromatography works because different compounds have different levels of attraction for the paper and the solvent.	
Chromatography involves three phases – a mobile phase, a stationary phase and a dynamic phase.	
Chromatography is a technique that can be used to create mixtures from their components.	
Chromatography gives you information about the quantity of the components in a mixture.	

NAILIT!

Remember that water isn't the only solvent that can be used for the mobile phase. Often, scientists will try different solvents until there is a good separation between the spots. Commonly used solvents include: ethanol, dichloromethane and ethyl ethanoate.

② **A student wanted to identify the inks used in a black pen. She set up the equipment as shown below.**

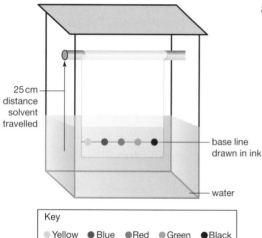

25 cm distance solvent travelled

base line drawn in ink

water

Key
Yellow ● Blue ● Red ● Green ● Black

a Suggest two errors in the way the student has set up the experiment. Explain the problems each of these errors would cause. (4 marks, ★★)

....

....

....

....

....

b The R$_f$ value for the yellow ink is 0.88. The R$_f$ value for the green ink is 0.84. Dot C has travelled 22 cm. Calculate the R$_f$ of dot C and identify its colour. (3 marks, ★★★)

....

....

MATHSKILLS

In the exam, you may need to rearrange the formula:

$$R_f = \frac{\text{Distance moved by spot}}{\text{distance moved by solvent}}$$

Distance moved by the spot = R$_f$ × distance moved by the solvent

Distance moved by the solvent = R$_f$ × distance moved by the spot

NAILIT!

Sometimes, solutes can have an elongated (stretched) spot, which can make it difficult to identify unknown substances. One of the skills involved choosing a mobile phase is choosing one which gives good, clear results for the substances you're looking at.

Scientific models of the atom

(1) **How did scientists describe the structure of the atom before electrons were discovered?**
(2 marks, ★★)

....

....

(2) **The plum pudding model was then suggested after the discovery of the electron. The image to the right shows a diagram of this model. Describe what the plum pudding model shows.**
(2 marks, ★★)

....

....

....

(3) **Further experiments by Rutherford tested the plum pudding model by firing alpha particles at gold foil. Instead of them all passing through the foil, some of them were deflected.**

a **What is the charge on an alpha particle?** (1 mark, ★)

....

b **Why did most of them pass through the gold foil?** (1 mark, ★★)

....

c **Why were some of the alpha particles deflected?** (1 mark, ★★)

....

d **What was the overall conclusion from this experiment?** (2 marks, ★★★)

....

....

e **Which sub-atomic particle did Chadwick prove existed in the nucleus?** (1 mark, ★★)

....

NAILIT!

The main fact that you need to know about the development of the atomic model is how Rutherford's scattering experiment changed scientists' ideas about the plum pudding model.

Atomic structure, isotopes and relative atomic mass

(1) **Complete the table of the relative charges and masses of the sub-atomic particles.** (3 marks, ★★)

Sub-atomic particle	Relative charge	Relative mass
	+1	
		Very small
Neutron		

NAILIT!

Learn the names of the sub-atomic particles, along with their relative masses and charges; this is often assessed in exam questions.

(2) **Explain why the overall charge of a magnesium atom is neutral.** (2 marks, ★★)

....

....

(3) **Element Z has a mass number of 184 and an atomic number of 74.**

a **Calculate the number of protons, electrons and neutrons in an atom of Z.** (2 marks, ★★)

....

....

DOIT!

You could be asked questions about any element in the periodic table. Pick random elements and calculate the number of protons, electrons and neutrons in each. This will also help to familiarise you with the periodic table.

b **Use the periodic table to identify the name of element Z.** (1 mark, ★★)

....

(4) **Use the words in the box below to complete the following passage about isotopes. You will not need to use all of the words, and some words may be used more than once.**

Isotopes of an element have the same .... number but a different .... number. This means that atoms of the same element have the same number of .... but different numbers of .... Two isotopes of carbon are C-12 and C-13. Both of these isotopes have .... protons; however, C-12 has .... neutrons and C-13 has .... neutrons. (3 marks, ★★)

| 12 | atomic | 7 | neutrons | electrons | 6 | mass | 13 | protons |

(5) **There are two naturally occurring isotopes of bromine, Br-79 and Br-81.**

Describe the similarities and differences between these two isotopes, referring to the number of sub-atomic particles in your answer. (3 marks, ★★★★)

....

....

....

....

(6) **The relative atomic mass of chlorine is 35.5. Chlorine exists as two isotopes, one of which is Cl-35. This makes up 75% of naturally occurring chlorine. Use this information to calculate the mass number of the other isotope of chlorine.** (3 marks, ★★★★★)

....

....

The development of the periodic table and the noble gases

1 Use your periodic table to answer the following questions. (4 marks, ★★)

a Carbon is in group .... of the periodic table.

b Potassium is in period .... of the periodic table.

c Why are phosphorous and nitrogen placed in the same group?

....

d Why are sulfur and silicon placed in the same period?

....

DO IT!

Early versions of the periodic table show the elements that had been discovered placed in order of increasing atomic weight. Why?

2 Mendeleev decided to arrange the elements according to their properties. The table below shows an early version of his periodic table.

Row	Group I	Group II	Group III	Group IV	Group V	Group VI	Group VII	Group VIII
1	H							
2	Li	Be	B	C	N	O	F	
3	Na	Mg	Al	Si	P	S	Cl	
4	K	Ca		Ti	V	Cr	Mn	Fe, Co, Ni, Cu

a What is the correct name for the horizontal rows in the periodic table? (1 mark, ★)

....

b Why did Mendeleev leave gaps? (1 mark, ★★)

....

c How are the elements arranged in the modern version of the periodic table? (1 mark, ★★)

....

d Suggest why it took a long time for the noble gases to be discovered. (1 mark, ★★)

....

3 The noble gases are found in group 0 of the periodic table, their boiling points are shown in the table below.

a What is the trend in boiling points? (1 mark, ★★)

....

b Predict the boiling point of krypton. (1 mark, ★★)

....

Noble gas	Boiling point/°C
He	−269
Ne	−246
Ar	−186
Kr	
Xe	−108
Rn	−62

Electronic structure

① **The diagram represents an element from the periodic table.**

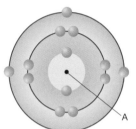

DO IT!

You are expected to be able to show the electronic structures of the first 20 elements (hydrogen up to calcium) by drawing out the atoms, or using the electronic configuration. Practise these so you are familiar with them.

NAIL IT!

Make sure you remember how many electrons can fit in each shell or energy level – up to 2 in the first, up to 8 in the second and up to 8 in the third.

a **What is the name of the part labelled A?** (1 mark, ★★)

....

b **What are the names of the sub-atomic particles found in A?** (2 marks, ★★)

....

....

The mass number of this element is 27.

c **Name the element represented by this diagram.** (1 mark, ★★)

....

d **How many neutrons does this element have?** (1 mark, ★★)

....

② **The electronic structures of six elements, A, B, C, D, E and F, are shown below.**

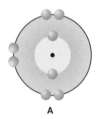

2,8,8,1

B

A

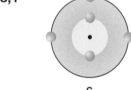

2,8

D

C

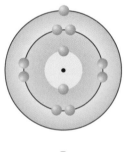

E

F

Use the correct letter or letters to answer each question.

a **Which atom represents an element in group 3?** (1 mark, ★)

b **Which element has the symbol O?** (1 mark, ★★)

c **Which two elements are in the same group?** (2 marks, ★★)

d **Which two elements are in period 4?** (2 marks, ★★)

e **Which element is a noble gas?** (1 mark, ★★)

f **Which element forms a 2⁻ ion?** (1 mark, ★★★)

Metals and non-metals

1 **Match up these words with their correct meanings.** (3 marks, ★)

Malleable	Makes a ringing sound when hit
Ductile	Can be hammered into shape
Sonorous	Can be drawn into wires

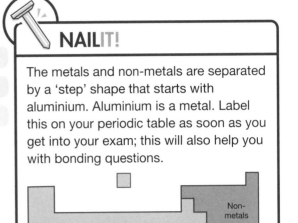

NAILIT!

The metals and non-metals are separated by a 'step' shape that starts with aluminium. Aluminium is a metal. Label this on your periodic table as soon as you get into your exam; this will also help you with bonding questions.

2 **Some elements in the periodic table are highlighted below.**

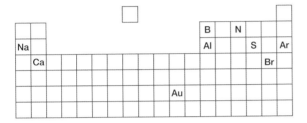

Choose the correct element to answer each question. (1 mark each)

a **Which element is in group 1?** (★) ....

b **Which element is used in jewellery?** (★) ....

c **Which element has a mass number of 32?** (★★) ....

d **Which element is a noble gas?** ....

e **Which element is a non-metal in group 3?** (★★★) ....

f **Which element is a non-metal in period 4?** (★★★) ....

g **Which element forms a 2$^+$ ion?** (★★★) ....

h **Which element forms a 3$^-$ ion?** (★★★★) ....

3 **Barium is a reactive element found in group 2 of the periodic table.**

a **Is barium a metal or a non-metal?** (1 mark, ★)

....

b **How many electrons does barium have in its outer shell?** (1 mark, ★)

....

c **Which two properties would you expect barium to have? Circle the correct answer.** (2 marks, ★★)

| low melting point | good electrical conductor | brittle | shiny |

Group 1 – the alkali metals

1. **Explain, using electron configuration, why all the group 1 metals have similar chemical properties.** (1 mark, ★★)

   ....

   ....

2. **Circle which group 1 metal is represented by the symbol K.** (1 mark, ★)

   | Lithium | Sodium | Potassium | Krypton |

3. **Circle which is the most reactive group 1 metal.** (1 mark, ★)

   | Sodium | Caesium | Lithium | Francium |

4. **The diagram shows the electronic structure of a group 1 metal.** (1 mark, ★★★)

   What is the symbol for this metal?

   | N | K | Na | Li |

   Symbol: ....

5. **A student observes the reaction of lithium with water.**

   State three observations the student would see during the reaction. (3 marks, ★★★)

   ....

   ....

   ....

6. **Potassium reacts with water in a similar way to lithium.**

   State two observations that would be different. (2 marks, ★★★)

   ....

   ....

   ....

Group 7 – the halogens

(1) **Circle the chemical symbol for fluorine.** (1 mark, ★)

Fl	Fr	F	Fe

(2) **Circle the most reactive halogen.** (1 mark, ★)

Bromine	Iodine	Chlorine	Fluorine

(3) **Circle the correct formula for a molecule of bromine.** (1 mark, ★★★)

Be	Br	B_2	Br_2

(4) **Circle which halogen has the electronic configuration 2,8,7.** (1 mark, ★★★)

Chlorine	Bromine	Fluorine	Iodine

NAILIT!

The halogens can react with other non-metals to form **covalent** substances. They can also react with metals to form **ionic** substances called halide (1-) ions.

When the halogens react, they change the ending of their name from **ine** to **ide**. Practise writing simple word equations to get used to this. For example:

sodium + chlorine → sodium chloride

(5) **A student watches the reaction between lithium and chlorine, and lithium and iodine.**

a **Which would be the most vigorous reaction? Explain why.** (1 mark, ★★)

....

b **Write a word equation for the reaction between lithium and chlorine.** (1 mark, ★★)

....

c **Write a balanced chemical equation for the reaction between lithium and iodine.**
(2 marks, ★★★★)

....

(6) **The reactivity of chlorine, bromine and iodine can be shown by carrying out reactions between these halogens and aqueous solutions of their salts, some of these reactions are shown below.**

	Chlorine	Bromine	Iodine
Potassium chloride	X	No reaction	
Potassium bromide	Orange solution formed	X	No reaction
Potassium iodide			X

a **Complete the table, stating any colour change that would take place.** (3 marks, ★★)

b **Write a word equation for the reaction between chlorine and potassium bromide.** (1 mark, ★★)

....

c **On a separate piece of paper, suggest an experiment that you could carry out to prove that iodine is more reactive than astatine. State what you would observe and write down a chemical equation and an ionic equation for this reaction.** (4 marks, ★★★★★)

Bonding and structure

(1) **Complete the diagram below by choosing the correct words which represent these changes of state.** (4 marks, ★)

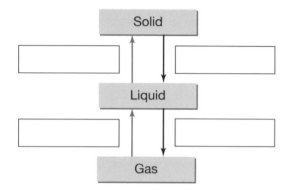

Condensing

Dissolving

Distillation

Freezing

Subliming

Boiling

Melting

NAILIT!

The **boiling point** is the temperature at which a liquid boils and turns into a gas, *or* condenses from a gas to a liquid.

The **melting point** is the temperature at which a solid melts, *or* when a liquid freezes and turns into a solid.

(2) **Water freezes at 0°C and turns into ice. It boils at 100°C and turns into water vapour.**
(2 marks, ★★)

a **What is the melting point of water?** ....

b **At what temperature will water vapour condense back into a liquid?** ....

(3) **Mercury, Hg, melts at –39°C and boils at 357°C. Use this information to predict the state of mercury at the following temperatures.** (3 marks, ★★★)

a **500°C** .... b **–40°C** ....

c **Room temperature, 25°C** ....

(4) **Air consists of a mixture of several different gases, some of which are shown in the table below.**

Gas	Boiling point/°C
Nitrogen	–196
Oxygen	–183
Argon	–186

The gases can be separated by fractional distillation; this involves cooling the air down and removing each gas as it condenses. (4 marks, ★★★)

a **Which gas has the highest boiling point?** ....

b **Which gas has the lowest boiling point?** ....

c **Which gas would condense first when air is cooled?** ....

d **Which gas has the strongest forces between its particles?** ....

Ions and ionic bonding

(1) **Complete the following passage using the words below. Some words may be used more than once.**

Magnesium is a metal which is found in group .... of the periodic table. This means it has .... electrons in its outer shell. When it reacts, it loses .... electrons and forms an ion with a .... charge. Fluorine is a non-metal which is found in group .... of the periodic table. When it reacts, it .... 1 electron to form an ion with a .... charge. When magnesium reacts with fluorine, it forms magnesium fluoride which has the formula .... (8 marks, ★★)

MgF	1	2	3	gains	Mg_2F	6
7	loses	MgF_2	1^-	2^-	1^+	2^+

NAILIT!

Use the periodic table when you tackle any questions about bonding. First of all, make sure you know where the metals and non-metals are found; this will help you to determine the **type** of bonding. Secondly, remember that the group number tells you **how many electrons** are found in the outer shell.

(2) **Match the compound to its correct formula.** (4 marks, ★★)

Potassium chloride

Magnesium oxide

Magnesium chloride

Aluminium fluoride

K_2Cl

MgO_2

$MgCl_2$

Al_3F

KCl

AlF_3

MgO

KCl_2

DOIT!

Practise writing out formulae by using the group numbers of the elements to find out the charge on the ions formed. Remember, **metals** form **positive ions (cations)** and **non-metals** form **negative ions (anions)**. Then, work out the number of each ion needed to make the charges add up to zero.

For example, potassium is in group 1 so forms an ion with a 1^+ charge, K^+.

Oxygen is in group 6 so forms an ion with a 2^- charge, O^{2-}.

K^+ $\qquad$ O^{2-}

There are 2 negative charges, but only 1 positive charge. Therefore, 2 positive charges are needed to cancel out the 2 negative charges which means we need to multiply the K^+ by 2.

$2 \times K^+$ $\qquad$ O^{2-}

Overall, the formula is K_2O.

(3) **Draw dot-and-cross diagrams (outer electrons only) to show the formation of the ionic compounds below. For each diagram, work out the formula of the compound formed.**

a **Lithium chloride** (3 marks, ★★)

b **Barium bromide** (3 marks, ★★★)

The structure and properties of ionic compounds

① **Tick three boxes that describe the correct properties of ionic compounds.** (3 marks, ★★)

High melting points	
Made of molecules	
Conduct electricity when solid	
Conduct electricity when molten or in solution	
Made of non-metals bonded together	
Made of ions	

② **From the diagrams below, give one substance A, B or C that:**

a **represents sodium chloride, NaCl.** (1 mark, ★) ....

b **represents magnesium chloride, MgCl$_2$.** (1 mark, ★★) ....

c **represents sodium oxide.** (1 mark, ★★★) ....

A   B   C

> **NAILIT!**
>
> Remember, ionic compounds only conduct electricity when molten or dissolved in water, because the ions are free to move, not the electrons. Make sure you use the correct charge carrier.

③ **Complete the following passage about the structure of ionic compounds, choosing the correct words from the box below.** (3 marks, ★★)

Ionic bonds are formed when .... react with .... Atoms either lose or gain

.... to become positive or negative particles called ions. The ions are held together in a

giant ionic .... by strong .... forces of attraction acting in all ....

magnetic	protons	metals	areas	electrostatic	molecules
directions	neutrons	lattice	non-metals	electrons	

④ **Potassium iodide is a substance that is often added to table salt in countries where people have little iodine in their diets. A deficiency of iodine can cause many long-term health problems but is also easily preventable. Use your ideas about structure and bonding to make predictions about the properties of potassium iodide.** (6 marks, ★★★★)

....

....

....

....

....

....

Covalent bonds and simple molecules

(1) **Which of the following substances are covalent? Tick the correct answers.** (2 marks, ★★)

NaCl	
CaO	
NH$_3$	
Potassium nitrate	
Water	

NAILIT!

Remember, covalent substances are only made from non-metals. Make sure you know where the non-metals are found in the periodic table!

(2) **The compounds drawn below all have covalent bonds.**

a **Complete the dot-and-cross diagrams below to show the covalent bonding in each molecule.** (6 marks, ★★)

Hydrogen

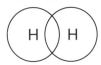

Methane

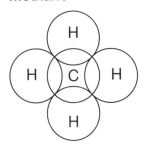

b **Write out the formula of each substance.** (2 marks, ★★)

Hydrogren ....

Methane ....

(3) a **Draw a dot-and-cross diagram to show the bonding in a molecule of nitrogen, N$_2$.**
(2 marks, ★★★★)

b **What type of covalent bond does it have?** (1 mark, ★★★★) ....

(4) a **Ethene is a hydrocarbon with the formula C$_2$H$_4$. Draw a dot-and-cross diagram to show its bonding.** (2 marks, ★★★★★)

b **What type of covalent bonds does it have?** (2 marks, ★★★★) ....

85

Diamond, graphite and graphene

① **The diagram below shows three giant covalent substances. Choose the correct letter to answer each question.** (2 marks, ★★)

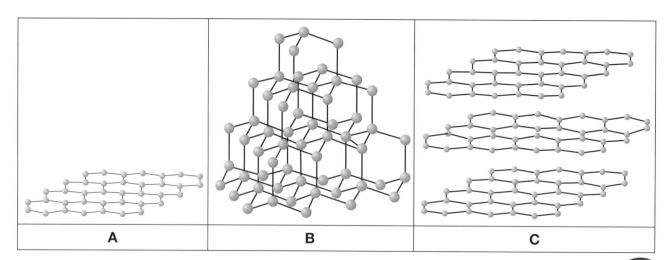

| A | B | C |

a **Which substance is graphene?** ....

b **Which substance has weak intermolecular forces?** ....

NAILIT!

The properties of diamond and graphite are often assessed in exams.

② **This question is about the properties of diamond and graphite.**

a **Use your knowledge about their structure and bonding to explain why diamond and graphite both have high melting points.** (2 marks, ★★★)

....

....

b **Explain why diamond is hard.** (2 marks, ★★★)

....

....

c **Although graphite is a non-metal, like metals it conducts electricity. Explain what feature both graphite and metals have that enable them to conduct electricity.** (1 mark, ★★★)

....

③ **Silicon dioxide (SiO_2) is the main component of sand. It has a giant covalent structure, shown below.**

a **SiO_2 does *not* conduct electricity. Suggest why.** (1 mark, ★★★)

....

b **Predict two further properties of SiO_2.** (2 marks, ★★★)

....

....

Fullerenes and polymers

1. **The diagram below shows four different substances made from carbon. Choose the correct letter to answer each question.** (4 marks, ★★)

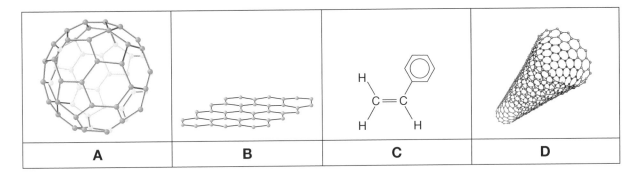

| A | B | C | D |

a **Which substance has a very high length to diameter ratio?** ....

b **Which substance could be used to make a polymer?** ....

c **Which substance is buckminsterfullerene?** ....

d **Which substance is made from a single layer of graphite?** ....

2. **The structures of fullerenes and nanotubes are unique, which gives them many uses. Explain how their structure makes them suitable for the following:**

a **Fullerenes can be used to deliver drugs to targeted areas inside the body.** (1 mark, ★★★)

....

b **Nanotubes make excellent catalysts.** (1 mark, ★★★)

....

3. **Polyethene is a polymer made from many ethene molecules joined together in a long chain.**

a **Which type of bonds are found in polymers?** (1 mark, ★)

....

The table below shows some of the properties of ethene and polyethene.

	Ethene	Polyethene
Melting point/°C	−169	Approximately 120
Size of molecules	Small	Large
State at room temperature	Gas	Solid

b **Use this information to explain why ethene is a gas at room temperature yet polyethene is a solid.** (3 marks, ★★★)

....

....

....

Giant metallic structures and alloys

DOIT!

The properties of metals depend on their structure and bonding. Practise drawing *labelled* diagrams to represent metallic bonding. This will help you to gain marks in exam questions.

NAILIT!

The difference in the properties between pure metals and alloys is all down to the *sizes* of the atoms or metal ions, and the *distortion* of the regular layers of atoms.

1. **Use the words in the box below to complete the following passage about metals. You will not need to use all of the words.** (4 marks, ★★)

Metals are .... structures.

The particles are arranged in ....

The outer shell electrons become detached from the rest of the atom and are said to be .... This means they are free to move throughout the whole metal.

Metallic bonding is strong because of the .... attraction between the positive metal ions and the electrons.

| layers | magnetic | giant | electrostatic | small | delocalised |

2. **Explain, with the aid of a labelled diagram, why metals are good electrical conductors.** (4 marks, ★★★★)

....

....

....

....

3. **Iron is the fourth most abundant element found in the Earth's crust, and has many different uses.**

   a **The melting point of pure iron is 1538°C. Explain this in terms of metallic bonding.** (2 marks, ★★)

   ....

   ....

   Pure iron is relatively soft, so is often mixed with other elements to form alloys. Steel is made when small amounts of carbon are added to iron.

   b **Explain why steel is harder than pure iron.** (2 marks, ★★★)

   ....

   ....

Quantitative chemistry

Conservation of mass and balancing equations

1. **Magnesium burns in oxygen to produce magnesium oxide.**

   a **Write a word equation for this reaction.** (2 marks, ★)

   .... → ....

   b **Identify the reactants and products in this reaction.** (2 marks, ★)

Reactants	Products

   The reaction can also be written in a balanced equation as:

   $2Mg + O_2 \rightarrow 2MgO$

   c **If 12g of magnesium reacts with 8g of oxygen, what is the mass of MgO product?** (2 marks, ★)

   ....

NAILIT!

Don't forget that in all chemical reactions, the mass before and after the reaction is the same.

Think of it as like making a cake – the amount of flour, sugar, butter and eggs doesn't change after you bake them – they just react and turn into something new!

WORKIT!

When sodium reacts with water it produces sodium hydroxide and hydrogen gas. Balance the equation.

Step 1 Write a word equation for the reaction and identify the reactants and products.

Reactants   Products

sodium   +   water   →   sodium hydroxide   +   hydrogen

Step 2 Write a chemical equation for the reaction.

Na + H_2O → $NaOH$ + H_2

Step 3 Count the number of atoms before and after the reaction.

$Na = 1$ → $Na = 1$

$O = 1$ $O = 1$

$H = 2$ $H = 3$

> We can see here that we end up with more hydrogen atoms than we started with – that's impossible!

Continued

WORKIT!

Step 4 Balance the equation by writing the number in front of the reactants or products, keeping count of the atoms as you go.

$$2Na \quad + \quad 2H_2O \quad \rightarrow \quad 2NaOH \quad + \quad H_2$$

$Na = 2$ $\rightarrow$ $Na = 2$

$O = 2$ $O = 2$

$H = 4$ $H = 4$

Step 5 Write the balanced equation.

$$2Na \quad + \quad 2H_2O \quad \rightarrow \quad 2NaOH \quad + \quad H_2$$

Balancing and interpreting equations are really important skills that will be useful elsewhere in the exam, so spend some extra time making sure you're happy with them before moving on.

---

(2) **The production of ammonia by reacting nitrogen and hydrogen is shown in the unbalanced equation below:** (4 marks, ★★★)

$$N_2(g) + H_2(g) \rightarrow NH_3(g)$$

a **Write a word equation for the reaction.**

....

b **Identify the number of atoms before and after the reaction in the unbalanced equation.**

	Reactants	Products
N		
H		

c **Write a balanced equation for this reaction.**

....

(3) **Write a balanced equation for the reaction of iron oxide (Fe_2O_3) with carbon monoxide to produce iron and carbon dioxide.** (2 marks, ★★★★)

....

NAILIT!

Double check that you've balanced the equation correctly – count the number of atoms again! Remember, the number of atoms in the reactants and the products should be the same – if they aren't, it isn't balanced.

Relative formula masses

① **Match the following terms to their definition.** (2 marks, ★★)

The relative atomic mass (symbol = A_r)	of a compound is calculated by adding up all the relative atomic masses of all the atoms present in the formula of the compound.
The relative formula mass (symbol = M_r)	of an element is the weighted average mass of its naturally occurring isotopes.
In equations, the relative formula masses of diatomic molecules, such as oxygen, bromine and nitrogen,	means that in a chemical reaction the sum of the relative formula masses of the reactants is equal to the sum of the relative formula masses of the products.
The law of mass conservation	are twice their relative atomic masses.

② **Find the A_r for the following elements.** (3 marks, ★★)

Carbon	Oxygen	Chlorine	Iron
12			

③ **A neutralisation reaction of sodium hydroxide and sulfuric acid is shown in the balanced equation:**

$2NaOH + H_2SO_4 \rightarrow Na_2SO_4 + 2H_2O$

a **Find the M_r for each of the reactants and products.** (4 marks, ★★)

NaOH	H_2SO_4	Na_2SO_4	H_2O

b **Calculate how much water is formed when 10 g of sulfuric acid reacts with excess sodium hydroxide.** (2 marks, ★★★★)

....

....

c **Calculate how much sodium hydroxide is needed to make 5 g of sodium sulfate.** (2 marks, ★★★★)

....

....

d **Suggest one reason why it is important for a company that produces sodium sulfate to know the mass of reactants.** (1 mark, ★★★★)

....

NAILIT!

- Remember that some elements are diatomic. HONClBrIF is one way to help you remember them.

- You will be given a periodic table in the exam – make sure you know which numbers refer to the relative atomic mass.

The mole and reacting masses

① **Calculate the number of moles for the following.** (4 marks, ★★)

a 2.3g of sodium ....

....

b 1.6g of CH_4 ....

....

c 0.2g of SO_2 ....

....

d 2.2g of CO_2 ....

....

② **Calculate the mass of the following.** (4 marks, ★★)

a 1.0 mol HCl ....

....

b 1.5 mol NaOH ....

....

c 0.3 mol Na_2CO_3 ....

....

d 0.5 mol $Al_2(SO_4)_3$ ....

....

③ **The labels on the containers of chemical substances in a laboratory have worn away and some of the information is missing. The information still visible has been recorded in the table below.**

Substance	A_r or M_r	Mass/g	Moles	Comments
Sodium	23.0	2.30	0.1	soft metal
		0.32	0.01	gas
CH_4		1.60		gas

a **Use the information available to complete the table.** (4 marks, ★★★)

   Another bottle contains hydrochloric acid (HCl) diluted in water. The label reads '50g HCl'.

b **Calculate the number of moles of HCl in the solution.** (2 marks, ★★★)

....

④ **Iron is an essential part of the human diet. Breakfast cereals often contain anhydrous iron(II) sulfate to supplement the iron from other sources in a person's diet. The formula for iron(II) sulfate is $FeSO_4$. Assume 1 mole of iron(II) sulfate produces 1 mole of iron.**

a **Calculate the M_r of $FeSO_4$.** (1 mark, ★★)

....

b **Calculate the mass of 0.25 moles of $FeSO_4$.** (1 mark, ★★★)

....

c **Calculate the mass of $FeSO_4$ needed to provide 7g of iron.** (2 marks, ★★★★)

....

d **Calculate the number of atoms of iron in 7g.** (2 marks, ★★★★)

....

(5) Calcium carbonate undergoes thermal decomposition to produce calcium oxide and carbon dioxide as shown in the equation below:

$CaCO_3(s) \rightarrow CaO(s) + CO_2(g)$

a Calculate the mass of calcium oxide produced if 25g of calcium carbonate decomposes. (2 marks, ★★★)

....

....

Carbon capture, storing carbon dioxide from the atmosphere in other forms, has been suggested as a way to reduce climate change caused by increased carbon dioxide in the atmosphere. Experiments have been conducted to find out whether calcium carbonate can be used in this way by reversing the thermal decomposition equation given above.

b Calculate the mass of calcium carbonate that would be produced by storing 500kg of carbon dioxide. (2 marks, ★★★)

....

....

(6) A pharmaceutical company produces tablets of the medicine paracetamol ($C_8H_9NO_2$), which contain 0.5g of paracetamol.

a Calculate the number of moles of paracetamol in each tablet. (2 marks, ★★★)

....

....

b The same company produces the medicine aspirin by the following reaction:

$$C_7H_5O_3 + C_4H_6O_3 \rightarrow C_9H_8O_4 + CH_3COOH$$

salicylic acid + ethanoic anhydride → aspirin + ethanoic acid

(M_r = 138)   (M_r = 180)

Calculate the number of moles of aspirin produced if 4g of salicylic acid is used. (2 marks, ★★★★)

....

....

c Calculate the number of molecules of salicylic acid that produce 0.5g of aspirin. (2 marks, ★★★★)

....

....

....

MATHS SKILLS

Use the formulae for your calculations:
$n = m/M_r$, $m = n \times M_r$; no. of particles = $n \times N_A$
N_A = Avogadro's number
Don't forget to put the units in your answer and use standard form (e.g. 6.5×10^{-5} instead of 0.000065) when appropriate.

Limiting reactants

> ### MATHS SKILLS
>
> - To identify the limiting reactant from a chemical equation, work out the number of moles of each reactant and compare this ratio with what is needed by looking at the ratio in the chemical equation for the reaction.
>
> - To convert the ratio in the equation to match the numbers you're told, find the factor by dividing one by the other, depending on the direction you're going. For the worked example above, the ratio is 4:5, which means that for every 4 units of NH_3 you needed 5 units of O_2. You knew the '4' units of NH_3 was 0.19, so to work out how much O_2 needed, simply divide 5 by 4 = 1.25 (i.e. 5 is 1.25 times bigger than 4!) and multiply that by 0.19 = 0.23.

(1) **After a reaction of magnesium and hydrochloric acid, there is magnesium left behind.**

    a Which is the limiting reactant? (1 mark, ★) ....

    b Which reactant was in excess? (1 mark, ★) ....

(2) **Hydrogen reacts with oxygen to produce water: $2H_2(g) + O_2(g) \rightarrow 2H_2O(l)$**

    If 1 mole of hydrogen is reacted with 1 mole of oxygen, determine the limiting reactant and the reactant in excess by matching the questions on the left to the correct answer on the right. (3 marks, ★★★)

How many moles of water can be produced by 1 mole of H_2?	1
How many moles of water can be produced by 1 mole of O_2?	2
Which is the limiting reactant?	1
How much H_2O is produced in the reaction?	O_2
Which reactant is in excess?	H_2
How many moles of O_2 is used in the reaction?	1

(3) **Copper reacts with oxygen in the air to produce copper(I) oxide. The reaction is shown in the equation below:**

    .... $Cu(s) +$ .... $O_2(g) \rightarrow$ .... $Cu_2O(s)$

    In an experiment to investigate this reaction, 80 g of copper was reacted with 50 g of oxygen.

    a Balance the equation. (2 marks, ★★)

    b Calculate the number of moles of the two reactants. (2 marks, ★★)

    ....

    ....

    c Identify the limiting reagent and explain your choice. (2 marks, ★★★)

    ....

    ....

Concentrations in solutions

(1) Two solutions are shown below in diagrams (1) and (2).

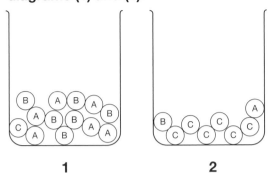

1   2

a Which of the two solutions has the highest concentration of solute A?

(1 mark, ★) ....

b Which of the two solutions has the highest concentration of solute C?

(1 mark, ★) ....

> ### MATHS SKILLS
>
> Concentration (in g/dm³ or mol/dm³) = amount in mol or mass in g/volume (in dm³).
>
> To convert from mol/dm³ to g/dm³, multiply the amount of the solute in 1 dm³ by its M_r.
>
> > For a 0.2 mol/dm³ solution of hydrochloric acid, HCl (M_r = 36.5):
> >
> > 0.2 moles × 36.5 = 7.3 g
> > so the concentration is 7.3 g/dm³
>
> We can also convert from g/dm³ to mol/dm³ by dividing by the M_r.
>
> > For a 5 g/dm³ solution of HCl:
> >
> > 5 g / 36.5 = 0.14 moles
> > so the concentration is 0.14 mol/dm³
>
> Remember that there are a thousand cubic centimetres in a cubic decimetre. So if you are given a volume in cubic centimetres, you need to divide by a thousand.

(2) A student dissolved sodium chloride (NaCl) into three beakers of water as shown in the table below.

Test	Mass of solute/g	Volume/dm³
1	5	0.020
2	10	0.025
3	20	0.035

M_r NaCl = 58.5

a Calculate the concentration of the solute in each of the three tests. (3 marks, ★★)

Test 1 .... g/dm³

Test 2 .... g/dm³

Test 3 .... g/dm³

b Calculate the number of moles of solute in each solution. (3 marks, ★★)

Test 1 .... moles

Test 2 .... moles

Test 3 .... moles

(3) The organisers of a swimming competition need to calculate how much cleaning agent to add to the pool to keep it free of harmful microorganisms. The pool contains 2.5×10^6 dm³ water and the instructions on the box of the cleaning agent state that the pool must contain 0.01 mol/dm³ of calcium oxychloride ($Ca(ClO)_2$) before swimming.

a Calculate the M_r of $Ca(ClO)_2$. (1 mark, ★★) ....

b Calculate the concentration of $Ca(ClO)_2$ required, in g/mol³. (1 mark, ★★★) ....

c Calculate the amount of cleaning agent, in g, that must be added for the pool to contain the correct concentration. Give your answer in standard form. (3 marks, ★★★★)

....

....

Metal oxides and the reactivity series

(1) **Magnesium reacts with oxygen to form a white solid.**

a **Write a word equation for this reaction.** (1 mark, ★★)

....

b **Write a balanced chemical equation for this reaction.** (2 marks, ★★★)

....

....

c **In this reaction, magnesium is oxidised. Explain what is meant by oxidation.** (1 mark, ★)

....

....

NAILIT!

More reactive metals will **displace** less reactive metals from metal salts.
This means that the metals swap places in the reaction. For example:

sodium + lead oxide → lead + sodium oxide

(2) **Use the reactivity series to predict the outcome of the following reactions.** (4 marks, ★★)

a **Aluminium + lead chloride →** ....

b **Silver + copper oxide →** ....

c **Calcium + zinc nitrate →** ....

d **Iron chloride + copper →** ....

(3) **A student has an unknown metal, X, and carries out some experiments in order to determine its reactivity. The student's results are in the table below.**

1	X + copper sulfate solution	A red/orange solid is formed
2	X + sodium sulfate solution	No reaction
3	X + magnesium sulfate	A silvery grey solid is produced
4	X + hydrochloric acid	X dissolves vigorously and a gas is produced

Metal	Reactivity
Copper	
Sodium	1
Magnesium	
X	

a **Use the student's results to place the metals in order of reactivity, with 1 being the most reactive and 4 being the least reactive. The most reactive is done for you.** (2 marks, ★★)

b **What is the name of the red/orange solid formed in experiment 1?** (1 mark, ★★★)

....

Extraction of metals and reduction

1. **Magnesium cannot be extracted from its ore by heating with carbon. Explain why.** (1 mark, ★★)

....

....

2. **Why does gold not need to be extracted from an ore?** (1 mark, ★★)

....

....

3. **Tin is extracted from its ore by heating it with carbon. The main tin ore is called cassiterite and it contains tin(IV) oxide, SnO_2.**

   a **Write a word equation for this reaction.** (2 marks, ★★★)

   ....

   ....

   b **Which substance is oxidised in this reaction?** (1 mark, ★★)

   ....

4. **Copper can also be extracted from its ore with carbon. Many copper containing ores contain copper(II) oxide, CuO.**

   a **Write a balanced chemical equation for this reaction. Include state symbols.**
   (2 marks, ★★★)

   ....

   ....

   b **Using the reactivity series, predict another element which could be used to extract copper from its ore. Suggest why this element is not used in practice.** (2 marks, ★★★)

   ....

   ....

   ....

   ....

DO IT!

Make sure that you always refer to the reactivity series when answering questions about metal extraction. Remember, any metal above carbon is extracted from its ore using electrolysis.

The blast furnace

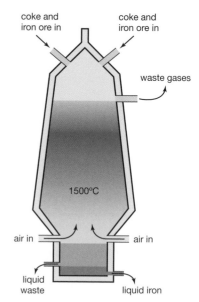

coke and iron ore in   coke and iron ore in

waste gases

1500°C

air in   air in

liquid waste   liquid iron

① **Iron is extracted from its ore in the blast furnace. The iron ore, which contains mostly iron(III) oxide, is mixed with coke (a form of carbon), limestone and air and heated to around 1500°C.**

There are several reactions that take place in the blast furnace. Although carbon can be used to extract iron from its ore, during this reaction, carbon monoxide (CO) is formed and this then reacts with the iron(III) oxide to form iron.

The first reaction is between carbon and oxygen to form carbon dioxide.

a Write a word equation for this reaction. (1 mark, ★)

....

The carbon dioxide then reacts with further carbon to form carbon monoxide.

b Write a balanced chemical equation for this reaction. Include state symbols.
(2 marks, ★★★★)

....

The following reaction then takes place.

Iron(III) oxide + carbon monoxide → iron + carbon dioxide

c What type of reaction is this? (1 mark, ★★)

....

d Balance the chemical equation for this reaction below. (2 marks, ★★★★)

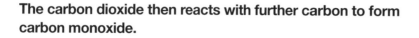

___Fe$_2$O$_3$ (s) + ___CO(g) → ___Fe (l) + ___CO$_2$ (g)

e How can you tell from this equation that the reaction is carried out at a high temperature?
(1 mark, ★★★)

....

The final stage of this reaction produces the waste product, calcium silicate (slag). This is formed when impurities such as sand (silicon dioxide) react with the limestone.

f What is the chemical formula for slag? (1 mark, ★★)

....

g On the diagram, label where the slag is formed. (1 mark, ★★)

NAILIT!

Learn the equations for each of the four stages in this metal extraction, and make sure you know which involve oxidation/reduction and which equation is an acid/base reaction.

The reactions of acids

1 State **one similarity** and **one difference** between bases and alkalis. (2 marks, ★★★)

....

....

....

2 Choose **two** chemicals from the table below that could be used to make the following salts. (3 marks, ★★)

a **Sodium chloride** ....

b **Potassium nitrate** ....

c **Copper sulfate** ....

Copper chloride	Sodium hydroxide	Sulfuric acid
Nitric acid	Chlorine	Potassium carbonate
Sodium sulfate	Hydrochloric acid	Copper oxide

3 Magnesium oxide and magnesium carbonate are both white solids that will react with dilute acids, including hydrochloric acid, HCl.

A student adds HCl to separate portions of magnesium oxide and magnesium carbonate and makes observations.

a **State one observation that the two reactions would have in common.** (1 mark, ★★)

....

b **State one observation that would be different.** (1 mark, ★★)

....

c **Write the word equation for the reaction between magnesium oxide and hydrochloric acid.** (1 mark, ★★)

....

d **What is the formula for magnesium carbonate?** (1 mark, ★★★) ....

4 Write chemical equations for these reactions, including state symbols. (6 marks, ★★★★)

a **Magnesium + hydrochloric acid** ....

b **Lithium oxide + sulfuric acid** ....

c **Copper(II) oxide + hydrochloric acid** ....

5 The reaction between calcium and hydrochloric acid is a redox reaction. This means that both oxidation and reduction take place at the same time.

a **Write an ionic equation for this reaction. Include state symbols.** (3 marks, ★★★★★)

....

b **State which species is oxidised and which species is reduced.** (2 marks, ★★★★)

....

The preparation of soluble salts

① **A sample of copper sulfate can be formed by reacting together solid copper carbonate and dilute sulfuric acid.**

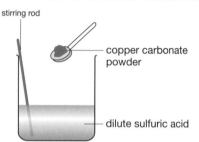

stirring rod
copper carbonate powder
dilute sulfuric acid

> **NAILIT!**
>
>
>
> The preparation of soluble salts can be summarised as follows:
>
> • heat acid (to increase the rate of reaction)
> • add insoluble base until no more reacts
> • filter excess base
> • allow solution to crystallise.
>
> This is the standard method regardless of which type of base is used.

a **Complete the word equation for this reaction.** (1 mark, ★★)

Copper carbonate + sulfuric acid → copper sulfate + ... + ...

b **State two observations that would be seen during this reaction.** (2 marks, ★★)

....

c **The copper carbonate needs to be added until it is in excess. Explain why this is necessary.** (1 mark, ★★)

....

d **How is the excess copper carbonate removed?** (1 mark, ★)

....

e **State another chemical that reacts with sulfuric acid to form copper sulfate.** (1 mark, ★★)

....

f **When soluble salts are prepared in this way, the percentage yield is generally less than 100%. Suggest one reason why.** (1 mark, ★★)

....

② **A soluble salt is formed in the reaction between calcium and nitric acid.**

Calcium + nitric acid → calcium nitrate + hydrogen

a **Write a balanced chemical equation for this reaction, including state symbols.** (3 marks, ★★★★)

....

b **A student carried out the experiment above and made 2.6 g of calcium nitrate. If the theoretical yield is 3.0 g, what is the percentage yield? Quote your answer to one decimal place.** (2 marks, ★★★)

....

....

③ **On a separate piece of paper, describe how to make a pure, dry sample of zinc chloride. Include an equation and a full equipment list.** (6 marks, ★★★★)

Oxidation and reduction in terms of electrons

(1) **Magnesium reacts with a solution of copper(II) chloride to form a solution of magnesium chloride and solid copper.**

   a **Write an ionic equation, including state symbols, for this reaction.** (3 marks, ★★★★)

   ....

   b **Which species is oxidised and which is reduced?** (1 mark, ★★★)

   ....

WORKIT!

Step 1   Write a balanced chemical equation, including state symbols.

$Mg(s) + CuCl_2(aq) \rightarrow MgCl_2(aq) + Cu(s)$

Step 2   Any aqueous solution will split up into its ions. Rewrite the equation to show this.

$Mg(s) + Cu^{2+}(aq) + 2Cl^-(aq) \rightarrow Mg^{2+}(aq) + 2Cl^-(aq) + Cu(s)$

Step 3   Cancel out any species that appear on both sides of the equation. These are **spectator ions** and don't take part in the reaction.

$Mg(s) + Cu^{2+}(aq) + \cancel{2Cl^-(aq)} \rightarrow Mg^{2+}(aq) + \cancel{2Cl^-(aq)} + Cu(s)$

Step 4   Rewrite the equation with the remaining ions.

$Mg(s) + Cu^{2+}(aq) \rightarrow Mg^{2+}(aq) + Cu(s)$

Step 5   Finish with a conclusion. The Mg has lost electrons and formed a positive ion, so according to OILRIG, it has been oxidised. The Cu^{2+} has gained electrons and has therefore been reduced.

(2) **Write ionic equations for the following reactions. In each case, state which species has been oxidised and which has been reduced.**

   a **Zinc(II) nitrate reacts with magnesium to form magnesium nitrate and solid zinc.**
     (4 marks, ★★★★★)

     ....

   b **Sodium reacts with a solution of zinc(II) chloride to form a solution of sodium chloride and solid zinc.**
     (4 marks, ★★★★★)

     ....

   c **Silver(I) sulfate reacts with copper to form copper(II) sulfate and silver metal.** (4 marks, ★★★★★)

     ....

   d **Calcium reacts with a solution of iron(III) chloride to form solid iron and a solution of calcium chloride.** (4 marks, ★★★★★)

     ....

NAILIT!

Writing ionic equations is tricky and you need to make sure you can write formulae correctly. You cannot always use the periodic table to work out the charges on metal ions, as the transition metals often form more than one ion. Here are some common ones.

Zinc – Zn^{2+} Iron(II) – Fe^{2+}

Copper – Cu^{2+} Iron(III) – Fe^{3+}

Silver – Ag^+

pH scale and neutralisation

(1) **Match each solution with its correct pH value and colour that universal indicator would change to. The first one is done for you.** (4 marks, ★★)

Solution	pH	Universal Indicator
Strong acid	13	Purple
Weak acid	2	Green
Strong alkali	9	Red
Weak alkali	7	Yellow
Neutral	5	Blue

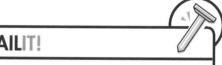

NAILIT!

All neutralisation reactions between an acid and an alkali can be simply represented by this ionic equation:

$H^+(aq) + OH^-(aq) \rightarrow H_2O(l)$

Always include this if you are asked about neutralisation; equations are an excellent way of gaining marks.

(2) **State the name of the ion that causes solutions to be alkaline.** (1 mark, ★) ....

(3) **State the formula of the ion that causes solutions to be acidic.** (1 mark, ★) ....

(4) **Which of these solutions has the greatest concentration of H⁺ ions? Tick one box.** (1 mark, ★★)

pH 3	☐
pH 1	

(5) **Which of these solutions has the lowest concentration of OH⁻ ions? Tick one box.** (1 mark, ★★)

pH 14	☐
pH 12	

(6) **Potassium sulfate (K_2SO_4) can be produced in the reaction between sulfuric acid and an alkali.**

a **State the name of the alkali that could be used.** (1 mark, ★)

....

b **Write a balanced chemical equation for this reaction.** (2 marks, ★★★★)

....

c **Write the ionic equation for this reaction.** (1 mark, ★★★)

....

(7) **Ammonia gas (NH_3) forms an alkaline solution when dissolved in water. Suggest the formulae of the two ions formed.** (2 marks, ★★★★★)

....

Strong and weak acids

WORKIT!

Hydrochloric acid, HCl, is a strong acid and ethanoic acid, CH_3COOH, is a weak acid. Write equations to show how they ionise in aqueous solution. (2 marks, ★★★)

Strong acids completely ionise (split up into ions) when they are in solution.

$$HCl(aq) \rightarrow H^+(aq) + Cl^-(aq)$$

Weak acids only partially ionise when they are in solution. This is represented by using the reversible arrow ($\rightleftharpoons$) in the equation.

Reversible reactions are discussed more on page 67.

$$CH_3COOH(aq) \rightleftharpoons CH_3COO^-(aq) + H^+(aq)$$

(1) **Write equations to show how the following acids ionise in solution.** (3 marks, ★★★)

   a **Nitric acid, HNO_3 (strong acid)**

   ....

   b **Methanoic acid, HCOOH (weak acid)**

   ....

   c **Sulfuric acid, H_2SO_4 (strong acid)**

   ....

(2) **Explain the difference between a weak acid and a dilute acid.** (2 marks, ★★★)

....

....

....

(3) **An acid with pH 3 has a hydrogen ion concentration of 0.001 mol/dm³.**

   a **Express this value in standard form.** (1 mark, ★★★)

   ....

   b **What is the hydrogen ion concentration of an acid with a pH of 1? Express your answer in standard form.** (3 marks, ★★★★★)

   ....

   ....

   ....

NAILIT!

Strong and concentrated do not mean the same thing!

Concentration refers to how much of a solute is dissolved in a solution. More solute means a **higher** concentration.

If an acid is strong, this means that it completely splits or **dissociates** into its ions in solution.

Electrolysis

(1) **Label the diagram choosing the correct words from the box below.** (3 marks, ★★)

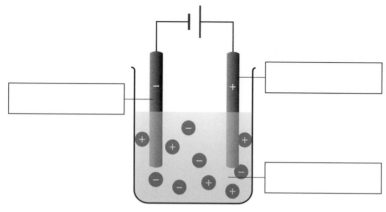

| cathode | electrolyte | electroplating | anode |

(2) **Why can ionic compounds conduct electricity when melted or in solution, but not when they are solids?** (2 marks, ★★)

....

(3) **Predict the products formed when these compounds undergo electrolysis.** (3 marks, ★★)

a **Molten zinc(II) chloride** ....

b **Molten silver iodide** ....

c **Molten copper(II) oxide** ....

(4) **Molten lead bromide undergoes electrolysis to form lead and bromine.**

a **Complete the half equations for this reaction.** (2 marks, ★★★) ◄——— Remember that half equations only show one species being oxidised or reduced.

   • **Pb^{2+} +** .... **→ Pb**

   • **$2Br^- → Br_2$ +** ....

b **Which species is oxidised and which is reduced?** (1 mark, ★★★)

....

DOIT!

Practise writing half equations for simple ionic compounds.

Step 1 Use the charges on ions to write a formula, e.g. K^+ and Cl^- forms KCl.

Step 2 Write out the half equations:

$K^+ → K$

$Cl^- → Cl_2$

Step 3 Balance any atoms:

$K^+ → K$ *already balanced*

$2Cl^- → Cl_2$ *2Cl⁻ needed*

Step 4 Add electrons to balance the charges.

$K^+ + e^- → K$

$2Cl^- → Cl_2 + 2e^-$

NAILIT!

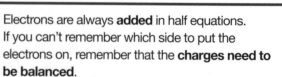

Electrons are always **added** in half equations. If you can't remember which side to put the electrons on, remember that the **charges need to be balanced**.

For example, during electrolysis of NaCl, Na^+ ions form Na metal.

$Na^+ → Na$

There is a **positive** charge on the **left-hand side**, which means that **one electron** needs to be added to the **right-hand side** to balance the charge.

$Na^+ → Na + e^-$

Electrolysis of copper(II) sulfate and electroplating

1 The diagram shows an experiment to show the apparatus used to electrolyse a solution of copper(II) sulfate. The electrodes are made of graphite and are inert.

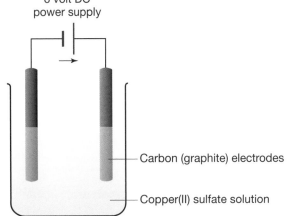

6 volt DC power supply

a **What is meant by the word 'inert'?** (1 mark, ★★)

....

b **What is the name of the electrolyte?** (1 mark, ★★)

....

c **Oxygen is produced at the anode (positive electrode). Describe how you would test for this gas.** (1 mark, ★)

....

— Carbon (graphite) electrodes

— Copper(II) sulfate solution

d **What would you see formed at the cathode (negative electrode)? Write an equation for this reaction.** (2 marks, ★★★★)

....

e **Copper(II) sulfate solution is blue. Explain what happens to the colour of the solution during this experiment.** (2 marks, ★★★)

....

f **A different reaction takes place if copper electrodes are used instead of graphite electrodes. State two differences that you would see.** (2 marks, ★★★★)

....

2 **Electroplating is an application of electrolysis that allows a thin layer of metal to be coated onto another, this could be to make them look nicer or increase protection. Bathroom taps are often plated in chromium which gives them a very shiny coating.**

a **In this reaction:**

i **What would the anode be made of?** (1 mark, ★★★)

....

ii **What would the cathode be made of?** (1 mark, ★★★)

....

b **Suggest a substance that could be used as the electrolyte.** (1 mark, ★★★)

....

c **Write a half equation to show what would happen at the cathode. Assume that the chromium ion formed is Cr^{3+}.** (2 marks, ★★★★★)

....

NAILIT!

Remember these rules for electroplating.
- The electrolyte must contain the metal ion that is being used to coat the object.
- The cathode must be the metal that is being used to coat the object.
- The anode must be the object that is being plated.

The extraction of metals using electrolysis

(1) Aluminium is extracted from its ore by electrolysis. The most common aluminium ore is called bauxite and this is purified to produce aluminium oxide, Al_2O_3. The aluminium oxide is heated to around 950 °C and dissolved in another aluminium compound called cryolite. The mixture then undergoes electrolysis and forms aluminium and oxygen.

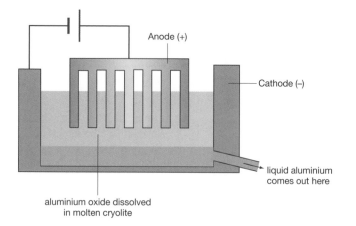

Anode (+)

Cathode (–)

liquid aluminium comes out here

aluminium oxide dissolved in molten cryolite

NAILIT!

This topic links with the **reactivity series** and **structure and bonding**. Make sure you can remember **why** ionic compounds can conduct electricity.

a Aluminium oxide has a high melting point. Use your ideas about structure and bonding to explain why. (2 marks, ★★★)

....

....

b Why does the aluminium oxide need to be heated? (1 mark, ★★)

....

c Why is cryolite added to the aluminium oxide? (2 marks, ★★★)

....

d The reaction that takes place at the anode is replaced with: $2O^{2-} \rightarrow O_2 + 4e^-$

This equation shows oxidation. Explain why. (1 mark, ★★)

....

e Aluminium is produced at the cathode. Write a half equation to show this reaction. (2 marks, ★★★)

....

f With the help of an equation, explain why graphite anodes require frequent replacing. (2 marks, ★★★)

....

....

g Aluminium was not discovered until around 200 years ago, yet there is evidence to suggest that iron was used by humans over 7000 years ago. Suggest why it took a long time for aluminium to be discovered. (1 mark, ★★)

....

....

Practical investigation into the electrolysis of aqueous solutions

Hypothesis: The product produced at the cathode when an aqueous solution undergoes hydrolysis depends on the reactivity of the metal in the salt solution.

A student carries out the following experiment with four different metal salt solutions, all of which have a concentration of $1\,mol/dm^3$. The salt solutions are:

- **Iron(III) chloride, $FeCl_3$(aq)**
- **Copper(II) chloride, $CuCl_2$(aq)**
- **Sodium chloride, NaCl(aq)**
- **Magnesium chloride, $MgCl_2$(aq)**

Method

- Measure out $100\,cm^3$ of iron(III) chloride solution in a measuring cylinder and pour into a beaker.
- Place two inert electrodes into the beaker and attach to a power pack.
- Set voltage to 4V, switch on the power pack and observe the product formed at the cathode.
- If a gas is produced, test to see if it is hydrogen.
- Repeat for the remaining salt solutions.

1 **a** **In the table below, state the variables in this experiment.** (4 marks, ★★★)

Independent variable	Dependent variable	Control variables

b **Describe how this experiment is valid.** (1 mark, ★)

....

2 **Describe the test for hydrogen gas.** (2 marks, ★★) ....

....

3 **a** **In the table below, predict the products that will be formed at the cathode.** (2 marks, ★★★)

Salt solution	Product produced at the cathode
$FeCl_3$	
NaCl	
$CuCl_2$	
$MgCl_2$	

b **Justify your predictions.** (2 marks, ★★★)

....

....

4 **All four solutions will produce the same product at the anode. Name this gas, and describe a test to identify it.** (2 marks, ★★★)

....

....

Exothermic and endothermic reactions

(1) **Explain what happens to the temperature of the surroundings during 'endothermic' and 'exothermic' reactions.** (2 marks, ★)

a **Endothermic** ....

....

b **Exothermic** ....

....

(2) **A student set up an experiment as shown in the image below. The initial temperature of solution was 23.7°C. At the end of the reaction the temperature was 15.4°C.**

a **Calculate the temperature change of the reaction and state whether the reaction is exothermic or endothermic.** (3 marks, ★★)

....

....

....

b **Another student repeated the experiment with different reactants. They recorded the temperature at the start and at the end of the reaction as shown below.**

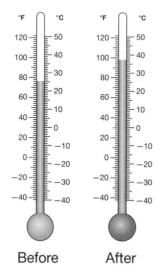

Before   After

i **Calculate the temperature change of the reaction.** (2 marks, ★★)

....

....

ii **State whether the reaction is endothermic or exothermic.** (1 mark, ★★)

....

NAIL IT!

Exothermic reactions include combustion (burning) reactions, most oxidation reactions and neutralisation reactions.

Endothermic reactions include *thermal decomposition* (breaking up of a compound using heat) and the reaction of citric acid with sodium hydrogen carbonate.

Practical investigation into the variables that affect temperature changes in chemical reactions

(1) **A student is comparing the temperature change in the reaction of iron with oxygen. She set up the experiment as shown in the diagram below.**

a **Label the diagram to identify the equipment the student used.** (4 marks, ★)

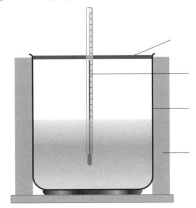

b **Suggest why the student wrapped the calorimeter in wool.** (2 marks, ★★)

....

....

The results of the experiment are shown below.

	Iron filings	Iron ball bearings	A large piece of iron
Initial temperature / °C	24.2	23.9	24.1
Final temperature / °C	60.1	37.3	24.3

c **What conclusions could be made from these results?** (2 marks, ★★)

....

....

d **Explain why it is important that the student kept the volume of air the same in all three tests.** (2 marks, ★★★)

....

....

(2) **On a separate piece of paper, describe how you would set up an experiment to investigate how the concentration of hydrochloric acid affects the temperature change during its reaction with calcium carbonate.** (6 marks, ★★★★)

Your answer should include:

* **an explanation for your choice of equipment**
* **the hypothesis you will be testing**
* **a prediction of what you think will happen and why**
* **how you would ensure valid results**
* **how you would record your results.**

NAILIT!

If asked why a student has kept a variable the same, it is usually not enough to simply say 'to ensure valid results' – you will typically be expected to explain what could happen if that variable was changed. For example, if a student is investigating the effect of particle size, it is important to keep the concentration the same, because increasing concentration can increase the rate of reaction and so would also affect the temperature change.

Reaction profiles

> ### NAILIT!
>
> One way to help you remember the energy changes in endo- and exothermic relations is to remember that **ex**othermic involves the **ex**it of energy to the surroundings – surrounding temperatures will increase, but the amount of energy in the products will reduce. The reverse is true for endothermic reactions.

1. **Fill the gaps to complete the sentence about reaction profiles for endothermic and exothermic reactions.** (4 marks, ★)

   A .... shows how the energy changes from reactants to products.

   In a reaction profile for an .... reaction the products are lower in energy than the reactants because .... is released to the surroundings during the reaction.

   In a reaction profile for an .... reaction the .... are higher in energy than the .... because energy is taken in from the .... during the reaction.

   Chemical reactions occur when reacting particles collide with enough energy to react. This energy is called the .... (E_a).

   | surroundings | energy | products | reaction profile |
   | reactants | activation energy | endothermic | exothermic |

2. **A student reacts barium hydroxide ($Ba(OH)_2.8H_2O(s)$) with ammonium chloride ($NH_4Cl(s)$) as shown in the balanced equation below:**

   $$Ba(OH)_2.8H_2O(s) + 2NH_4Cl(s) \rightarrow 2NH_3(g) + 10H_2O(l) + BaCl_2(s)$$

   The student predicts that the reaction will be exothermic.

   a **Use the reaction profile diagram below to suggest whether the student's prediction is correct. Explain your answer.** (3 marks, ★★★)

   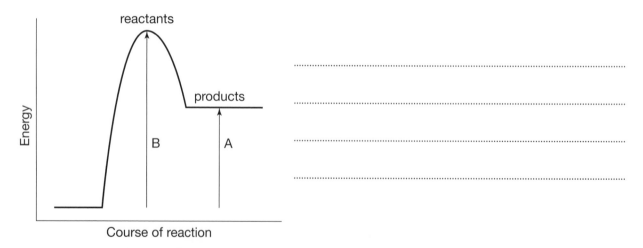

   ....

   ....

   ....

   ....

   b **Identify what is shown on the diagram by labels A and B.** (2 marks, ★★)

   i **A** ....

   ii **B** ....

   c **On a separate piece of paper, draw a diagram to show how a catalyst might change the reaction profile.** (2 marks, ★★★)

The energy changes of reactions

(1) **1 mole of hydrogen and 1 mole of chlorine react to form 2 moles of hydrogen chloride gas, as shown below.**

Bond	Bond energy (kJ per mol)
H–H	436
Cl–Cl	243
H–Cl	432

H–H + Cl–Cl → 2 × (H–Cl)

a **Calculate the amount of energy required to break both the H–H and Cl–Cl bonds.**
(2 marks, ★★)

H–H ....

Cl–Cl .... **Sum (bond breaking)** ....

b **Calculate the amount of energy released as the H–Cl bonds are formed.** (2 marks, ★★)

....

c **Suggest whether the reaction is exothermic or endothermic.** (1 mark, ★★★)

....

d **Calculate the energy change of the reaction.** (1 mark, ★★★)

....

(2) **Two moles of hydrogen bromide produce one mole of hydrogen and bromine gas.**

$2HBr(g) \rightarrow H_2(g) + Br_2(g)$

Bond	Bond energy (kJ per mol)
H–Br	366
Br–Br	193
H–Cl	432

a **Draw the bonds present in the molecules.** (3 marks, ★★)

b **Calculate the energy change of the reaction and identify whether the reaction is endothermic or exothermic.** (3 marks, ★★★★)

....

....

....

Ways to follow a chemical reaction

(1) **A student wants to investigate how the size of marble chips affects the rate of reaction with hydrochloric acid. The chemical equation for the reaction is:**

$CaCO_3(s) + 2HCl(aq) \rightarrow CO_2(g) + H_2O(l) + CaCl_2(s)$

a **Identify the independent variable in this experiment.** (1 mark, ★)

....

b **What else does the student need to record to be able to calculate the rate of the reaction?** (1 mark, ★)

....

c **Suggest what the student could use as the dependent variable in the experiment. Explain your answer.** (2 marks, ★★)

....

d **Suggest what variables the student would need to control to ensure the investigation results were valid.** (2 marks, ★★)

....

....

(2) **In an experiment to investigate the effect of concentration on the rate of reaction, a student is given sodium thiosulfate ($Na_2S_2O_3$) and $2\,mol/dm^3$ hydrochloric acid (HCl). The chemical equation for the reaction is:**

$2HCl(aq) + Na_2S_2O_3(aq) \rightarrow 2NaCl(aq) + SO_2(g) + S(s) + H_2O(l)$

The student marks a sheet of paper with an X and places it under the flask in which the reaction will take place.

a **Suggest what the student is using to identify the progress of the reaction.** (1 mark, ★)

....

b **Identify the independent variable in the experiment.** (1 mark, ★)

....

c **What variables should be controlled to ensure the experiment is valid?** (2 marks, ★★)

....

d **Explain how this experiment could be improved to reduce errors.** (2 marks, ★★★)

....

....

(3) **On a separate piece of paper, describe how you would use the equipment listed below to investigate how the concentration of hydrochloric acid affects the rate of its reaction with magnesium. Explain how you will ensure the experiment is valid.** (6 marks, ★★★)

- magnesium ribbon
- hydrochloric acid
- safety goggles
- conical flask
- bung and delivery tube to fit conical flask
- trough or plastic washing-up bowl
- measuring cylinder
- clamp stand, boss and clamp
- stop clock

Calculating the rate of reaction

(1) **Describe how you could calculate the rate of a reaction from the amount of product formed.** (1 mark, ★)

....

(2) **For each of the graphs below, describe what is shown in terms of the rate of reaction.**
(4 marks, ★★)

a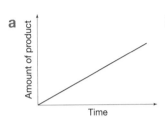

b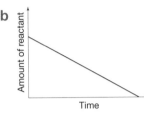

c

d

....

(3) **In a reaction between magnesium and hydrochloric acid, hydrogen gas is given off. The volume of hydrogen was recorded every 10 seconds, as shown in the table.**

Time/s	0	10	20	30	40	50	60	70	80	90	100	110	120
Volume of H_2/cm^3	0	21	39	55	67	76	84	91	95	97	98	99	99

a **Write a balanced chemical equation for the reaction.** (1 mark, ★)

....

b **Calculate the mean rate of the reaction in cm³/s.** (2 marks, ★★)

....

c **On a piece of graph paper draw a graph of the results.** (3 marks, ★★)

d **Draw a tangent to the curves on your graph at 30s, 60s and 90s.** (3 marks, ★★★)

NAILIT!

To calculate the rate of reaction you can either use the amount of reactant used:

$$\text{Mean rate of reaction} = \frac{\text{Amount of reactant used up}}{\text{Time taken}}$$

Or the product formed:

$$\text{Mean rate of reaction} = \frac{\text{Amount of product formed}}{\text{Time taken}}$$

e **Calculate the rate of reaction at 30s, 60s and 90s from the tangents of your graph.**
(3 marks, ★★★★)

....

....

f **Calculate the rate of the reaction in moles/second of hydrogen gas produced at 30s and 60s.** (4 marks, ★★★★)

....

....

The effect of concentration on reaction rate and the effect of pressure on the rate of gaseous reactions

(1) **Fill the gaps to complete the sentence.** (3 marks, ★)

For a reaction to happen, particles must .... with sufficient .... The minimum amount of .... that particles must have for a specific reaction is known as the

.... The rate of a reaction can be increased by increasing the .... of collisions and increasing the .... of collisions.

| frequency   activation energy   energy   collide | (some words are used more than once) |

(2) **A student planned to investigate the effect of concentration on the rate of reaction. The student predicted that the rate of reaction would increase as the concentration increased.**

Give two reasons why the student's prediction is correct. Tick two boxes. (2 marks, ★★)

There are more particles	
The particles have more energy	
The particles have a larger surface area	
The frequency of successful collisions increases	
The particles have greater mass	

(3) **A student investigated how pressure affects the rate of reaction between two gases.**

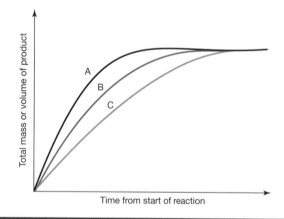

a **Identify which curve represents the lowest pressure.** (1 mark, ★★) ....

b **Identify which curve represents the highest pressure.** (1 mark, ★★) ....

NAILIT!

Remember that concentration is the number of moles of a substance per unit of volume.

- If you increase the moles but keep the volume the same, you've increased the concentration. Increasing the concentration means it is more likely that the particles will collide successfully.

- Similarly, if you keep the same number of moles but decrease the volume, you've also increased the concentration.

- Concentration = number of moles/volume

For gases, increasing pressure has the same effect – and you can increase the pressure by reducing the size of the container or increasing the number of particles.

(4) Another student investigated the reaction between marble chips and hydrochloric acid. The student collected the carbon dioxide (CO_2) given off and recorded the amount at intervals of 10 s. The results are shown below.

Time (s)	0	10	20	30	40	50	60	70
Volume of CO_2 (cm^3)	0.0	1.4	2.4	2.9	3.5	3.9	4.1	4.1

a **Plot this data on a graph, including a line of best fit.** (3 marks, ★★)

b **Use your graph to describe how the rate of the reaction changes with time.** (2 marks, ★★)

....

....

c **The reaction eventually stops. Pick the correct explanation for this.**
Tick one box. (1 mark, ★★★)

The catalyst has been used up	
The particles do not have enough energy	
The pressure reduces	
One (or more) of the reactants has been used up	
The temperature reduces	

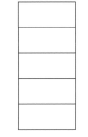

d **Sketch on your graph what you would expect to see if the concentration of hydrochloric acid was halved.** (2 marks, ★★★★)

e **Explain, in terms of particles, the reason for this difference.** (3 marks, ★★★★)

....

....

....

Rates of reaction – the effect of surface area

(1) **A student is investigating how surface area affects the rate of the reaction of calcium carbonate (CaCO₃) and hydrochloric acid (HCl).**

A
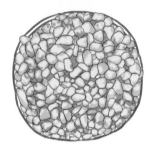

B

a **Identify which sample of calcium carbonate has the larger surface area.** (1 mark, ★) ....

b **Predict which you think will give the fastest rate of reaction.** (1 mark, ★★) ....

c **Explain, in terms of particles, your answer to (b).** (2 marks, ★★)

....

....

d **Marshmallows are made primarily of sugar. They are produced by mixing finely powdered sugar, water, gelling agent and flavourings. When exposed to a flame, marshmallows burn slowly.**

Explain why factories producing marshmallows often have strict rules in place to prevent explosive fires. (2 marks, ★★★)

....

....

....

(2) **A pharmaceutical company produces medicine in the form of effervescent tablets that dissolve in water. As the tablet dissolves, carbon dioxide bubbles are produced. Following feedback from patients, the company want to investigate how they can reduce the time it takes for the medicine to dissolve.**

a **Suggest how the company could vary the surface area of the tablets.** (2 marks, ★★)

....

....

b **The company recorded the loss of mass as a tablet dissolved in a beaker of water, as shown in the graph. Sketch onto the graph what you would expect to find if the tablet were crushed into powder.** (1 mark, ★★★)

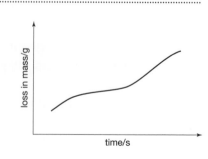

c **Suggest another method the company could use in their experiment to follow the rate of the reaction.** (2 marks, ★★)

....

....

The effects of changing the temperature and adding a catalyst

1 **A student wanted to investigate the effect of temperature on the rate of a reaction. The student put 10 cm³ of sodium thiosulfate (Na₂S₂O₃) in a beaker with 10 cm³ of hydrochloric acid and recorded the time it took for a cross to become obscured. The student predicted that the rate of reaction would increase with increasing temperature.**

a Give **two** reasons why the student's prediction is correct. (2 marks, ★)

....

b At 20°C the student found that it took 40 s for the cross to disappear. Predict how long it would take for the cross to disappear at 40°C. (2 marks, ★★)

....

2 **The Haber process produces ammonia (NH₃) by passing nitrogen and hydrogen over iron.**

a State the role of iron in this reaction. (1 mark, ★★)

....

b Explain how iron increases the rate of the reaction. (2 marks, ★★★)

....

c Complete the diagram below by labelling the line representing the reaction with and without iron. (2 marks, ★★★)

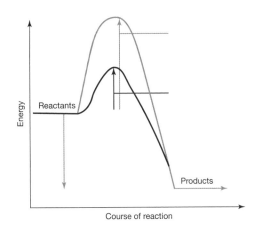

3 **Hydrogen peroxide (H₂O₂) decomposes at room temperature to produce water and oxygen, as shown in the balanced equation below:**

$$2H_2O_2\,(aq) \rightarrow 2H_2O(l) + O_2\,(g)$$

a How could you measure the rate of the reaction? (1 mark, ★★★)

....

b Manganese oxide (MnO₂) can be used as a catalyst to increase the rate of decomposition of hydrogen peroxide. Catalase is an enzyme found in the liver where it also increases the decomposition of hydrogen peroxide. On a separate piece of paper, explain how you would set up an experiment to investigate which is more effective at increasing the rate of decomposition. State how you would ensure valid results in your answer. (4 marks, ★★★★)

An investigation into how changing the concentration affects the rate of reaction

1. You are given sodium thiosulfate ($Na_2S_2O_3$) and hydrochloric acid (HCl) and asked to investigate how changing the concentration of sodium thiosulfate or hydrochloric acid affects the rate of reaction. The chemical equation for the reaction is:

   ....HCl(aq) + ...$Na_2S_2O_3$(aq) → ....NaCl(aq) + ...SO_2(g) + ...S(s) + ...H_2O(l)

   a **Balance the chemical equation above.** (1 mark, ★)

   b **Suggest a suitable hypothesis for the investigation.** (1 mark, ★★)

   ....

   c **Make a prediction for your investigation. Explain your prediction.** (3 marks, ★★★)

   ....

   ....

   ....

   d **Describe the method you would use to test your hypothesis. Suggest how you would ensure the experiment was valid.** (4 marks, ★★★)

   ....

   ....

   ....

   ....

   e **Explain how a change in temperature could affect your results.**
   (2 marks, ★★★)

   ....

   ....

   ....

   ....

   f **Evaluate two different methods you could use to measure the progress of the reaction.** (4 marks, ★★★)

   ....

   ....

MATHS SKILLS

- You should be comfortable developing hypotheses and making predictions.
- The hypotheses in these reactions will always be that increasing concentration of a reactant increases the reaction rate.
- Your prediction should include whether or not you think the hypothesis is true, and an explanation, i.e. I think the hypothesis is true because...
- When answering questions about valid results it's always a good idea to explain why it is important to keep a particular variable the same, in terms of what might happen if it changed. For example, in an investigation about the effect of concentration on the rate of reaction, it's important to keep the temperature the same, because increasing temperature also increases the rate of reaction.

....

....

....

Reversible reactions

1 The decomposition of ammonium chloride is a reversible reaction:

ammonium chloride $\rightleftharpoons$ ammonia + hydrogen chloride

$$NH_4Cl(s) \rightleftharpoons NH_3(g) + HCl(g)$$

a What symbol tells you that the reaction is reversible? (1 mark, ★)

> **NAILIT!**
>
> Relatively few reactions are reversible – for example, most combustion reactions are generally irreversible!

....

b Which of the following statements about reversible reactions is correct? **Tick one** box. (1 mark, ★)

Reversible reactions can go both forwards and backwards in certain conditions.	
All reactions are reversible to some extent.	
Reversible reactions stop when they reach equilibrium.	
If the forward reaction is endothermic, the backward reaction must also be endothermic.	

> **NAILIT!**
>
> When a reversible reaction reaches a dynamic equilibrium the reaction does not stop. The forwards reaction is simply happening at the same rate as the backwards reaction. The concentration of reactants and products stays the same.

c Explain what is meant by the term **dynamic equilibrium.** (2 marks, ★★)

....

....

2 A student heats limestone ($CaCO_3$) to produce lime (CaO) and carbon dioxide, as shown below:

$$CaCO_3 \rightleftharpoons CaO + CO_2$$

The reaction is reversible. The student collects the carbon dioxide in an upturned measuring cylinder in a trough of water.

> **NAILIT!**
>
> Remember that for reversible reactions if the forward reaction (left to right) is exothermic, the backward reaction (right to left) must be endothermic.

a Explain what is meant by the term **reversible reaction.** (2 marks, ★★)

....

b Determine whether the backwards reaction is endothermic or exothermic. Explain your answer. (3 marks, ★★★)

....

....

c Explain why, after some time, the volume of carbon dioxide stops increasing and remains the same. (3 marks, ★★★★)

....

....

The effect of changing conditions on equilibrium

① **Complete the sentence about dynamic equilibrium below.** (1 mark, ★)

At dynamic equilibrium, the rate of the forward reaction is ....

....

② **Give three factors that can be changed that may change the position of equilibrium.** (3 marks, ★)

a ....

b ....

c ....

> **NAILIT!**
>
> If the temperature is increased the equilibrium will shift in favour of the reaction which is accompanied by a decrease in temperature. This means that if the backward reaction is endothermic, like in the Haber process, then more reactants are formed.

③ **Define Le Chatelier's Principle.** (3 marks, ★★)

....

....

....

④ **In the Haber process, nitrogen and hydrogen produce ammonia, a valuable product which has many uses. The process is shown in the reaction shown below:**

> **NAILIT!**
>
> If you increase the concentration of one of the products then the system will try to lower its concentration by forming more reactants.

$$\sim 400°C$$
$$\sim 200 atm \text{ pressure}$$
$$\text{Iron catalyst}$$
$$N_2(g) + 3H_2(g) \rightleftharpoons 2NH_3(g) \text{ (+ heat)}$$

a **Describe what would happen if the temperature was increased.** (3 marks, ★★★)

....

....

b **Suggest a possible reason the reaction isn't carried out at room temperature.**
(1 mark, ★★★)

....

....

c **Explain the effect that the iron catalyst has on the reaction.**
(3 marks, ★★★)

> **NAILIT!**
>
> A catalyst has no effect on the position of equilibrium. It speeds up how quickly equilibrium is reached.

....

....

d **Explain why the Haber process is carried out at high pressure.**
(2 marks, ★★★★)

....

....

Organic chemistry

NAILIT!

The trends in the physical properties of alkanes are linked to the number of carbon atoms they have.

As the number of carbon atoms increases, boiling points and viscosity increase, the colour darkens and flammability decreases.

Viscosity is a measure of how easily fluids flow.

(1) **Explain each of the following facts about alkanes.**

   a **Alkanes are hydrocarbons.** (1 mark, ★)

   ....

   b **Alkanes are described as saturated.** (1 mark, ★★)

   ....

   c **Alkanes form a homologous series.** (2 marks, ★★★)

   ....

(2) **State the formulae for the following alkanes.** (4 marks, ★★)

   a **Alkane with 20 carbon atoms.** ....

   b **Alkane with 18 hydrogen atoms.** ....

(3) **Complete the dot-and-cross diagram to show the bonding in ethane.** (2 marks, ★★)

DOIT!

Remember the general formula for alkanes, C_nH_{2n+2}. You can then use this to predict the formula of any alkane if you are given the number of carbon or hydrogen atoms.

(4) **Heptane is an alkane which contains seven carbon atoms.**

   a **Draw out its displayed formula.** (1 mark, ★★)

   b **State its molecular formula.** (1 mark, ★★) ....

(5) **Which of these alkanes is the most flammable? Tick one box.** (1 mark, ★★)

CH_4	
C_3H_8	

(6) **Which of these alkanes has the highest boiling point? Tick one box.** (1 mark, ★★)

Propane	
Pentane	

(7) **Which of these alkanes is the most viscous? Tick one box.** (1 mark, ★★)

C_2H_6	
C_4H_{10}	

Fractional distillation

① Crude oil is separated into fractions by fractional distillation. Fractions are mixture of hydrocarbons which contain similar numbers of carbon atoms, and therefore have similar physical properties.

Describe how fractional distillation separates crude oil into fractions. (4 marks, ★★★★)

NAILIT!

Note: use the key words **heat**, **evaporate**, **condense** and **boiling points** when describing fractional distillation.

....

....

② Two of the fractions produced during fractional distillation are in the table below.

Name of fraction	Use	Example of alkane in this fraction	Molecular formula of alkane	Boiling point of alkane/°C
Petroleum gases	Household fuels	Methane	CH_4	−162
Kerosene		Dodecane		214

Kerosene contains an alkane called dodecane, which has 12 carbon atoms.

a **State a use for kerosene.** (1 mark, ★★) ....

b **What is the molecular formula for dodecane?** (1 mark, ★★) ....

c **Explain why dodecane has a higher boiling point than methane.** (1 mark, ★★)

....

WORKIT!

Balance the chemical equation to show the **complete combustion** of butane, C_4H_{10}.

$C_4H_{10} + O_2 \rightarrow CO_2 + H_2O$

Step 1 Balance the carbon atoms. There are 4 in butane, so this means 4 × CO_2

$C_4H_{10} + O_2 \rightarrow 4CO_2 + H_2O$

Step 2 Balance the hydrogen atoms. There are 10 in butane, which means 5 × H_2O

$C_4H_{10} + O_2 \rightarrow 4CO_2 + 5H_2O$

Step 3 Finally, balance the oxygen atoms. There are now 9 in total. Remember, you have O_2, so you need to halve 9. It's ok to use a fraction – half of 9 is 9/2 or 4½

$C_4H_{10} + 4½O_2 \rightarrow 4CO_2 + 5H_2O$

③ Write balanced chemical equations to show the complete combustion of:

a **Ethane** (2 marks, ★★★) ....

b **Propane** (2 marks, ★★★) ....

c **Pentane** (2 marks, ★★★) ....

Cracking and alkenes

(1) Explain why alkenes are described as **unsaturated hydrocarbons.** (2 marks, ★★★)

....

....

NAILIT!

- Learn the products for the addition reactions for alkenes.
- Alkene + hydrogen → **alkane**
- Alkene + steam → **alcohol**
- Alkene + halogen → **dihaloalkane (an alkane with two halogens attached to it)**

(2) Alkenes undergo addition reactions with hydrogen, steam and halogens.

a Write out the structural formula for these reactions, ensuring that the organic reactants and products are fully displayed.

   i **Pentene + hydrogen** (2 marks, ★★★) ....

   ii **Butene + steam** (2 marks, ★★★) ....

   iii **Propene + chlorine** (2 marks, ★★★) ....

b **Explain why the addition reactions of alkenes show 100% atom economy.** (1 mark, ★★)

....

(3) Complete these equations to show the missing substances. (5 marks, ★★★)

a $C_8H_{18} \rightarrow C_5H_{12} +$ ....

d $C_{14}H_{30} \rightarrow C_4H_{10} + C_6H_{12} +$ ....

b $C_{18}H_{38} \rightarrow C_3H_6 +$ ....

e $C_{14}H_{30} \rightarrow C_8H_{18} + 2$ ....

c .... $\rightarrow C_4H_8 + C_9H_{20}$

(4) Decane is an alkane with ten carbon atoms. Two possible products when it undergoes cracking are hexane (C_6H_{14}) and an unknown compound Z, which decolourises bromine water.

a **What is the formula for decane?** (1 mark, ★) ....

b **Suggest a use for hexane.** (1 mark, ★★) ....

c **Why does compound Z decolourise bromine water?** (1 mark, ★★) ....

d **Suggest a use for compound Z.** (1 mark, ★★) ....

e **Work out the formula for compound Z and use this to construct the overall chemical equation for the cracking of decane.** (1 mark, ★★★)

....

Testing for gases

(1) **Match the gas to its test and result if it is present. Chlorine has been done for you.** (3 marks, ★)

Hydrogen	a glowing splint put into a test tube of the gas	is extinguished with a 'pop'
Oxygen	bubble the gas through a solution of limewater	produces solid calcium carbonate, turning the limewater cloudy
Carbon dioxide	expose to litmus or UI paper	colour change and bleaches the paper
Chlorine	a lighted splint put into a test tube of the gas	relights

(2) **For each of the following, identify the gas being tested.** (4 marks, ★★)

a **The gas turns limewater turns cloudy.** ....

b **The gas bleaches litmus paper.** ....

c **The gas extinguishes a lighted splint with a pop.** ....

d **The gas relights a glowing splint.** ....

NAILIT!

Chlorine gas is toxic – reactions involving the production of it should be done in small quantities and in a fume cupboard.

(3) **For the following reactions, describe the test that could be used to confirm the gases produced.** (4 marks, ★★)

a $CH_4 + 2O_2 \rightarrow CO_2 + 2H_2O$ ....

b $Mg + H_2SO_4 \rightarrow MgSO_4 + H_2$ ....

c $CO_2 + H_2O \rightarrow C_6H_{12}O_6 + O_2$ ....

d $HCl + MnO_2 \rightarrow MnCl_2 + 2H_2O + Cl_2$ ....

NAILIT!

Hydrogen is actually a very flammable gas and can cause explosions. The pop you hear is actually a tiny explosion!

(4) **A student sets up an experiment using limewater to test the gases produced by a lit candle.**

Explain what the student will observe, and how they could find out whether the candle produces other gases. (6 marks, ★★★)

NAILIT!

You are expected to remember each of the tests for gases.

- Carbon dioxide – limewater
- Oxygen – relight
- Hydrogen – pop
- Chlorine – bleach

....
....
....
....
....
....

The composition and evolution of the Earth's atmosphere

1　**a** Tick **two** processes that reduced the amount of carbon dioxide in the atmosphere. (2 marks, ★)

Carbonate rock formation	
Respiration by animals	
Fossil fuel combustion	
Fossil fuel formation	

b What reduced the amount of water vapour in the atmosphere? (1 mark, ★★)

....

....

....

c Explain how this affected the amount of carbon dioxide in the atmosphere? (2 marks, ★★)

....

d Photosynthesis by algae, bacteria and later, plants, is thought to have significantly reduced the amount of carbon dioxide in the atmosphere. Write the balanced chemical equation for the reaction. (2 marks, ★★)

....

2　Some students set up an experiment to investigate what percentage of air is oxygen, as shown in the diagram below.

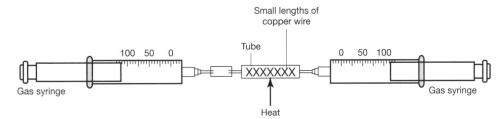

$100\,cm^3$ of air is drawn into the syringe. When heated, the oxygen in the air reacts with the copper in the tube. At the end of the experiment, the volume of gas in the syringe had reduced to $78.5\ cm^3$. The equation for the reaction is:

.........$Cu + O_2 \rightarrow$.........CuO

a Balance the chemical equation. (1 mark, ★)

b Calculate the percentage of oxygen in the $100\,cm^3$ sample of dry air. (1 mark, ★★)

....

....

c Explain why it is important to allow the apparatus to cool before recording the result. (2 marks, ★★)

....

....

....

Climate change

① It is known that some gases are greenhouse gases that have the potential to increase global temperatures. It is also known that human activity has increased the amount of some of these greenhouse gases in the atmosphere. To understand the possible consequences, scientists have created climate models that they use to try to predict future changes to the Earth's climate.

a Give **one** reason why it is difficult to create models to predict future climate change. (1 mark, ★)

....

b Describe what is meant by the term **peer review.** (1 mark, ★★)

....

c Identify **two** greenhouse gases. (2 marks, ★)

....

d Describe how human activity has increased the amount of these two gases in the atmosphere. (4 marks, ★★)

....

....

....

....

② The graph below shows how temperatures and the proportion of CO_2 have changed over the last 400 000 years.

a Suggest **two** conclusions you could make from the data in the graph. (2 marks, ★★★)

....

....

b One theory about climate change is that temperatures on Earth have always changed with natural increases and decreases in the amount of CO_2 in the atmosphere and that the current situation is no different. Use the data in the graph and your knowledge to **evaluate** this theory. (4 marks, ★★★★)

....

....

....

....

The carbon footprint and its reduction

1 **Match the method of reducing the carbon footprint to the description of how it works.**
(3 marks, ★★)

Alternative energy	Removing the carbon dioxide given out by power stations by reacting it with other chemicals. The product of this reaction can then be stored deep under the sea in porous sedimentary rocks.
Energy conservation	Plants take in carbon dioxide as they grow, when they are burned they only release the same amount of carbon dioxide. This makes them carbon neutral.
Carbon Capture and Storage (CCS)	Renewable energy sources such as solar cells, wind power and wave power do not rely on the burning of fossil fuels.
Carbon taxes	Reducing the amount of energy used by using energy-saving measures such as house insulation, using devices that use less energy, reduces the demand for energy.
	Penalising companies and individuals who use too much energy by increasing their taxes reduces the demand for energy.
Carbon offsetting	Removing carbon dioxide from the air using natural biological processes such as photosynthesis. This is achieved by planting trees and increasing marine algae by adding chemicals to the oceans.
Using plants as biofuels	

2 The table shows the annual carbon footprint (in tonnes per person) of some countries in 1990 and 2011.

a **Suggest two reasons that countries such as the USA and Qatar have carbon footprints much higher than China or India.** (2 marks, ★★)

....

....

b **Describe how the carbon footprint in the UK has changed since 1990.**
(1 mark, ★)

Country	Carbon footprint (tonnes/person) 1990	Carbon footprint (tonnes/person) 2011
Qatar	25.2	44.0
USA	19.1	17
UK	10	7.1
Greece	7.2	7.6
New Zealand	7.1	7.1
China	2.2	7.2
India	0.7	1.2

....

c **Explain why some countries have seen an increase in their carbon footprints since 1990.** (3 marks, ★★★)

....

....

Atmospheric pollutants

1 **Match the pollutant with its effects and ways to reduce its release in the atmosphere.**
(4 marks, ★★)

| Soot | | Dissolves in clouds to cause acid rain and causes respiratory problems | Ensure complete combustion of fossil fuels |

| Carbon monoxide | | A toxic gas which binds to haemoglobin in the blood, preventing the transport of oxygen around the body | Desulfurisation of petrochemicals before combustion |

| Sulfur dioxide | | Global dimming and lung damage | Ensure complete combustion of fossil fuels |

| Oxides of nitrogen | | Dissolves in clouds to cause acid rain and causes respiratory problems | Catalytic converters used after combustion |

2 **The table below shows information about the pollutants emitted by cars which use diesel and petrol fuels.**

Fuel	Relative proportion of CO_2	Relative proportion of SO_2	Relative amount of particulate matter	Relative amount of oxides of nitrogen
Diesel	80	40	100	30
Petrol	100	10	0	20

a **Compare the pollutants from cars using petrol as their fuel to those using diesel.** (3 marks, ★★)

....

....

....

b **Electric cars emit no pollutants directly and are powered by batteries that are recharged by plugging them into an electrical plug socket. Suggest how powering these vehicles may still release pollutants into the atmosphere.** (2 marks, ★★)

....

....

3 **The use of coal to produce electricity has in recent decades reduced in many countries. However, with reducing oil supplies, some countries are considering building new coal power stations. The chemical reaction for the complete combustion of coal is:**

$4C_{240}H_{90}O_4NS + 1053O_2 \rightarrow 960CO_2 + 174H_2O + 4HNO_3 + 4H_2SO_4$

a **Calculate the number of moles of carbon dioxide released when 8 moles of coal is burned in an excess of oxygen.** (2 marks, ★★)

....

b **In the 1950s, thousands of people in London died during the 'London Smog'. Many of these deaths were due to high levels of sulfur dioxide in the atmosphere released by the burning of fossil fuels such as coal. Using the balanced equation above, explain how burning coal can also cause damage to limestone buildings, trees and plant crops.** (2 marks, ★★★)

....

....

Using resources

Finite and renewable resources, sustainable development

(1) **Fill the gaps to complete the sentence about finite and renewable resources.** (5 marks, ★)

The .... used by chemists to make new materials can be divided into two categories – .... and .... resources will run out. Examples are fossil fuels and various metals. .... resources are ones that can be replaced at the same rate as they are used up. They are derived from plant materials.

.... meets the needs of present development without depleting natural resources for future generations.

natural resources	finite	renewable	sustainable development

(some words are used twice)

(2) **State four characteristics of a sustainable process.** (4 marks, ★)

....

....

....

....

> **NAILIT!**
>
> Look over your notes on atom economy and percentage yield as you may be asked to compare the sustainability of reactions in terms of quantitatively using them.

(3) **Explain how the use of catalysts helps make chemical reactions more sustainable.** (2 marks, ★★)

....

....

(4) **Two companies produce a plastic used to manufacture goods. Company A uses a method where they expect to produce 25 kg. Company B uses a method where they expect to produce 19 kg. Company A actually produces 22 kg and Company B actually produces 18 kg.**

  a **Calculate the percentage yield for both companies.** (2 marks, ★★)

  ....

  ....

  ....

  b **Suggest which company uses the more sustainable method.** (1 mark, ★★)

  ....

  ....

  ....

  ....

> **NAILIT!**
>
> Sustainable processes:
> - have reactions with high atom economy with as few waste products as possible;
> - use renewable resources from plant sources;
> - have as few steps as possible to eliminate waste and increase the yield;
> - use catalysts to save energy.

Life cycle assessments (LCAs)

(1) Explain what is meant by the term life cycle assessment. (2 marks, ★)

....

....

(2) List the stages of a life cycle assessment. (2 marks, ★)

....

....

(3) a Complete the table of the life cycle assessments of paper and plastic shopping bags. (4 marks, ★★)

Stage of LCA	Plastic bag	Paper bag
Source of raw materials		Come from trees
Production	Simple process involving no chemical change	
Use	Reusable	
End of life	Decompose slowly but produce less	Decompose quickly but generate more ....

b Use the information in the table to compare the life cycle assessments of the paper and plastic shopping bags. (2 marks, ★★★)

....

....

....

(4) A supermarket that supplies its customers with plastic carrier bags ran the following advert:

'Our carrier bags are environmentally friendly as their manufacture produces no harmful pollutants. They're also reusable.'

Explain why the advert is misleading. (2 marks, ★★★)

....

....

....

Alternative methods of copper extraction

1. a **Complete the flow chart below to show how copper ores that are rich in copper can be extracted.** (1 mark, ★★)

copper rich ores → [....................] ⋯⋯ → [....................] → copper

b **Suggest a reason why the copper produced by smelting may need to undergo electrolysis.** (1 mark, ★★)

....

2. **Tick two potential problems when using these processes.** (2 marks, ★)

Smelting and electrolysis use a lot of energy	☐
Copper-rich ores are scarce	☐
Copper is less reactive than iron	☐
Copper is used in many products	☐
Electrolysis is not necessary	☐

> **NAILIT!**
>
> Copper is a widely used metal – it is in coins, electrical wiring and motors, because it conducts heat and electricity well.

> **NAILIT!**
>
> Copper-rich ores are scarce because copper is so widely used. Using traditional methods for ores that are low in copper is uneconomical – it costs more than the value of the copper produced. Developing alternative processes is an active area of research.

3. a **Tick three alternative methods that can be used to extract copper from low-grade ores.** (3 marks, ★)

Distillation using heat	☐
Bioleaching using bacteria	☐
Phytomining using plants	☐
Displacement using silver	☐
Displacement using iron	☐

> **NAILIT!**
>
> This is another topic where it's useful to know the order of reactivity of metals!

b **Identify one advantage and one disadvantage for each of these methods.** (3 marks, ★★)

i Method ....

Advantage: .... Disadvantage: ....

ii Method ....

Advantage: .... Disadvantage: ....

iii Method ....

Advantage: .... Disadvantage: ....

Making potable water and waste water treatment

① **State what is meant by the term potable water.** (1 mark, ★)

....

② **Explain why potable water can't be described as 'pure water'.** (2 marks, ★)

....

③ **The flow chart below shows the different stages in the production of potable water.**

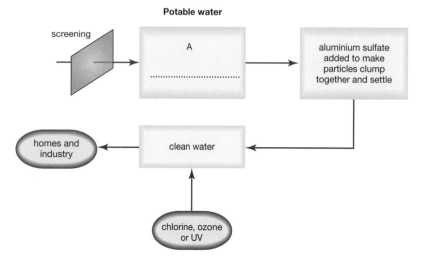

Potable water

a **Fill in the gap in the box marked 'A' to identify what happens at that stage of potable water production.**
(1 mark, ★)

b **Suggest why chlorine, ozone or UV is used in this process.** (1 mark, ★★)

....

....

④ **One way to obtain potable water from salt water is by distillation.**

a **Identify one other way to obtain potable water from salt water.** (1 mark, ★)

....

b **Explain why distillation requires energy to heat the salt water.** (2 marks, ★★)

....

....

⑤ **The flow chart below shows how waste water is treated.**

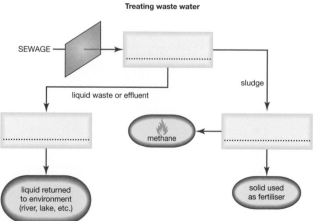

Treating waste water

a **Complete the diagram to identify the stages of waste water treatment.**
(4 marks, ★★)

b **Suggest what additional treatment may be needed for industrial waste before it can be released into the environment.** (1 mark, ★★★)

....

....

Ways of reducing the use of resources

① There are many benefits to reusing and recycling materials like glass, plastic and metal.

a **Tick two** statements which are not benefits of reusing glass bottles. (2 marks, ★)

Reduces use of limited raw materials to make glass bottles	
Reduces use of glass bottles	
Reduces demand for energy from limited resources	
Melting glass bottles to form new products requires energy	
Reduces use of limited raw materials to make other glass products	

NAILIT!

Remember that steel is an alloy of iron with specific amounts of carbon and other metals.

b **Tick three** statements which are processes involved in recycling metals. (3 marks, ★)

Separation	
Distillation	
Reforming	
Demineralisation	
Melting	
Cracking	

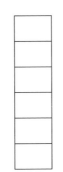

NAILIT!

Extracting metals from their ores is energy intensive. Look back at the metals topic to see how metals are extracted and how the reactivity of a metal impacts the amount of energy required to extract it.

② The table below shows data about the extraction and recycling of iron and aluminium.

	Iron		Aluminium	
	Extraction	Recycling	Extraction	Recycling
Relative energy use	70	30	95	5
Relative CO_2 emissions	70	30	95	5
Relative impact on ore deposits	100	0	100	0
Comments	Magnetic		Reactive	

a **Suggest why iron is easy to separate from other metals.** (1 mark, ★)

....

b **Describe how recycled iron can reduce the amount of raw materials required to produce steel.** (2 marks, ★★)

....

....

c **Explain why increasing the amount of aluminium that is recycled is important.** (3 marks, ★★★)

....

....

The Haber process

(1) **What is the product of the Haber process? Tick one box.** (1 mark, ★)

Ammonia	
Nitrogen	
Nitrates	
Nitrites	

(2) **Write a balanced chemical equation for the reaction.** (2 marks, ★)

....

....

(3) **Which of these describes the Haber process best? Tick one box.** (1 mark, ★★)

The reaction is reversible and the forward reaction is exothermic. This means that the backward reaction is endothermic.	
The reaction is reversible and the forward reaction is endothermic. This means that the backward reaction is exothermic.	
The reaction is not reversible and the reaction is endothermic.	
The reaction is not reversible and the reaction is exothermic.	

(4) **Describe the conditions of the Haber process.** (3 marks, ★★)

....

....

(5) **Explain the compromised conditions used in the Haber process.** (6 marks, ★★★)

....

....

....

....

(6) **The graph below shows the percentage yield of ammonia changes with pressure at different temperatures.**

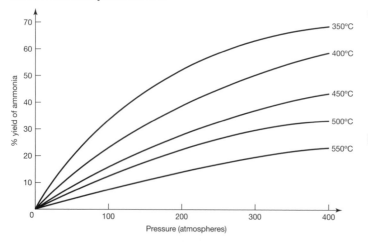

a **Explain why the percentage yield of ammonia is higher at higher pressure.** (2 marks, ★★)

....

....

b **Explain why 350°C is described as a 'compromise'.** (2 marks, ★★)

....

....

c **Determine the percentage yield of ammonia at:**

i **300 atmospheres and 400°C** (1 mark, ★★★) ....

ii **200 atmospheres and 350°C** (1 mark, ★★★) ....

Energy

1 **Complete the gaps with the following words. The words can only be used once.** (3 marks, ★★★)

A system is an object, or group of objects. The .... in a system is a numerical .... that tells us whether certain .... in the system could, or could not, happen. The total .... of energy in a system is always the .... no matter what changes happen in the system, but the energy available can be .... in different parts of this system.

amount	form	different	energy	changes
same	redistributed	kinetic	decreases	value

2 **Match the following energy stores to where they are found. Two have been done for you.** (3 marks, ★★)

1 Gravitational potential	**a** Fuel
2 Kinetic	**b** A position in the gravitational field
3 Thermal	**c** In a stretched or compressed spring
4 Nuclear	**d** In a warm object
5 Magnetic	**e** In two separated magnets that attract/repel
6 Elastic potential	**f** In two separated charges that attract/repel
7 Electrostatic	**g** Large unstable nuclei such as plutonium and uranium
8 Chemical	**h** In a moving object

3 **Complete the flowchart below for someone making a cup of tea at a campsite with a saucepan and butane burner.** (5 marks, ★★)

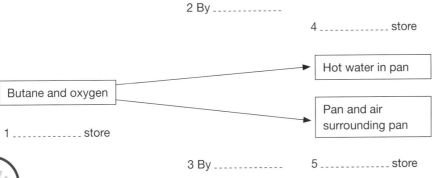

2 By ....

4 .... store

Butane and oxygen

Hot water in pan

Pan and air surrounding pan

1 .... store

3 By ....   5 .... store

DO IT!

Think about different situations and the changes in the energy stores that take place. Can you identify the useful energy stores or pathways? For example, a boy flicking an elastic band, a girl climbing up some stairs, or a sky diver on his descent.

NAILIT!

Use a mnemonic to learn the energy stores: **T**hermal, **N**uclear, **E**lectrostatic, **C**hemical, **G**ravitational potential, **E**lastic potential, **M**agnetic. The first letter of the mnemonic is the first letter of each energy store: **T**homas **N**ever **E**ats **C**arrots **G**ranny **E**ats **M**any.

Changes in energy stores: kinetic energy

① a **Write the equation used to calculate the kinetic energy of a moving object.** (1 mark, ★★)

....

b **Write the unit for the energy in a kinetic store.**
(1 mark, ★★)

....

② **A car of mass 1000 kg is moving at 10 m/s. Calculate the car's energy in the kinetic store.** (2 marks, ★★★)

....

....

WORKIT!

How to tackle a question where you would normally rearrange the equation at the beginning.

Calculate the speed of a 6000 kg bus with 3.7 MJ of energy in the kinetic store. (4 marks, ★★★)

Step 1 $E_k = 0.5 \times m \times v^2$ ◄——————— Write the formula but don't try to rearrange. Write 0.5 instead of $\frac{1}{2}$.

Step 2 Substitute in the values you are given.

$3\,700\,000 = 0.5 \times 6000 \times v^2$ (1) ◄——— Leave v^2 alone!

Step 3 Multiply out right-hand terms 0.5 and 6000.

$3\,700\,000 = 3000 \times v^2$ (1) ◄——— To get v^2 on its own divide both sides by 3000.

Step 4 $\dfrac{3\,700\,000}{3000} = \dfrac{3000}{3000} \times v^2$

Step 5 Swap v^2 to the left-hand side and take the square root of both sides. Remember → $\sqrt{v^2} = v$ → $v = \sqrt{1233} = 35\,m/s$ (1)

The bus is going at 35 m/s which is approximately 70 mph. It should slow down! (1)

For those who are good at rearranging equations: $v = \sqrt{\dfrac{2 \times E_k}{m}} = \sqrt{\dfrac{2 \times 3\,700\,000}{3000}} = 35\,m/s$

③ **A train is travelling at a speed of 10 m/s and has 0.8 MJ of energy in the kinetic store. Calculate the train's mass.** (4 marks, ★★★★)

....

....

....

....

Changes in energy stores: elastic potential energy

① **State the elastic potential energy equation.** (1 mark, ★★★)

....

....

② **A spring has a spring constant k = 10 N/m.**

A force is applied to stretch the spring. The spring's length increases from 5 cm to 25 cm.

Calculate the energy in the elastic potential store of the spring. (4 marks, ★★★★)

....

....

....

Metre rule

Spring

Slotted mass

③ **A force of 2.5 N is applied to a spring. The spring's length increases from 10 cm to 20 cm.**

Calculate the spring constant of the spring. Express your answer in N/m. (4 marks, ★★★)

....

....

....

....

④ **A fisherman has a fish on the end of his rod, and is trying to reel it in.**

His fishing rod line has 20 J of energy in the elastic potential store. The spring constant of the line is 10 kN/m.

Calculate the extension of the line in cm. (4 marks, ★★★★★)

....

....

....

 **NAILIT!**

In calculation questions, always write the equation first. Then substitute in the values from the question. You might get some marks just for showing you know the equation and can substitute in the correct values.

NAILIT!

Formulas for kinetic energy and elastic potential energy both include the fraction $\frac{1}{2}$ in the formula. Remember to enter it as 0.5 on a calculator when trying to work out a problem.

Changes in energy stores: gravitational potential energy

(1) **State the gravitational potential energy equation.** (1 mark, ★★★)

....

....

....

DO IT!

Memorise the gravitational potential energy equation. Write it out over and over again.

Use (g = 10 N/kg) for all questions.

(2) **Calculate the (energy) gain in the gravitational potential store of a power drill when a power drill of 4 kg is lifted upwards 4 m by a man climbing a ladder.** (2 marks, ★★★)

....

....

....

NAILIT!

Remember that weight is a force and
weight = mass × gravitational field strength.
Do you notice any similarity between the formula for work done and gravitational potential energy?

(3) **Calculate the (energy) gain in the gravitational potential store when a mass of 40 kg is lifted upwards 500 cm by a forklift.** (2 marks, ★★★)

....

....

....

(4) **Calculate the height fallen by a ball of mass 300 g if the energy in the gravitational store decreases by 90 J.** (4 marks, ★★★★)

....

....

....

....

Energy changes in systems: specific heat capacity

Specific heat capacities to be used in questions:

Water: 4200 J/kg °C   Ethanol: 2400 J/kg °C

Rubber: 2000 J/kg °C   Air: 1000 J/kg °C

Copper: 390 J/kg °C

1 a **Write a definition for specific heat capacity.** (1 mark, ★★)

....

....

   b **State the equation for specific heat capacity.** (1 mark, ★★)

....

   c **Write the unit for specific heat capacity.** (1 mark, ★★)

....

2 **Two objects of the same mass are heated up on a hotplate for the same amount of time.**

   One is made of copper, the other of steel.

   The copper object rises in temperature from 25°C to 35°C.

   The temperature of the iron object increases only from 25°C to 30°C.

   Using ideas about specific heat capacity, explain why this happens. (3 marks, ★★★★)

> **NAILIT!**
>
> Remember specific heat capacity is a measure of how much energy is required to raise the temperature of 1 kg of a substance by 1°C. Metals require less energy to change their temperature than non-metals. Use this to consider why metals feel colder than non-metals.

....

....

....

3 **A teacher uses a Bunsen burner to heat some ethanol in a beaker.**

   The energy supplied by the burner is 1.5 kJ.

   The temperature increases from 25°C to 35°C.

   Find the mass of ethanol in kg that was heated.
   (4 marks, ★★★★)

> **DOIT!**
>
> Think about why a fruit pie feels quite cool on the outside but when you bite into the filling it burns your tongue. Try to explain why this happens. It has something to do with specific heat capacity.

....

....

....

....

Power

(1) Bill and Ted went to the gym. They argued about who was the most powerful. They decided on three tests in the gym to see who was correct. First, they bench-pressed 30 kg for 60 seconds. Next they timed how many step-ups they could do in 60 seconds. Finally, they did kettle bell raises for 60 seconds. Their results are shown in the table.

Activity	Bill	Ted
Bench press	50 repetitions in 60 s Uses 7.5 kJ in total Power	42 repetitions in 60 s Uses 6.3 kJ in total Power ....
Step-ups	89 repetitions in 60 s Uses 17.8 kJ in total Power	100 repetitions in 60 s Uses 20 kJ in total Power ....
Kettle bell raises	60 raises in 60 s Uses 7.2 kJ in total Power	67 raises in 60 s Uses 8.04 kJ in total Power ....

power = energy transferred ÷ time

a Calculate the power of each man for each activity and add to the table above. (6 marks, ★★★)

b Who was the most powerful overall? (2 marks, ★★★)

....

(2) A television has a power rating of 50 watts.

It is switched on for $7\frac{1}{2}$ hours.

Calculate the energy transferred in this time. (2 marks, ★★★)

....

....

(3) A forklift works at 100 kW of power.

The forklift requires 2200 kJ of energy to lift a heavy crate onto a higher loading platform.

Calculate the time taken for the forklift to load the crate onto the platform. (3 marks, ★★★★)

....

....

....

Energy transfers in a system

1. **State the conservation of energy law.** (2 marks, ★★★)

   ....

   ....

2. **Look at the table.**

   Complete the table by giving examples of devices where electricity can be transferred into each of the energy stores.
   (3 marks, ★★★)

Electricity changes into:	Example
Gravitational potential store	
Vibrational store	
Thermal store	

3. **For each of the following statements, write down the changes in energy stores that take place.** (4 marks, ★★★★)

   a **A person base-jumping off the Eiffel Tower** ....

   b **A gas fire** ....

   c **Shooting a stone from a catapult** ....

   d **Boiling water in an electric kettle** ....

WORKIT!

Describe the changes in the way energy is stored if a rocket is fired. Explain the journey until it runs out of fuel. (3 marks, ★★★)

Before the rocket is launched the chemical ◄— store is full. (1)

> Remember to break your answers into short sentences. This will make it easier for the examiner to mark.

At the instant the fuel is lit the chemical store begins to empty and kinetic and thermal stores fill. (1)

As the rocket goes higher its gravitational store increases. The kinetic store will also keep increasing until the rocket runs out of fuel. If the fuel is burned at the same rate, the thermal store will remain fairly constant, but some of the thermal energy store will be dissipated to the surroundings. (1)

NAILIT!

Do not confuse energy resources with energy stores.

Energy resources are: nuclear, coal, gas, oil, geothermal, tidal, wind, wave, biofuels, and hydroelectric.

Think of your own mnemonic to learn the ways of generating energy.

DOIT!

Practise the mnemonic you have learned. Can you remember what every letter stands for? **T**homas **N**ever **E**ats **C**arrots **G**ranny **E**ats **M**any.

Efficiency

① a **State the efficiency equation.** (1 mark, ★★★)

....

b **State the two ways of stating a value of efficiency.** (2 marks, ★★★★)

....

....

② **Complete the table below. The first example has been done for you.** (3 marks, ★★★)

Device or situation	Initial energy store	Final energy store
Catapult	Elastic	Kinetic
A go-kart freewheeling down a hill		
A car going uphill		
A growing plant		

③ **An MP3 changes 500 joules of energy via electrical work to 360 joules of useful energy stores. How efficient is it?** (2 marks, ★★★★)

....

....

....

④ **What is the efficiency of a van that requires 5000 joules of energy from its chemical store to transfer 900 joules to its kinetic store?** (2 marks, ★★★★)

....

....

....

NAILIT!

An energy transfer will never be 100% efficient in practice. In a laboratory or practical situation some energy is always dissipated, increasing the thermal store of the air around us.

National and global energy resources

1 The table below lists some renewable and non-renewable sources of energy.

Source	Renewable?	Requires burning
Geothermal Power	Yes	No
Coal		
Biofuels	Yes/No	Yes
Oil		
Uranium		
Wave Power		
Solar Farms		
Wind Power		
Hydroelectricity		

Complete the table above to show whether each source:

a **Is renewable.** (4 marks, ★★)

b **Needs to be burned.** (1 mark, ★★★)

2 **Why are biofuels identified as both renewable and non-renewable?** (1 mark, ★★★★)

....

....

3 **The graph below shows how the power output from a wind turbine changes with wind speed.**

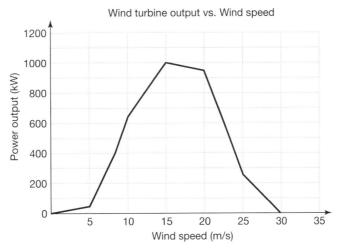

Wind turbine output vs. Wind speed

a **At what wind speed is the power at a maximum?** (2 marks, ★★★)

....

....

b **If this maximum power output was constant, how many of these wind turbines would be needed to provide a total power output of 10 MW?** (2 marks, ★★★)

....

....

c **Why is it unlikely that a wind farm would produce a constant power output?** (1 mark, ★★★)

....

....

Standard circuit diagram symbols

(1) **Name and draw a component in the box that matches the description.** (4 marks, ★★★★)

1 Used to measure current	(A) Ammeter
2 Changes resistance with light intensity	
3 Only lets current flow in one direction	
4 Can be used to vary resistance	
5 A safety component that melts when the current gets too high	

(2) **A student wants to get the *I–V* characteristic for a filament lamp.**

a **Draw a circuit diagram to show the components they would use.** (2 marks, ★★★★★)

b **Explain the method they would use to carry out the experiment.** (6 marks, ★★★★★)

....

....

....

....

....

....

NAILIT!

Remember that a cell and a battery are both power supplies, but a battery is two or more cells joined together.

DOIT!

The only way to learn the circuit symbols is to keep drawing and redrawing them. Use a ruler and a 5p or 1p coin to draw ammeters, voltmeters, light dependent resistors and diodes.

Electrical charge and current

1 **State the equation linking charge, current and time.** (1 mark, ★★)

....

2 **Complete the following sentences.** (6 marks, ★★★)

.... is the name given to the flow of negatively .... particles around a

closed circuit. These particles are called .... Because of their charge they are

attracted to the .... terminal of a cell or .... In books we refer to the

opposite direction and call this .... current flow. This is where the current flows from

the positive to negative terminal of the power supply.

conventional	charged	electrons	positive	current
energy	alternating	protons	negative	battery

3 **Use the formula that links charge, current and time to complete the table.** (4 marks, ★★★)

Charge (C)	Current (A)	Time (s)
10	10	1
40	2	
10	2	
100		500
	6	150

DOIT!

Make a mnemonic to learn difficult symbols such as Q for charge. An example is: the **Q**ueen is in **C**harge. Remember if you make your own, you will remember them much more easily.

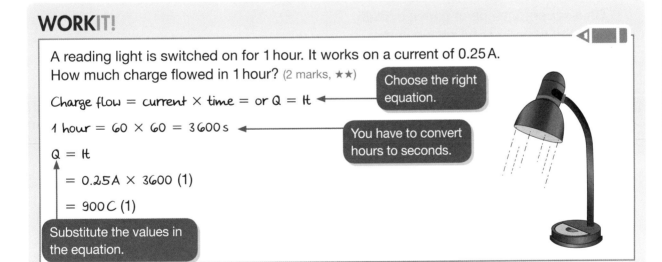

WORKIT!

A reading light is switched on for 1 hour. It works on a current of 0.25 A. How much charge flowed in 1 hour? (2 marks, ★★)

Choose the right equation.

Charge flow = current × time = or Q = It

1 hour = 60 × 60 = 3600 s

You have to convert hours to seconds.

Q = It

= 0.25 A × 3600 (1)

= 900 C (1)

Substitute the values in the equation.

 NAILIT!

Success in the electricity topic hinges on learning all the circuit symbols and then learning the formulas, symbols and units. Keep testing yourself over and over again. Repetition is the key.

Current, resistance and potential difference and resistors

(1) a **State the equation linking potential difference, current and resistance.** (1 mark, ★★)

....

b **What is this equation called?** (1 mark, ★★)

....

c **What condition needs to be present for it to work?** (1 mark, ★)

....

(2) **The diagram below shows part of an electric circuit.** (4 marks, ★★★★)

Complete the circuit diagram by adding:

a **A variable resistor in series with the battery.**

b **A fixed resistor in series with the battery.**

c **A voltmeter that measures the potential difference across the fixed resistor.**

d **An ammeter in series that measures the total current in the series circuit.**

(3) **On a separate piece of paper, explain how the experimental set-up in the question above could be used to find the resistance of the fixed resistor.** (6 marks, ★★★★)

Include the following: how equipment is used, which measurements are taken, and how results are analysed to plot a graph.

(4) **Calculate the total resistance in the following resistor combination.** (2 marks, ★★★)

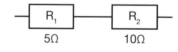

R₁ 5Ω   R₂ 10Ω

....

....

(5) **The resistance vs temperature graph for one type of electrical component is drawn below.**

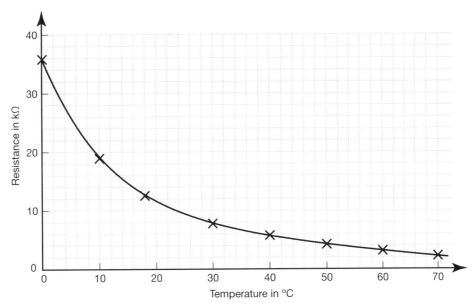

a **What component would have this relationship?** (1 mark, ★★)

....

b **Complete the diagram to show a circuit that can be used to make a results table of resistance vs temperature for the device.** (4 marks, ★★★★)

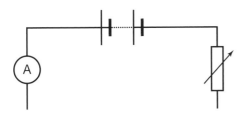

NAILIT!

Use the correct circuit symbol for each component that you add to the diagram.

c i **What other measuring device would you need to gather the data for the graph, and how would you control the temperature?** (2 marks, ★★★)

....

....

ii **Use the graph to find out the resistance of the device at 10°C.** (2 marks, ★★★)

....

....

iii **How could the device be used in a practical application?** (1 mark, ★★★)

....

Series and parallel circuits

1 Draw series circuits in the three boxes below with the following instructions. A complete circuit that contains:

   a **One bulb, one cell and a switch.** (2 marks, ★★)

   b **Two cells (connected together correctly) and three bulbs. Connect an ammeter to measure the circuit current.** (3 marks, ★★★)

   c **A battery, thermistor and bulb. Connect a voltmeter to measure the potential difference of the thermistor.** (4 marks, ★★★★)

a	b	c

2 Draw parallel circuits in the boxes below with the following instructions. A complete circuit that contains:

   a **One battery, two bulbs in parallel and a switch that switches off both bulbs.** (2 marks, ★★)

   b **One battery, three bulbs in parallel and a switch that only switches off one bulb.** (2 marks, ★★★★)

   c **A battery, bulb and thermistor in series and a bulb connected in parallel with the thermistor.** (2 marks, ★★★★)

a	b	c

3 Explain why all the lights in a house can be switched off separately in different rooms.
(2 marks, ★★★)

....

....

....

Mains electricity: direct and alternating potential difference (dc/ac)

(1) **a What do the terms dc and ac stand for?** (2 marks, ★★★)

....

b Describe the difference between ac and dc. (2 marks, ★★★)

....

....

(2) **Explain why we have to use ac for domestic supply.** (4 marks, ★★★★)

....

....

....

(3) **What type of potential difference is being supplied in the diagram to the right? What is the potential difference's value if each square represents 2V?** (2 marks, ★★★★)

....

....

....

(4) **An ac source is connected to an oscilloscope. The waveform of the alternating potential difference from the source is displayed on the oscilloscope screen to the right.**

The Y-gain setting of the oscilloscope is 5V/square. Determine the amplitude of the alternating potential difference. (2 marks, ★★★★★)

....

....

....

NAILIT!

Small portable devices generally run on dc, for example, laptops, torches, and mobile phones.

Larger domestic appliances or heaters usually run on ac, for example fridges, ovens, freezers, and toasters.

DOIT!

Learn the definitions for ac and dc, and explain the difference using a diagram. In one of them the current travels in one direction. In the other the current changes direction 50 times every second. Which is which?

Mains electricity

(1) **Complete the gaps using the words below.** (3 marks, ★★)

The .... supplied to our homes is called .... electricity and it is an ....
current supply. This type of current .... direction many times per second. In fact the
current goes forwards and back .... times per second. This means it has a ....
of 50 Hz.

frequency	changes	fifty	alternating	mains	one hundred
electricity	direct	wavelength	charge	domestic	

(2) **Complete the labels on the following diagram of the plug.** (4 marks, ★★★)

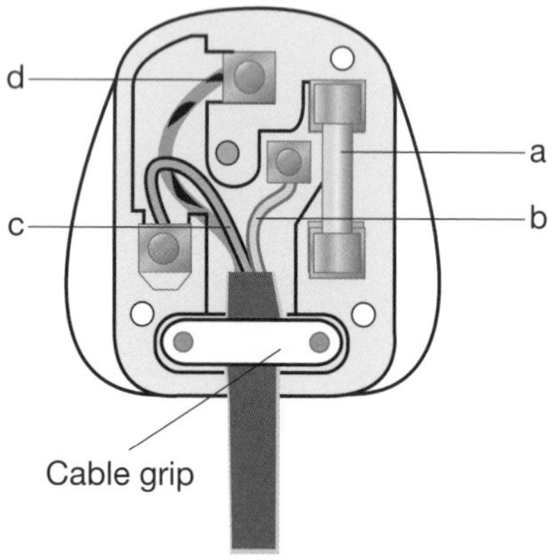

Cable grip

a ....

b ....

c ....

d ....

DO IT!

Practise drawing the inside of a plug and make an effort to remember the colour and main job of each cable.

(3) **Explain the role of the following in mains electricity and give the typical potential difference values for them when the circuit is working correctly.**

a **Earth wire** (1 mark, ★★★) ....

....

b **Live wire** (1 mark, ★★★) ....

....

c **Neutral wire** (1 mark, ★★★) ....

....

(4) a **Explain why a live wire may be dangerous even if a switch in the live circuit is open.** (2 marks, ★★★)

....

....

b **Explain why it is not necessary to connect an earth wire to a device that has a plastic casing.** (2 marks, ★★★)

....

....

NAILIT!

Sockets and the cases of plugs are generally made out of hard plastic. Plastic is used because it is a very good electrical insulator and can be moulded to completely surround the cables.

Electric power (with electrical devices)

(1) **State three formulas for calculating power.** (3 marks, ★★★)

....

....

....

(2) **A 20 V battery supplies 2 A through a resistor. Calculate the power dissipated in the resistor.** (3 marks, ★★)

....

....

....

(3) **A torch has a current of 0.1 A and has a resistance of 100 Ω. What is its power rating?** (2 marks, ★★★)

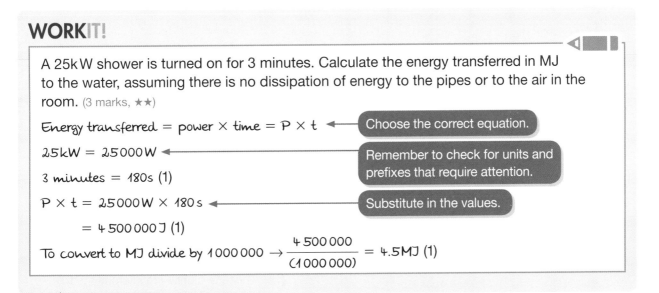

....

....

(4) **A 10 kW electric fire consumes 36 MJ of energy.**

How long is it on for in seconds and hours? (3 marks, ★★★★)

....

....

....

WORKIT!

A 25 kW shower is turned on for 3 minutes. Calculate the energy transferred in MJ to the water, assuming there is no dissipation of energy to the pipes or to the air in the room. (3 marks, ★★)

Energy transferred = power × time = P × t ◄——— Choose the correct equation.

25kW = 25000W ◄———

3 minutes = 180s (1)

Remember to check for units and prefixes that require attention.

P × t = 25000W × 180s ◄——— Substitute in the values.

$\qquad$ = 4500000 J (1)

To convert to MJ divide by 1000000 → $\dfrac{4\,500\,000}{(1\,000\,000)}$ = 4.5MJ (1)

Energy transfers in appliances

(1) **State two formulas for calculating energy.** (2 marks, ★★)

....

....

(2) **Complete the following sentences. Each word can only be used once.** (3 marks, ★★★)

Everyday electrical .... are designed to bring about .... transfers. The .... of energy an appliance .... depends on how .... the appliance is switched on for and the .... of the appliance.

amount	transfers	long	energy	charge
appliances	power	heat	symbols	size

(3) a **A 20 V internet digital radio is switched on and a charge of 500 C flows. How much energy is transferred?** (2 marks, ★★★)

....

....

b **The radio above had a constant current of 2 A. How long was the radio switched on for?** (2 marks, ★★★)

....

....

(4) **An electric toothbrush operates at 12 V and draws a current of 2 A. It is used for 2 minutes. Calculate:**

a **The toothbrush's resistance.** (3 marks, ★★)

....

....

b **The charge flowing through the toothbrush in 2 minutes.** (3 marks, ★★★)

....

....

c **The energy supplied to the toothbrush in 2 minutes.** (3 marks, ★★★)

....

....

....

NAILIT!

Remember the unit for energy is the joule, and the unit for power is the watt.

1 watt is also equivalent to 1 joule/second. This is because:

$$\text{Power} = \frac{\text{energy}}{\text{time}} = \frac{E}{t}$$

So sometimes you might see J/s instead of W. These two units are interchangeable.

The National Grid

(1) **Label a to f in the diagram below with the following words.** (3 marks ★★)

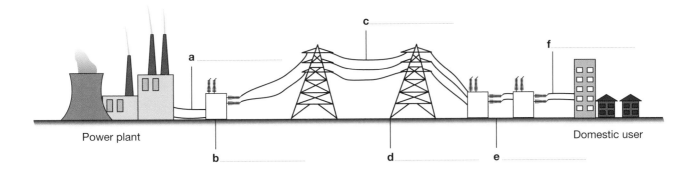

Power plant   Domestic user

230 V	60 Hz	675 kV	2.3 kV	pylon
step-up transformer	step-down transformer	step-up transducer	underground cables	step-down transducer

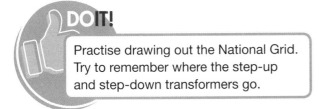

DO IT!

Practise drawing out the National Grid. Try to remember where the step-up and step-down transformers go.

NAIL IT!

You don't need to remember the exact values of potential difference except for domestic supply which is 230 V at 50 Hz.

(2) **Explain how increasing the potential difference in power transmission reduces power losses. You could refer to the equations $P = I^2 R$ or $P = VI$.** (3 marks, ★★★★)

....

....

....

....

③ **A student tries to make a model of the National Grid, it looks like the circuit below.**

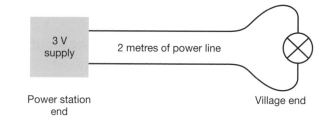

3 V supply

2 metres of power line

Power station end

Village end

a **Explain why the bulb is very dim when the circuit is set up like this.** (1 mark, ★★★)

....

....

b **He improves the design and sets up a circuit like the one below. Why is the bulb now bright? Explain the roles of transformers A and B in the circuit.** (4 marks, ★★★★)

3 V supply

Transformer A

Transformer B

....

....

....

....

....

NAILIT!

Remember that to transfer electrical energy over long distances we need to step-up the potential difference to a higher value. The **power** is constant and we can use the power formula $P = IV$ to explain that if **voltage** goes up, current goes down. If we then put a really small current into another formula for power, $P = I^2 R$. The power losses through heating of the cable are much smaller. Think about it. Try squaring a really small number (a number less than 1) using your calculator and see what happens.

Static charge and electric fields (1)

1. The picture shows an investigation of static electricity. A girl rubs a balloon on her head so the balloon gains a negative charge. She then holds the balloon close to her head, and her hair rises.

   a **Explain, in terms of moving charges, how the balloon becomes negatively charged.** (2 marks, ★★★)

   ....

   ....

   b **Explain why the girl's hair rises.** (2 marks, ★★★)

   ....

   ....

   c **Later the balloon is placed against a wall and it stays 'stuck' to the wall. Explain why.** (2 marks, ★★★)

   ....

   ....

   d **Explain why the balloon won't stay there for as long if the air is damp.** (1 mark, ★★★★)

   ....

NAILIT!

Success in statics questions is mostly about using the following key words with confidence: electrons, friction, insulator, conductor, earth, positive, negative, like, unlike, repel, attract, discharge, and so on.

Remember that in the question it is always something to do with the movement of electrons from one place to another!

Write the answer in short sentences and focus on using key words.

WORKIT!

Explain why the powder paint that leaves a spray paint machine spreads out.

How can static electricity be used to make the paint stick to a car body? (3 marks, ★★)

Friction between the paint and plastic paint nozzle transfers electrons from paint to paint nozzle. The paint powder is now positively charged. (1)

The positively charged paint repels itself as like charges repel. The paint spreads out evenly. (1)

The car is connected to an earth cable so compared to the paint is negatively charged. The positive paint is attracted to the negatively charged car. (1)

Static charge and electric fields (2)

(1) **Complete the following sentences. Each word can only be used once.** (3 marks, ★★★)

A .... object creates an .... field around itself. For example, a car can become charged because of .... removing electrons from it and .... them to dust particles as the car is moving through .... This would leave the car with a .... electric field.

charged	friction	electric	uncharged	transferring
positive	air	force	conduction	negative

(2) a **Draw a diagram of the electric field pattern around the proton below.** (2 marks, ★★)

(P)

b **Another proton is brought towards the first proton. Sketch the field lines.** (3 marks, ★★★★)

(P) (P)

(3) **Use ideas about fields to explain how a lightning rod works.** (3 marks, ★★★★)

....

....

....

DO IT!

Practise drawing field lines for these situations:

- positively or negatively charged objects on their own
- two positively charged objects
- two negatively charged objects
- two objects with opposite charges.

NAILIT!

- Electric field lines always go from positive to negative.
- Field lines never cross.
- The further apart the field lines, the weaker the field.
- The closer together the field lines, the stronger the field.

Particle model

Particle model of matter and density of materials

(1) Complete the sentences. Some of the words can be used more than once. (6 marks, ★★★)

The formula for density is .... divided by .... and the standard SI unit is

.... Sometimes the values are very large so .... are used instead. A density of

.... kg/m³ is equal to the density of .... g/cm³. This is also the density of water.

1000	kg/m³	force	1	g/cm³
area	newtons	mass	1 000 000	volume

(2) A metal block has a volume of 0.005 m³ and mass of 56.5 kg.

a Calculate the density of the metal block in kg/m³. (2 marks, ★★★)

....

b Convert the density to g/cm³. (1 mark, ★★★★)

....

(3) A large wooden block has a volume 8000 cm³ and density of 600 kg/m³.

Calculate the mass of the wooden block in kg. (3 marks, ★★★★)

....

....

(4) A small stone of mass of 18 g is lowered into a measuring cylinder.

The water level increases from 20.0 to 27.5 ml.

Calculate the density of the stone in g/cm³. (4 marks, ★★★★)

Measuring cylinder

Water

Stone

....

....

NAIL IT!

Don't get confused with conversions between m³ → mm³ and m³ → cm³ and vice versa.

Remember 1 m = 100 cm   or   1 m = 1000 mm

$1 m^3 = 1 m \times 1 m \times 1 m = 1 m^3$

$1 m^3 = 100 cm \times 100 cm \times 100 cm = 1 000 000 cm^3$ (or $10^6 cm^3$)

$1 m^3 = 1000 mm \times 1000 mm \times 1000 mm = 1 000 000 000 mm^3$ (or $10^9 mm^3$)

DO IT!

Make an effort to learn the symbol and units for density. The symbol is ρ and is pronounced 'rho' and it is from the Greek alphabet. The units for density are generally g/cm³ or kg/m³. Make sure you can convert between the two.

Changes of state and internal energy

(1) **Marbles in a box are a good model to represent the molecules in a solid, liquid and a gas. Explain which box best represents each state of matter and briefly explain why.**
(6 marks, ★★★★)

A   B   C

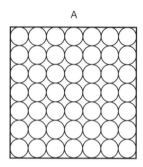 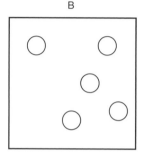 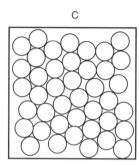

A ....

B ....

C ....

(2) **Explain why the temperature of a window increases when water condenses onto its surface.** (3 marks, ★★★★)

....

....

(3) **What term describes the type of change when ice melts and becomes water? Tick one box.** (1 mark, ★★)

Physical	
Chemical	
Sublimation	
Radiation	

NAILIT!

Practise drawing the diagrams for liquids, solids and gases. Remember to do the following:

- Draw particles as circles and make them all approximately the same size.

- The particles in solids are ordered in straight rows and are touching on all sides. The gaps between them are very small.

- The particles in liquids are still touching, but are not as organised and look a little chaotic. They still fill the container and no gaps are bigger than the particles themselves.

- For gases draw very few atoms that are far apart.

Changes of temperature and specific latent heat

(1) State the formula for specific latent heat. (1 mark, ★★)

....

....

(2) The following diagram represents energy supplied in kJ by a heater to increase the temperature of water from below 0°C to above 100°C.

What happens to the energy of the particles of the solid/liquid in each state-change as more energy is supplied by heating? (6 marks, ★★★★)

....

....

....

....

....

....

(3) Calculate the energy in kJ required to melt 100 g of ice. The specific latent heat of fusion for ice is 334 000 J/kg. (3 marks, ★★★★)

....

....

....

Particle motion in gases (1)

(1) Complete the gaps with the words below. (6 marks, ★★★)

The molecules of gas are in constant .... motion. The average ....
energy of the .... is proportional to temperature on the .... scale.
Changing the temperature of a gas in a container of fixed volume will change the ....
exerted on the sides of the ....

kinetic	random	Celsius	container	kelvin
ordered	gravitational potential		particles	pressure

(2) This diagram shows a sealed box filled with oxygen molecules.

Describe the motion of the molecules. (2 marks, ★★)

....

....

....

(3) Define internal energy. (2 marks, ★★★)

....

....

....

WORKIT!

This diagram shows the kinetic energy of the different gas molecules in a sealed container.

Some of the gas condenses on a cool side of the container.

Referring to the graph explain why the temperature of the remaining gas would initially increase. (4 marks, ★★)

The slower moving molecules would condense onto the surface more readily, as they would require less energy to change from a gas into a liquid. (1)

Molecules with higher kinetic energy (E_k) would remain. (1)

The kinetic energy, or E_k of molecules, is proportional to temperature (in kelvins). (1)

As more higher speed molecules remain, the average temperature will go up. (1)

Graph axes: y-axis — Number of molecules; x-axis — Kinetic energy (Slow, Average, Fast)

DOIT!

Remember that when doing these calculations, unless you are calculating a temperature change, it is always necessary to convert degrees Celsius (°C) into kelvin (K). ◄

A helpful rhyme to learn the conversion is 'K is C plus 273' for K = °C + 273.

Particle motion in gases (2)

(1) State the equation that links pressure and volume in gases. (1 mark, ★★★)

....

(2) The initial temperature of a gas trapped in a container is –23°C. The container is heated and the final temperature of the gas is 477°C.

a **Calculate the temperature change in °C and then state it in kelvins.** (2 marks, ★★★)

....

....

b **What is the change in kinetic energy of the particles in the gas?** (2 marks, ★★★★)

....

....

(3) A gas has an initial volume of 120 cm³ at a pressure of 75 kPa.

Assume that the temperature remains constant.

Calculate the final volume of this gas if pressure is increased to 225 kPa. (3 marks, ★★★★)

....

....

....

(4) When a bicycle pump is used to pump up a tyre, the pump starts to feel warm. Explain why this happens. (3 marks, ★★★★)

....

....

....

NAILIT!

Work done = energy transferred

If we do work on a gas it increases the internal energy of the gas molecules, and this leads to an increase in temperature (remember, E_k is proportional to temperature).

DO IT!

Make sure you learn the units for pressure. The standard unit is the pascal, abbreviated to Pa, which is equivalent to N/m².

The structure of the atom (1)

(1) **Complete the following sentences.** (3 marks, ★★)

  a The atom is composed of 3 subatomic particles: ...., ... and

  ....

  b The centre of the atom is called the .... and contains .... and

  ....

  c An atom contains the same number of .... and .... and has a

  .... charge.

(2) **The diagram shows a simplified helium atom. Insert on the diagram the missing names of the subatomic particles.** (3 marks, ★★)

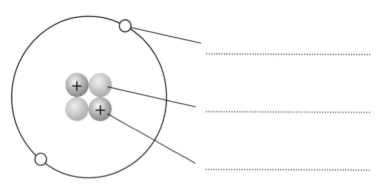

(3) **Complete the table below.** (4 marks, ★★)

Particle	Symbol	Relative mass	Charge
Proton	p		+1
Neutron	n	1	
Electron	e⁻		

NAILIT!

Ideas about the atom have evolved over the centuries. Make sure that you understand the basics of each model.

(4) **Describe our current understanding of the nuclear model of the atom. Make particular reference to the following: radius, size of atom, electron arrangement and mass of atom.** (6 marks, ★★★★)

....

....

....

....

....

The structure of the atom (2)

(1) **State how many protons, neutrons and electrons there are in the atoms below.** (6 marks, ★★★)

⁷Li₃	⁹Be₅	⁶³Cu₂₉

Protons ....

Neutrons ....

Electrons ....

²³Na₁₁	³⁹K₁₉	¹⁵²Eu₆₃

Protons ....

Neutrons ....

Electrons ....

(2) **Complete the sentences below. Some words may be used twice.** (6 marks, ★★★)

An .... is an atom with the same number of .... and a different number

of ....

.... have the same chemical properties as the atom. If the .... number

is altered, the .... changes.

isotope	electrons	protons	different	neutrons	isotopes
	electron	ion	ions	atomic	element

(3) **Circle true (T) or false (F) for the following statements.** (4 marks, ★★★★)

a **To form an ion you have to remove a proton from an atom.**   T   F

b **An ion can be formed by gaining or removing an electron.**   T   F

c **Metal atoms lose electron(s) to form positively charged ions.**   T   F

d **Non-metal atoms lose electrons to form negatively charged ions.**   T   F

Developing a model of the atom

(1) In the early part of the 20th century, scientists thought that the atom was like a 'plum pudding'. They used this model to explain the internal structure of the atom.

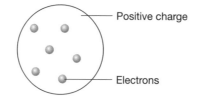

Plum pudding model

Describe the main features of the plum pudding model that were put forward to explain the internal structure of the atom. (3 marks, ★★★★)

....

....

....

(2) **An experiment, designed to investigate the 'plum pudding' model, involved firing alpha particles at thin gold foil leaf.**

The diagram shows the main paths, A, B and C, of several thousand alpha particles. The results are expressed as percentages.

Explain what each of the paths A, B and C tells us about the atom. Your ideas should reference why the plum pudding model was wrong. (6 marks, ★★★★★)

Path A: Very small deflection of 0 to 4 degrees was taken by approximately 62% of the alpha particles.

Path B: Small to medium sized deflection of 4 to 30 degrees were taken by approximately 38%.

Path C: Large deflection of more than 120 degrees or backscattering was taken by only 0.01% of the alpha particles.

Gold nucleus

....

....

....

....

....

....

....

....

....

Radioactive decay and nuclear radiation

1 **Fill in the missing words in the paragraph below, using words from the box.** (6 marks, ★★★)

Some atomic nuclei are .... The nucleus emits .... as it changes to

become more stable. This is a .... process called radioactive ....

Activity is the rate at which a source of .... nuclei decays. Activity is measured in

.... (Bq).

| decay | becquerel(s) | stable | random | radioactive |
| waste | radiation | unstable | fusion | fission |

2 **Complete the table below about alpha, beta and gamma radiation.** (3 marks, ★★★)

Radiation type	What it is made of?	What stops it?	Ionising effect
Alpha			Highly ionising
Beta		A few millimetres of aluminium	
Gamma	High energy EM wave		

3 **The following diagram shows how beta radiation can be used to make sure paper is made with a fairly constant thickness.**

a **Why is beta suitable for this task, and not alpha or gamma?** (2 marks, ★★★)

....

....

....

b **How does feedback ensure that paper is of uniform thickness?** (2 marks, ★★★)

....

....

NAILIT!

The unit for activity is the becquerel. The becquerel is equivalent to 1 disintegration, or decay of one nucleus, per second. Activity cannot be detected directly but can be estimated with a Geiger–Muller tube, which measures count-rate. Count-rate can also be stated as 'number of counts per minute, hour, day or year'. Whereas activity is always in Bq – nuclear disintegrations **per second**. Count-rate and activity are not always the same because the Geiger–Muller tube has a dead time in which it doesn't detect some nuclear disintegrations.

DO IT!

Alpha (α), beta (β) and gamma (γ) are the three kinds of radiation. For each one make sure you learn:

- What is it composed of?
- What stops it?
- How heavily ionising is it?
- Is it affected by magnetic fields?

Remember that there are two types of beta radiation: negative and positive.

Nuclear equations

(1) **Uranium-238 eventually decays to the stable isotope lead-208.**

All the steps in this process can be shown on a diagram. This is called a decay chain and the process takes several billion years. An example is shown below:

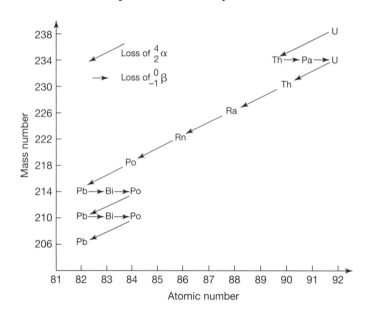

Use the mass number and atomic number references in the above decay chain to complete the following nuclear decay equations. Complete the mass and atomic number for each particle.

a $^{214}_{82}Pb \rightarrow \boxed{}Bi + \boxed{}_{-1}e$ (2 marks, ★★★)

b $^{214}_{84}Po \rightarrow \boxed{}Pb + \boxed{}He$ (2 marks, ★★★★)

c $^{230}_{90}Th \rightarrow$ (4 marks, ★★★★★)

DO IT!

You do not need to remember specific nuclear equations but you do need to be able to balance the mass and atomic numbers for nuclear equations for alpha (α) and beta (β) decays.

Complete the following example and state if it is an example of beta (β) or alpha (α) decay.

$$^{238}_{92}U \rightarrow \quad Th \; \boxed{} \quad \boxed{}\boxed{}$$

To check your atomic and mass numbers refer back to graph of mass number vs atomic number.

NAILIT!

Changes take place in the atomic and mass numbers during alpha (α) and beta (β) decay, but not during gamma (γ) decay. In nuclear equations, make sure that the atomic numbers and mass numbers balance on each side of the equation.

Half-life of radioactive elements

(1) **Write a definition for the term half-life.** (2 marks, ★★★)

....

....

....

DO IT!

Learn the definition for half-life from memory. It often comes up in exams

(2) **A body was found in a bog in rural Ireland.**

A sample of bone from the body was analysed using radio-carbon dating techniques.

Once a living thing dies, the carbon-14 in its body decays. Carbon-14 has a half-life of 5700 years.

Consequently, archaeologists can use any material containing carbon to determine the age, such as bone, wood or leather.

a **If a bone contained $\frac{1}{4}$ of the expected carbon-14, how old would it be?** (3 marks, ★★★★)

....

....

....

b **If a bone contained $\frac{1}{16}$ of the expected carbon-14, how old would it be?** (3 marks, ★★★★)

....

....

c **Draw a sketch of the graph of the half-life. Assume an initial count-rate of 4000 cpm.**
(4 marks, ★★★★)

NAIL IT!

If you are a Higher Tier student remember that you need to be able to express the net decline of radioactive isotopes as a **ratio.**

Hazards and uses of radioactive emissions (1)

(1) **There are two main ways in which people can be exposed to radiation.**

State the two ways they can happen and the effects of radiation on body tissue.
(6 marks, ★★★★)

....

....

....

....

(2) **a** **What protective measures can be taken to protect those who regularly come into contact with radioactive sources?** (5 marks, ★★★★)

....

....

....

....

....

b **Why is it important for findings on the effects of radiation on humans to be published?**
(2 marks, ★★★★)

....

....

(3) **This pie chart shows the main sources of background radiation in the UK. Each source contributes to the average yearly radiation dose.**

a **What is meant by background radiation?**
(1 mark, ★★)

....

....

Food and drink

Human activity (including medical)

Cosmic rays

Rocks and soil

Inhaled (radon gas)

Sources of background radiation

b **Suggest why an astronaut is likely to get a higher dose of background radiation than the average person.** (2 marks, ★★★)

....

....

....

DO IT!

Some background radiation is artificial but most is natural. Make sure you know three examples of each.

Hazards and uses of radioactive emissions (2)

1. The table below shows the different half-lives and type of decay for several radioactive isotopes.

Radioactive isotope	Decay type	Half-life
Radium-226	Alpha	1600 years
Bismuth-214	Beta	20 minutes
Lead-210	Beta	22 years
Polonium-210	Alpha	138 days
Bismuth-210	Alpha, beta and gamma	5 days
Radon-222	Alpha	3.8 days

The initial count-rate of a sample of rock containing bismuth-214 is 4000 counts/minute. How many counts/minute would be detected 1 hour later? (2 marks, ★★★)

....

....

2. Radium-226 decays into radon-222 via alpha decay. A rock is found that once had a large deposit entirely made of radium-226. Now an eighth of the deposit is the original radium-226 but seven eighths of this part of the rock is filled with radon-222 gas.

a How many half-lives have passed? (2 marks, ★★★★)

....

....

b How long has passed since all of the original radium-226 was present? (2 marks, ★★★)

....

....

DOIT!

Radioactive isotopes have many applications in our day-to-day lives: smoke alarms, treating cancer, destroying bacteria, detecting metal or paper thickness, as tracers and dating. Study these examples and make flashcards to help you remember.

WORKIT!

A safe level of radon-222 gas is 20 Bq. A house's basement contains trapped radon-222 gas which has an activity of 320 Bq. Building changes are made and radiation levels are checked by physicists. If no radon enters or leaves the basement, how long would it take the trapped radon-222 to reach safe levels? (3 marks, ★★)

The original activity is 320 Bq and the safe activity is 20 Bq. (1)

$320 \rightarrow 160 \rightarrow 80 \rightarrow 40 \rightarrow 20$ ◄── How many times do you have to halve 320 to reach 20?

It had to be halved 4 times. (1)

This means 4 half-lives have elapsed.

4 half-lives = 4 × 3.8 days

= 15.2 days (1)

Hazards and uses of radioactive emissions (3)

Radioactive isotope	Decay type	Half-life
Technetium-99	Gamma	6 hours
Xenon-133	Gamma	5 days
Strontium-90	Beta	28 years
Americium-241	Alpha	433 years
Protactinium-234	Beta	80 seconds

Answer questions 1 and 2 using the table above, and make reference to half-life and decay type in your answers.

1 **Which type of radioactive isotope is used to investigate whether a person's liver is functioning correctly? Why is this type chosen?** (3 marks, ★★★★)

....

....

....

2 a **Cobalt-60 is the most commonly used isotope to treat brain tumours. If it wasn't available, which type of radioactive isotope from the table would be the most suitable to kill cancer cells? Explain why.** (3 marks, ★★★★)

....

....

....

b **Cobalt-60 has a half-life of over 5 years. Why is this an advantage over the radioactive isotope you chose in part a?** (1 mark, ★★★)

....

3 **Explain why the use of radiation to destroy cancerous cells is classed as a 'high risk method' for the treatment of cancer. What are the risks of chemotherapy and radiotherapy?** (4 marks, ★★★)

....

....

....

....

....

Forces

1 **Tick which of the following quantities is a vector.** (1 mark, ★★★)

Speed	
Distance	

Energy	
Velocity	

2 **Draw lines to match the words to their definitions.** (4 marks, ★★★★)

1 Speed	**a** Has magnitude but no direction.
2 Velocity	**b** Has both magnitude and direction.
3 A scalar quantity	**c** Change in distance per unit time.
4 A vector quantity	**d** Change in displacement per unit time.

3 **A boy is pulling a trolley along the ground. Moving the trolley requires him to exert a force on the trolley. The arrow represents the force. What two pieces of information does the vector tell you about the force?** (2 marks, ★★★)

....

....

4 **An electrostatic force is a non-contact force.**

a **Describe the difference between a contact force and a non-contact force.** (2 marks, ★★★)

....

....

b **State two other non-contact forces.** (2 marks, ★★)

....

....

NAILIT!

You need to be able to break a vector down into its vertical and horizontal components. This can be done graphically or by using trigonometry.

DOIT!

Learn the definition for scalar and vector and a couple of examples of each. Being asked to define vectors and scalars and provide examples of each is a common exam question.

Gravity

(1) **State the formula and unit for weight.** (2 marks, ★★★)

....

(2) **Two students, Karen and Jane, are talking about mass and weight.**

> Mass and weight are not the same and have different units.

Karen

> Mass and weight are the same and are both measured in kg.

Jane

Explain which one of the students is correct. Compare mass and weight in your answer. (6 marks, ★★★★)

....

....

....

....

....

(3) **An astronaut has a mass of 75 kg. He visits the Moon.**

The Moon has gravitational field strength of 1.6 N/kg

Calculate the astronaut's weight on the Moon. (2 marks, ★★)

....

....

....

 DO IT!

Learn the difference between mass and weight. This is one of the most common misunderstandings in physics. Don't be the person who gets it wrong!

NAILIT!

Gravitational field strength is proportional to the mass of the planet the astronaut is on and inversely proportional to his or her distance from the centre of the planet.

The greater the mass → the greater the field strength.

The further from the centre of the planet → the lower the field strength.

Resultant forces

① **Match the left side to the right side to complete the sentences below.** (4 marks, ★★)

1 A resultant force is	**a** one force that is the sum of all forces acting.
2 A force is	**b** the resultant force is zero.
3 When forces are balanced	**c** an object's motion or its shape.
4 A force can affect	**d** a push or a pull.
5 The unit of force is	**e** the newton (N).

② **Calculate the resultant force acting on each of the three boxes.** (3 marks, ★★★)

(Arrows are not to scale and are only to indicate direction of the force.)

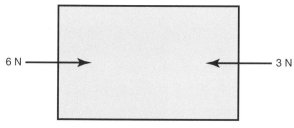

6 N →   ← 3 N

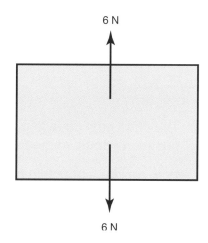

6 N

6 N

a ....

b ....

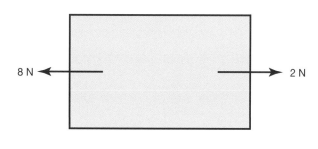

8 N ←   → 2 N

c ....

 **NAILIT!**

Remember that if an object is moving with constant velocity, or if it is stationary, the vector forces must be all balanced. Make sure you are familiar with all the different forces. Here are a few examples: normal contact force, weight, drag, friction and upthrust.

 DOIT!

Practise drawing free body diagrams. Make sure you can do this for objects that are in water, on a solid surface or falling through air.

Work done and energy transfer

(1) **State the formula for work done.** (2 marks, ★★)

....

(2) **Which of the following units can be used for work done, as well as J or joules.** (1 mark, ★★★)

W	
Nm	

N/m	
J/s	

(3) **a A child pushes a go-kart with a force of 30 N. The go-kart moves 4 m along the floor. Calculate the work done on the go-kart.** (3 marks, ★★★)

....

....

....

....

b The child now does 240 J of work on the go-kart and pushes with the same force as in part a.

How far does the child have to push the go-kart to do 240 J of work? (3 marks, ★★★★)

....

....

....

....

c Would the temperature of the go-kart change? Explain your answer. (2 marks, ★★★)

....

....

....

....

DOIT!

Learn the formula and units for work done. Remember work done is equivalent to energy transfer. Does this help you remember the unit for work done?

NAILIT!

Remember that the symbol for the displacement is **s**, and it is often used for distance as well.

Forces and elasticity

(1) A student investigates by how much the extension of a spring changes when he suspends different slotted masses from it.

The student finds that the spring's extension increases by the same length each time an additional slotted mass is added, as long as he only adds one mass at a time. **Explain why.** (2 marks, ★★)

....

....

....

Ruler

Spring

Masses

(2) a **Label the axes below, and sketch a graph to show the behaviour of a spring under tension/when a force is applied to it.** (3 marks, ★★★)

NAILIT!

To change the shape of an object by stretching, bending or compressing, there have to be at least two forces present.

DOIT!

Make sure you are familiar with all the key words in this topic. What is the difference between elastic and inelastic deformation?

b **How could you work out the spring constant from the graph of results?** (2 marks, ★★★★)

....

....

....

(3) The student uses the same experimental procedure but this time hangs slotted masses from an elastic band.

They conclude that the elastic band's extension is not always proportional to the force applied and undergoes inelastic deformation.

Explain what is meant by the term *inelastic* deformation. (2 marks, ★★★)

....

....

....

Distance, displacement, speed and velocity

1 **A bird flies from point A on one fence to point B on another. It travels a route that is 18 m long in total.**

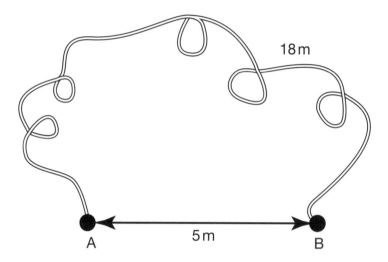

The diagram shows the route it took to get from A to B.

The 5 m route is the shortest way to get from A to B.

a **State the term used for the 18 m route:** .... (1 mark, ★★★)

b **State the term used for the 5 m route:** .... (1 mark, ★★★)

2 **Label the following distance time graphs with the following words.** (3 marks, ★★★)

steady speed	acceleration	deceleration

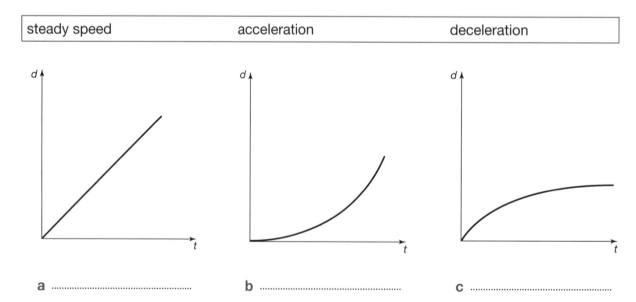

a ....   b ....   c ....

3 The following distance–time graph shows a car journey.

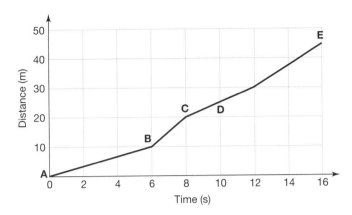

a What is the total distance travelled on the journey? (1 mark, ★★★)

....

b Work out the speed from A to B on the graph. (3 marks, ★★★)

....

....

c Without making a calculation, how can you tell that the speed from B to C is higher than A to B? (2 marks, ★★★★)

....

....

....

4 Match the following to their typical speeds. One has already been done for you.
(4 marks, ★★★)

1 An aeroplane	**a** 5 m/s
2 Olympic sprinter	**b** 30 m/s
3 Cheetah	**c** 200 m/s
4 Mouse	**d** 10 m/s
5 Snail	**e** 0.02 m/s

NAILIT!

Learn the difference between distance and displacement. It's a classic exam question and comes up all the time.

DOIT!

Practise drawing distance–time graphs and make sure you know how to represent the following: stationary or at rest, low steady speed, high steady speed, acceleration and deceleration.

Acceleration

(1) **A car goes on a journey and the velocity–time graph below is made of a short part of the journey. Use the graph to answer the following questions.**

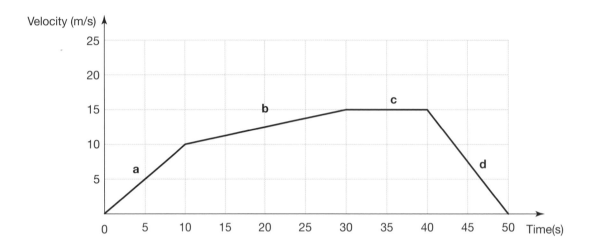

a **Calculate the acceleration during part a.** (2 marks, ★★)

....

....

b **Calculate the acceleration during part b.** (3 marks, ★★★★)

....

....

....

c **Describe the car's motion in part c.** (1 mark, ★★★★)

....

....

(2) **Using the graph in question 2, calculate the distance travelled during parts a and b of the journey.** (3 marks, ★★★★)

....

....

....

Equations of motion

These equations will be used in the following questions.

- final velocity = initial velocity + acceleration × time ($v = u + at$)

- distance = $\frac{1}{2}$ (initial velocity + final velocity) × time ($s = \frac{1}{2}(u + v)t$)

- (final velocity)^2 = (initial velocity)^2 + 2 × acceleration × distance ($v^2 = u^2 + 2as$)

- distance = initial velocity × time + $\frac{1}{2}$ × acceleration × time^2 ($s = ut + \frac{1}{2}at^2$)

The equations apply for motion with constant acceleration.

They are sometimes referred to as the **SUVAT** equations.

> **DO IT!**
>
> Learn what the letters of **S U V A T** stand for. Keep writing them down and testing yourself until you know them off by heart.

(1) **A sports car accelerates from 0 m/s to 50 m/s in 7 seconds on a race track.**

   a **Calculate its acceleration.** (3 marks, ★★★)

   ....

   ....

A cheetah is watching a gazelle and walking slowly and quietly through a bush.

Suddenly the cheetah accelerates from 2 m/s to 35 m/s. This takes 3 seconds.

   b **Calculate the acceleration of the cheetah.** (3 marks, ★★★)

   ....

   ....

   c **Compare of the acceleration of the cheetah and the sports car. Is anything surprising about the values?** (2 marks, ★★★)

   ....

   ....

   ....

NAIL IT!

It is really important that you can rearrange the equations to work out the answers to the problems. Remember to write each stage carefully.

WORKIT!

A car speeds up along a straight race track from rest to 32 m/s in 16 s.

Calculate its acceleration and the distance it moves in this time.

Step 1 Choose the correct equation.

$$a = \frac{v - u}{t}$$

Step 2 Substitute in the values.

$$\frac{32 - 0}{16} = 2 \text{ m/s}$$

Step 3 Choose the c

Step 4 Substitute in the values.

Correct equation.

$$s = ut + 0.5at^2$$

$(0 \times 16) + (0.5 \times 2 \times 162) = 256 \text{ m}$ ⟵ Remember the unit.

Note that it may be possible to use a different equation to get the correct answer.

② **A train stops at a station. When the train departs it accelerates at 1 m/s² to reach a maximum speed of 60 m/s. The train then maintains this top speed for 1 hour.**

a **Calculate how long it takes the train to reach its top speed.** (3 marks, ★★★★)

....

....

....

③ **A skateboarder stands at the top of a ramp of length 30 m, and then accelerates down it. At the bottom of the ramp the speed of the skateboarder is 15 m/s.**

a **Calculate the acceleration of the skateboarder on the ramp.** (4 marks, ★★★★)
Use the equation:

$$v^2 = u^2 + 2as$$

....

....

....

b **Calculate the time it takes the skateboarder to reach the bottom of the ramp.**
(3 marks, ★★★★)

....

....

....

Newton's laws of motion

(1) **Complete the sentences with the missing words.** (3 marks, ★★)

The .... of an object will only change if there is a .... force acting on it.

When a car is at a .... speed the driving force and .... forces of friction and

.... are equal and act in .... directions.

| steady | resistive | opposite | resultant | velocity |
| drag | balanced | high | upthrust | low |

(2) **State Newton's second law in words. Use an equation in your answer.** (4 marks, ★★★★)

....

....

....

....

(3) **Newton's first law is sometimes called the law of inertia. Define inertia.** (1 mark, ★★★★)

....

....

(4) **A boy jumps out of a boat. When he jumps out of the boat he pushes on the boat with a force of 100 N.**

a **The boat also pushes on the boy. Draw an arrow on the diagram to show the direction and size of this force.** (1 mark, ★★★)

....

....

....

← 100 N

b **Explain why you chose the value you did as your answer to part a.** (2 marks, ★★★)

....

....

c **Which of Newton's laws applies in this situation?** (1 mark, ★★★★)

....

....

(5) **A 100 kg box has two forces acting on it. The forces are acting in opposite directions.**

10 N acts to the left. 15 N acts to the right.

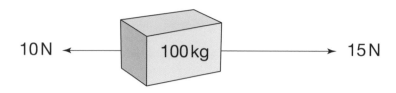

10 N ← 100 kg → 15 N

a **Work out the resultant force on the box.** (1 mark, ★★)

....

....

b **The box was initially at rest. Which way will it move?** (1 mark, ★★)

....

c **Calculate the acceleration of the box.** (3 marks, ★★★★)

....

....

....

WORKIT!

A car of mass 1200 kg accelerates from rest to 20 m/s in 10 s.

a Calculate the car's acceleration. (2 marks, ★★★)

$a = \dfrac{v - u}{t}$ ← Choose the correct equation and substitute in the values from the question.

$a = \dfrac{20 - 0}{10}$ (1) ← Remember, from rest means 0 m/s.

$a = 2 \text{ m/s}^2$ (1) ← Remember to state your answer in the correct units.

b Calculate the resultant force acting on the car. (2 marks, ★★★)

$F = ma$

$F = 1200 \times 2$ (1)

$F = 2400 \text{ N}$ (1)

DOIT!

Make sure you learn each of Newton's three laws. The basic idea of each law is actually very simple.

NAILIT!

Newton's third law is the best known law, but probably the least understood. Remember the forces act in pairs but **never cancel each other out**. They are the same type of force but act on different objects.

Stopping distance

(1) **Complete the following equation.** (2 marks, ★★★)

Stopping distance = ... + ...

(2) **The following graph shows how braking distance and thinking distance are affected by speed.**

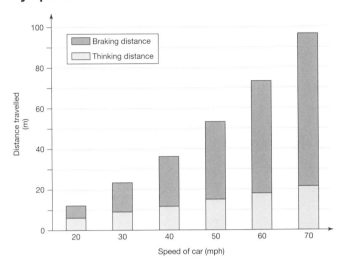

a **State two other factors that affect braking distance.** (1 mark, ★★)

....

b i **Using the graph, describe the relationship between thinking distance and speed.**
(1 mark, ★★★)

....

ii **Using the graph, describe the relationship between braking distance and speed.**
(2 marks, ★★★★)

....

....

(3) **A student explains a simple experiment to compare the reaction times of different students in her class.**

One student drops the ruler.

The other student has to catch it as quickly as possible.

The shorter the distance that the ruler falls through the fingers, the shorter the reaction time of the student. Repeat the experiment twice and take an average.

Another student says: 'This experiment could be changed to see if texting on a mobile phone affects reaction time'. On a separate piece of paper, explain how this new experiment would be conducted. (6 marks, ★★★)

Momentum (1)

(1) **Which of the following is the unit for momentum?** (1 mark, ★★)

m/s
kg m/s
kg/ms
m/s²

(2) **State the formula for momentum.** (1 mark, ★★)

....

(3) **A 1000 kg car is driving along a racing track with a velocity of 400 m/s.**

Calculate its momentum. (3 marks, ★★★)

....

....

....

(4) **A 3500 g labrador is running at 10 m/s.**

Calculate the dog's momentum. (4 marks, ★★★★)

....

....

NAILIT!

Momentum has two units. Make sure you learn them both so you don't get caught out in exams.

NAILIT!

Momentum is a vector, so it has both magnitude and direction.

Momentum (2)

1 **Complete the following sentence with the missing words.** (2 marks, ★★★)

In a _____ system (in which no _____ forces act) the total momentum before an event

is equal to the total momentum after the event. This is called the _____ of _____ law.

external	moments	momentum	conservation
internal	closed	released	sum

2 **A speeding truck is approaching a stationary car at traffic lights.**

  a **Calculate the momentum of the truck.** (2 marks, ★★★)

....

....

40 m/s →

0 m/s

Truck 2000 kg

Car 800 kg

  b **In an inelastic collision the two vehicles crumple together.**

  Calculate the velocity of the truck and car as they move off joined together. (3 marks, ★★★★)

....

....

....

3 **Two cars have a head-on collision, their speeds and mass are shown in the diagram. Assume momentum is conserved in the collision.**

Both cars crumple together in an inelastic collision.

40 m/s →   ← 30 m/s

800 kg   1000 kg

Calculate the velocity and direction of the cars as they move off together. (6 marks, ★★★★★)

....

....

....

NAILIT!

When a force acts on an object that is moving, or able to move, a change in momentum occurs.

DOIT!

Make sure that you are confident with collision, recoil and explosion questions.

Momentum (3)

1. Explain, using physics ideas, why a crumple zone may prevent the driver in an accident from being killed during a collision. (6 marks, ★★★★★)

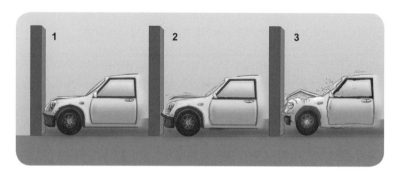

....

....

....

2. A cricket ball of mass 200 g is struck with a force of 180 N for a period of 0.005 s.

   Calculate the change in momentum. (3 marks, ★★★)

....

....

3. A golf ball of mass 50 g is struck with a force of 200 N for a period of 0.005 s. Calculate:

   a The change in momentum. (2 marks, ★★★)

....

....

....

   b The speed of the golf ball immediately afterwards. (3 marks, ★★★★)

....

....

....

DOIT!

$F = ma$ is equivalent to

$$F = \frac{m\Delta v}{\Delta t}$$

Can you demonstrate how?

NAILIT!

$F = \dfrac{m\Delta v}{\Delta t}$ is an important equation. It helps us to understand why increasing the time of impact by using crumple zones, for example, can reduce the forces suffered by the driver or passenger in a car collision.

Waves

Transverse and longitudinal waves

1. **Water ripples on a surface of a lake are an example of which type of wave?** (1 mark, ★★)

Longitudinal
Transverse

☐

EM waves
Rarefaction

☐

2. a **What is a longitudinal wave?** (2 marks, ★★★)

....

....

   b **Give an example of a longitudinal wave.** (1 mark, ★★)

....

....

   c **Draw a diagram of a longitudinal wave.** (2 marks, ★★★)

3. **A student is interested in waves.**

   She takes a slinky and shakes it up and down while a classmate is holding the other end.

   She observes this:

Direction of wave

Vibration of coils

   a **What type of wave does she observe? Explain your answer.** (3 marks, ★★★)

....

....

   b **What could she do with the slinky to make a different type of wave?** (2 marks, ★★★)

....

....

   c **Compare the two wave types. State their differences.** (2 marks, ★★★★)

....

....

DO IT!

Learn at least two examples of each type of wave.

NAILIT!

Waves can be either longitudinal or transverse. Make sure that you know the differences between them.

Properties of waves

(1) **Define the following:**

a **Amplitude** (2 marks, ★★★)

....

....

b **Frequency** (2 marks, ★★★)

....

....

c **Wavelength** (2 marks, ★★★)

....

....

(2) **The figure below shows an oscilloscope trace of a musical note.**

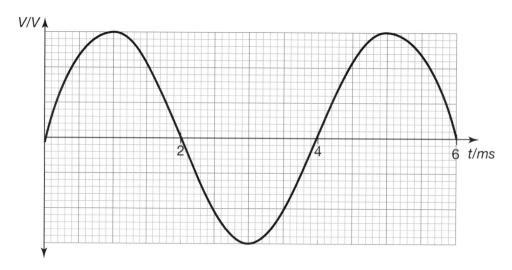

Work out the following:

a **The time period of the wave.** (2 marks, ★★★)

....

b **The frequency of the wave.** (2 marks, ★★★)

....

c **The amplitude of the wave. Each cm square represents 1 V.** (2 marks, ★★★)

....

Reflection and refraction

① **A wave approaches a boundary. Which three things could happen?** (3 marks, ★★★★)

....

....

....

② **The diagram below shows a wave front approaching a hard flat surface.**

Complete the diagram to show reflection taking place. (3 marks, ★★★)

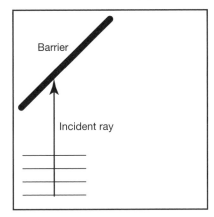

③ **The light ray is moving from air into glass blocks a and b.**

Assume no reflection takes place.

Complete the path of the light rays:

   i **entering**

  ii **travelling through**

 iii **leaving the glass blocks**

On each diagram label the normal and direction of the rays.

a (3 marks, ★★★)

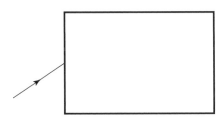

b (3 marks, ★★★★)

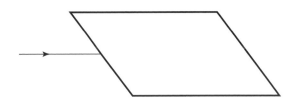

NAILIT!

Remember to add a normal when drawing ray diagrams.

If the wave is travelling from a less dense medium into a denser medium, it slows down and bends towards the normal. If it travels from a denser to less dense medium, it speeds up and bends away from the normal.

DOIT!

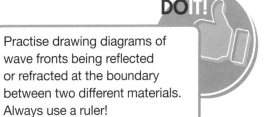

Practise drawing diagrams of wave fronts being reflected or refracted at the boundary between two different materials. Always use a ruler!

Sound waves (1)

(1) What is the normal audible frequency range for humans? (2 marks, ★★★)

....

....

(2) A loudspeaker plays music. The sound waves reach the outer ear.

With reference to the diagram to the right, explain how a human can 'hear' music.

(6 marks, ★★★★)

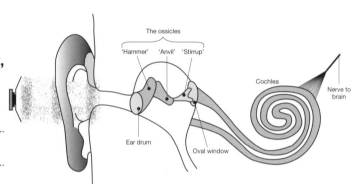

....

....

....

....

(3) A tuning fork is struck against a microphone connected to an oscilloscope.

The sound wave can be seen on an oscilloscope screen.

Each horizontal square on the oscilloscope trace represents 1 ms.

Each vertical square represents 1 V.

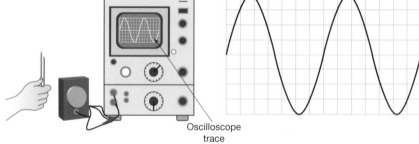

Oscilloscope trace

a What is the time period of the wave? (2 marks, ★★★★)

....

b Calculate the frequency of the wave. (2 marks, ★★★)

....

c What is the amplitude of the wave? (2 marks, ★★★★)

....

DOIT!

Practise drawing diagrams of sound waves. Use the words **compression** and **rarefaction** in your labels to explain the ideas of low and high pressure air. Label the wavelengths.

NAILIT!

Sound behaves in a similar way to other mechanical waves. The wave transfers energy through matter such as solids, liquids and gases. The matter vibrates but does not actually move from one place to another.

For example, a wave travelling in water moves from one place to another, but the water doesn't. Each point on the water wave moves up and down perpendicularly to the direction of the wave.

Sound waves (2)

① **Define the term 'ultrasound'.** (2 marks, ★★★)

....

....

② **State two uses or applications of ultrasonic waves.** (2 marks, ★★★)

....

....

③ **Seismograph stations all over the world can detect P-waves and S-waves in the event of an earthquake.**

The diagram below shows the epicentre of an earthquake and the detection of P-waves and S-waves at different seismograph stations locations around the world.

Epicentre

1
2
3
4
a
b

P- and S-waves
P-waves only

a **What is a P-wave? What type of wave is it?**
(4 marks, ★★★)

....

....

b **What is an S-wave? Describe what type of wave an S-wave is.** (4 marks, ★★★)

....

....

c **Explain why the waves that reach points 1, 2, 3 and 4 curve gradually as they pass through the Earth.** (4 marks, ★★★★)

....

....

....

DO IT!

Make sure you know the difference between a P-wave and an S-wave. Which is transverse and which is longitudinal?

d **Explain why only P-waves can be detected at points a and b.** (2 marks, ★★★)

....

....

NAILIT!

Ultrasound can be used to measure distances without having to cut something open. Partial reflections of ultrasound take place at boundaries of different materials. It is possible to use an oscilloscope to work out the time it takes for the pulse reflection to return to the transducer. If the speed of ultrasound is known in the material, then you can calculate the distance to the different boundary. This technique can be used for many applications, for example, finding flaws in metal casings and measuring the size of eyeballs.

Electromagnetic waves

(1) Match the following EM spectrum waves to the application/use. (6 marks, ★★★)

1 Radio waves	**a** Fibre optics and communication
2 Microwaves	**b** TV and radio
3 Infrared	**c** Heaters and cooking food
4 Visible light	**d** Sun tanning
5 Ultra violet	**e** Medical imaging and treatments
6 X-rays + gamma rays	**f** Satellite communications and cooking food

(2) State three properties of electromagnetic waves. (3 marks, ★★★)

....

....

(3) Radio waves and microwaves are both used in communications.

Radio waves can be used to transmit television and radio programmes.

Microwaves are used for mobile phones and Wi-Fi.

The different properties of microwaves and radio waves make them suitable for these applications.

MICROWAVE

IONOSPHERE

RADIO

On a separate piece of paper, explain why microwaves and radio waves are suitable for these different applications. Include reference to the diagram above. (6 marks, ★★★★)

(4) Which of the following can be produced by oscillations in electrical circuits? (2 marks, ★★★★)

Ultraviolet waves	
Sound waves	

Gamma waves	
Radio waves	

(5) Ultraviolet, X-rays and gamma rays can have hazardous effects on human tissue. Describe two factors that determine the extent of the effect. (2 marks, ★★★★)

....

....

Emission and absorption of infrared radiation

(1) **If an object radiates and absorbs radiation at the same rate what does this tell you about the object's temperature?** (1 mark, ★★★)

It is increasing			It is constant		
It is decreasing			It is impossible to know		

(2) A student carries out an experiment on the absorption and emission of infrared radiation.

He paints one can white and another black.

He then fills them both with the same amount of boiling water.

He records the temperature change with a thermometer for each can 15 minutes later.

NAILIT!

All objects emit infrared radiation, the hotter the object the more radiation it emits.

The student records that the black can's temperature goes down by 15 °C, but the white can's temperature goes down by only 5 °C. **Explain why.** (3 marks, ★★★★)

....

....

....

....

....

(3) The student modifies the experiment and places an infrared heater equally spaced from both cans. He then fills both cans with cold water. He turns on the heater and records the temperature change after 15 minutes.

a **Would the temperature of the water in each can increase or decrease by the same amount? Explain your answer.** (3 marks, ★★★★)

....

....

....

....

....

b **Describe the limitations of the experiment.** (3 marks, ★★★)

....

....

....

....

WORKIT!

The student was only interested in finding out about absorption and emission of infrared radiation. What other factors may have affected his experiment? (1 mark, ★★)

The experiment will also be affected by conduction and convection. (1)

4. **An object has an increasing temperature. Which of the following statements is true?** (1 mark, ★)

Absorption and emission of infrared are at the same rate	
Absorption and emission of infrared are at different rates	
Absorption of infrared is greater than emission of infrared	
Emission of infrared is great than absorption of infrared	

5. **Explain the factors that determine the temperature of the Earth.** (6 marks, ★★★★)

....

....

....

....

....

....

Electromagnetism

① **Complete the sentence. The poles of a magnet are the places where:** (1 mark, ★★)

the magnetic fields are the strongest	
the field lines are the furthest apart	
the magnetic fields are the weakest	
flux lines overlap	

② **a What is an induced magnet?** (2 marks, ★★★)

....

....

> **NAILIT!**
>
> Make sure you learn that magnetic materials are iron, steel, cobalt and nickel.

b What kind of force always exists between a permanent and an induced magnet? (1 mark, ★★★)

....

c Describe a simple test to check if a material is an induced or permanent magnet. (3 marks, ★★★★)

....

....

....

③ **Draw the field lines on the following magnet combinations.** (6 marks, ★★★★)

a

b

N   S

N   S

S   N

N   S

> **DOIT!**
>
> The direction of a magnetic field at any point is given by the direction of the force that would act on another north pole placed at that point. Remember north pole really means north-seeking pole.

Electromagnetism

(1) **A student builds the circuit to the right. The circuit contains a dc power supply and a switch. He places a plotting compass near the wire.**

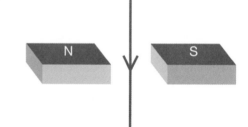

Switch

Compass

Power supply

2V

a **When he closes the switch to complete the circuit what will he observe?** (2 marks, ★★★)

....

....

b **The student reverses the battery connection then closes the switch. What will he observe now?** (2 marks, ★★★)

....

....

(2) **The diagrams show a wire carrying current in the direction indicated by the arrow.**

For each wire sketch the magnetic field that would be induced.
(6 marks, ★★★★)

Current

Current

(3) **A current-carrying wire is placed between the two magnets below.**

The current direction is indicated with an arrow.

N

S

a **Draw an arrow on the wire to show the direction in which it will experience a force.** (1 mark, ★★★★)

b **What is the name given to this effect?** (1 mark, ★★★★)

....

c **What changes could be made to make the wire move with a greater force?**
(3 marks, ★★★★)

....

....

NAILIT!

A wire shaped into a coil that carries a current is called a solenoid. A solenoid has the same magnetic field pattern as a bar magnet. The field inside a solenoid is strong and uniform (that is, the field lines are parallel and the same distance away from each other). If you place a core inside the solenoid, you have created an electromagnet.

Motor effect

(1) **Add the following labels to the electric motor diagram below. Some labels are used more than once.** (6 marks, ★★★★)

force	split-ring-commutator	rotating coil	dc power supply	brush

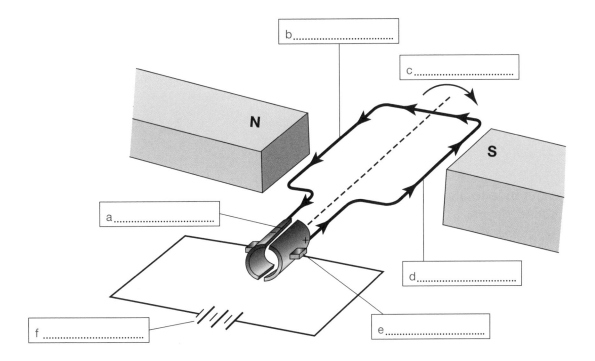

(2) a **Explain the function of a split-ring commutator in a dc motor.** (2 marks, ★★★★)

....

....

b **Explain the role of the brushes in an electric motor.** (2 marks, ★★★★)

....

....

NAILIT!

Learn the different parts of the dc motor. Make sure you know the difference between a split-ring commutator and slip rings. Do you know why a split-ring commutator is used in a dc motor?

NAILIT!

Learn Fleming's left-hand rule. It comes up all the time. Remember that the left-hand rule is for motors.

③ **The diagram below shows a student's design for a loudspeaker.**

The student will plug his MP3 player into the loudspeaker.

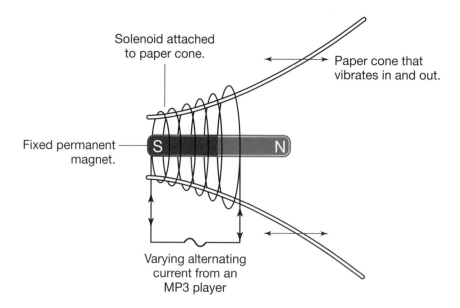

Solenoid attached to paper cone.

Paper cone that vibrates in and out.

Fixed permanent magnet.

S   N

Varying alternating current from an MP3 player

With reference to the diagram, explain how the loudspeaker converts an electrical signal into sound waves. (6 marks, ★★★★)

....

....

....

....

....

....

NAILIT!

A loudspeaker uses the motor effect to convert variations in the current to the pressure variations in sound waves. You need to be able to explain how a loudspeaker works. Remember to use bullet points and explain it stage by stage.

Transformers

① **The diagram to the right shows an old-fashioned carbon microphone.**

If the carbon powder is compressed by pressure, its resistance changes.

a **With reference to the diagram, explain why the current changes when a person talks into the microphone.** (3 marks, ★★★★)

....

....

b **With reference to the diagram, explain why a changing current makes the metal plate vibrate back and forth.** (3 marks, ★★★★)

....

....

....

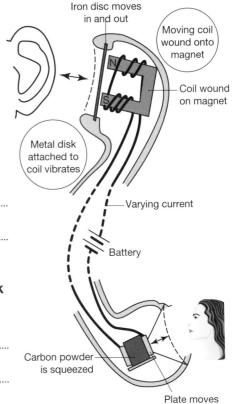

Iron disc moves in and out

Moving coil wound onto magnet

N

S

Coil wound on magnet

Metal disk attached to coil vibrates

Varying current

Battery

Carbon powder is squeezed

Plate moves in and out

c **With reference to the diagram, explain why the coil is wound onto a magnet.**
(2 marks, ★★★)

....

② **The following diagram shows a transformer.**

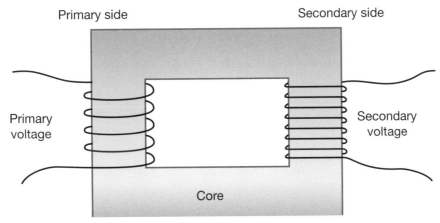

Primary side

Secondary side

Primary voltage

Secondary voltage

Core

What type of transformer is shown in the diagram? Explain your answer. (2 marks, ★★★)

....

....

(3) **Transformers are used in ac transmission.**

a **Explain how a transformer works.** (6 marks, ★★★★)

....

....

....

....

....

b **Explain why a transformer can only be used with ac, and not dc.** (3 marks, ★★★)

....

....

....

WORKIT!

A transformer is used in a laboratory. The voltage input to the primary coil is 230 V. The primary coil has 200 turns and the secondary coil has 1000 turns.

a Calculate the potential difference output of the secondary coil. (2 marks, ★★★)

$$\frac{V_p}{V_s} = \frac{n_p}{n_s}$$ ⟵ Choose the correct equation

$$\frac{230}{V_s} = \frac{200}{1000} \rightarrow V_s = \frac{230 \times 1000}{200} = 1150 \ (1)$$ ⟵ Substitute in the values

Express answer with correct units $V_s = 1150$ V (1)

b If current in the primary is 3 A calculate the current in the secondary coil. Assume the transformer is 100% efficient. (2 marks, ★★★)

$$V_s I_s = V_p I_p \rightarrow 1150 \times I_s = 230 \times 3 \ (1)$$ ⟵ Remember to select the right equation and substitute in the values

$$I_s = \frac{230 \times 3}{1150}$$

$$= 0.6 \text{ A} \ (1)$$

c Explain why this current would be more suitable for transmission. (1 mark, ★★★)

Current is lower, so power losses would be lower. (1)

NAILIT!

Make sure that you know how to rearrange the transformer equations.

$$\frac{V_p}{V_s} = \frac{n_p}{n_s}$$

NAILIT!

Remember that transformers only work with ac. Transformers are very useful because when potential difference is stepped up, the current goes down. This can be explained with this formula: $V_s I_s = V_p I_p$. This means that there are less power losses in transmission. (This can be explained with the formula $P = I^2 R$.)

1.1 **The image below shows a plant cell.**

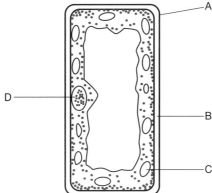

a **Label the parts of the cell A–D.** (4 marks)

A ....

B ....

C ....

D ....

b **What is the function of structure C?** (2 marks)

....

c **The ribosomes are not shown on the image. What type of microscope is needed to see small structures such as ribosomes?** (1 mark)

....

d **What is the maximum magnification and resolution of the microscope described in (c)?** (2 marks)

Magnification ....

Resolution ....

e **The cell is actually 10 µm in diameter, but in the image it is shown at 25 mm in diameter. Calculate the magnification.** (2 marks)

Magnification = ...

1.2 a The cell on the previous page is a specialised plant cell. How did the cell become specialised? Tick **one** box. (1 mark)

Mitosis	
Differentiation	
Meiosis	
Transpiration	

b Describe **two** ways in which the plant cell is different to an animal cell. (2 marks)

....

....

1.3 a Draw the cell cycle and label each stage. (2 marks)

b Describe what is happening at each stage of your cell cycle diagram. (4 marks)

....

....

....

....

....

1.4 a An investigation was carried out to see the effect of a drug called paclitaxel on mitosis. One onion root tip was treated with paclitaxel and another was not. After four hours, the number of cells in mitosis in each root tip was counted. The investigation was repeated three times. The results are shown in the table below.

	Number of cells in mitosis			Mean number of cells in mitosis
	1	2	3	
Root tip treated with paclitaxel	3	4	2	
Root tip without paclitaxel	44	51	46	

    i **What was the dependent variable in this investigation?** (1 mark)

....

    ii **What was the independent variable in this investigation?** (1 mark)

....

b **Calculate the mean value for each row and complete the table.** (2 marks)

....

c i **Describe the results of the investigation.** (2 marks)

....

....

    ii **Suggest a reason for these results.** (1 mark)

....

    iii **Why was the investigation carried out three times? Tick one box.** (1 mark)

To make the results more valid	
To make the results more reliable	
To make the results more accurate	

    iv **Suggest how this experiment could be improved.** (2 marks)

....

....

2.1 **Potatoes contain a lot of starch. A slice of potato is placed in a concentrated salt solution for 4 hours.**

a **The mass of the potato decreased from 5.0 g to 4.4 g. Calculate the percentage change in mass.** (2 marks)

.... %

b **Explain why the mass of the potato decreased.** (2 marks)

....

....

c Describe on a cellular level the effect of osmosis on the potato cells in the concentrated salt solution. (2 marks)

....

....

d Which food test could be used to test if the potato contained starch? (1 mark)

....

2.2 a The table below shows the results of the food tests being carried out on several unknown solutions.

Unknown solution	Sugar test	Starch test	Protein test
A	Blue	Orange	Blue
B	Blue	Blue-black	Blue
C	Green	Orange	Lilac
D	Green	Orange	Blue

i Which unknown solution could have been milk? (1 mark) ....

ii Explain your answer to (i). (2 marks)

....

....

b How is starch used in plant cells? (1 mark)

....

c A student suggests that A is sucrose. Could they be right? (1 mark)

....

d What further test could you do to test if solution A is sucrose? (2 marks)

....

....

e What type of enzyme breaks down starch in the human digestive system? Tick one box. (1 mark)

Lipase	
Protease	
Carbohydrase	

f   **Write a word equation to show how starch is broken down into smaller molecules.**
(2 marks)

....

2.3   **The image below shows a human heart.**

a   **What blood vessel is labelled A? Tick one box.** (1 mark)

Pulmonary artery	
Aorta	
Pulmonary vein	

b   **Where does A take the blood to?** (1 mark)

....

c   **Why does the blood go through the heart twice?** (2 marks)

....

....

d   **What is that type of circulation called?** (1 mark)

....

e   **Draw onto the image where the heart's pacemaker can be found.** (1 mark)

f   **Explain why it is important that the ventricles of the heart contract a short time after the atria contract.** (2 marks)

....

....

2.4 a The coronary arteries supply the heart with oxygen. Explain what will happen to the heart if the coronary arteries become blocked. (2 marks)

....

....

b How could this type of artery blockage be treated? (1 mark)

....

c Suggest **two** risk factors for coronary heart disease. (2 marks)

....

....

3.1 a Tuberculosis is caused by a bacterium. Give **three** differences between a bacterium and a eukaryotic cell. (3 marks)

....

....

....

b What type of drugs are used to treat tuberculosis? (1 mark)

....

3.2 Vaccination programs are being used worldwide to get rid of tuberculosis. The graph below shows the number of cases from tuberculosis in Madagascar between 1990 and 2015.

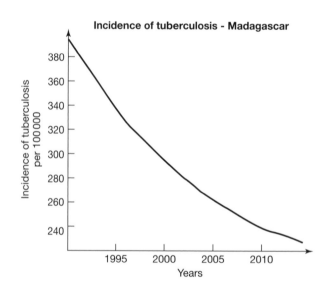

a **Which of the following statements is true? Tick one box.** (1 mark)

Fewer people died from tuberculosis in 2015, compared to 2010.	
In 1995, 340 people caught tuberculosis.	
There were fewer incidences of tuberculosis in 2015 compared to 2010.	

b **Describe how vaccination works.** (3 marks)

....

....

....

c **Suggest why tuberculosis is still prevalent in Madagascar.** (3 marks)

....

....

....

d **Explain what would happen to the immunity of the population if 90% or more people were vaccinated against tuberculosis.** (3 marks)

....

....

....

3.3 **Painkillers are a type of drug that inhibits pain.**

a **Give one example of a painkiller.** (1 mark)

....

b **New drugs are being discovered all the time. Name two sources of new drugs.**
(2 marks)

....

....

c A new painkiller is discovered and the scientist wants to be able to give it to the general public. What testing does the new drug have to go through first? (6 marks)

....

....

....

....

....

....

4.1 Some students are investigating the effect of light intensity on the rate of photosynthesis in pondweed. They placed a lamp at different distances from the pondweed. The students placed the pondweed underneath a glass funnel under water and measured the volume of oxygen given off using a measuring cylinder. The results are shown in the table.

Distance of lamp from pondweed	Volume of oxygen collected in 5 minutes (cm³)	Rate of reaction (cm³ min⁻¹)
0	15.0	3.0
20	12.5	
40	6.5	
60	6	
80	6.0	

a Calculate the rates of reaction in the table. (4 marks)

b Correct any mistakes in the table. (2 marks)

....

....

c What is the independent variable in this investigation? (1 mark)

....

d **What is the dependent variable in this investigation?** (1 mark)

....

e **Name two variables that must be kept controlled throughout the investigation.** (2 marks)

....

....

f **How could the students make their data more reliable?** (1 mark)

....

4.2 a **Draw the expected shape of a graph when the rate of reaction of photosynthesis is plotted against increasing carbon dioxide levels.** (2 marks)

b **Explain the shape of the graph.** (2 marks)

....

....

c **Draw another line on the graph to show how the shape of the graph would change if the light intensity was increased.** (2 marks)

....

....

d **Explain why you have drawn the graph in this way.** (2 marks)

....

....

For an additional practice paper and the mark schemes for these, visit: www.scholastic.co.uk/gcse

Chemistry Paper 1

1.1 **The three states of matter can be represented by the simple particle model.**

a **Match each diagram to the correct state of matter.** (3 marks)

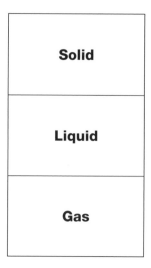

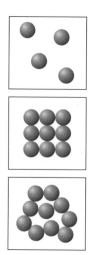

The temperature at which a substance changes from a liquid to a solid is known as the **freezing point.** This can be investigated by heating a solid until it melts and then recording the temperature at regular intervals as it cools.

Some results of an experiment are shown below.

Time/minutes	Temperature/°C
0	80
1	76
2	73
3	72
4	72
5	72
6	72
7	71
8	68
9	64
10	60

b **Choosing a suitable scale, plot these points on graph paper.** (3 marks)

c **Join up the points with a line and state the freezing point of this solid.** (2 marks)

d **State one limitation of the simple particle model when it is used to explain changes of state.** (1 mark)

....

1.2 Lithium reacts with chlorine to form lithium chloride.

a What is the correct formula for lithium chloride? Tick **one** box. (1 mark)

Li_2Cl	
$LiCl_2$	
$LiCl$	
Li_2Cl_2	

b Lithium also reacts with water to form an alkaline solution.

Identify the ion responsible for making the solution alkaline. Tick **one** box.
(1 mark)

OH^+	
H^+	
H^-	
OH^-	

c The formula for lithium oxide is Li_2O.

What is its relative formula mass? Tick **one** box. (1 mark)

14	
30	
22	
39	

1.3 Lithium exists as two stable isotopes, ^6_3Li and ^7_3Li.

Complete the table below to show the number of sub-atomic particles
in each isotope. (3 marks)

Isotope	Number of protons	Number of electrons	Number of neutrons
^6_3Li			
^7_3Li			

1.4 The most abundant isotope of lithium is ^7_3Li, which accounts for 92.5% of naturally
occurring lithium.

a Calculate the percentage abundance of the ^6_3Li isotope. (1 mark)

....

b Use the information to work out the relative atomic mass of lithium to one
decimal place. (3 marks)

....

....

2.1 **The table below shows some of the properties of calcium, chlorine and calcium chloride.**

Substance	Formula	Type of bonding	Melting point	Electrical conductivity
Calcium	Ca		842	Good
Chlorine	Cl_2		−102	Does not conduct
Calcium chloride	$CaCl_2$		772	Conducts only when molten or in solution

a **Complete the table to show the type of bonding in these substances.** (3 marks)

....

....

b **Explain why calcium can conduct electricity.** (2 marks)

....

....

c **Complete the dot-and-cross diagram to show the bonding in a molecule of chlorine.**
(2 marks)

d **Use your ideas about structure and bonding to explain the melting points of calcium, chlorine and calcium chloride.** (6 marks)

....

....

....

....

....

2.2 In a reaction, 5g of sodium reacts with an excess of oxygen to form sodium oxide.

The balanced chemical equation for this reaction is as follows:

$$4Na(s) + O_2(g) \rightarrow 2Na_2O(s)$$

a Explain what happens, in terms of electrons, when sodium reacts with oxygen. You can include diagrams in your answer. (4 marks)

....

....

....

b Sodium oxide does not conduct electricity when solid, but will when molten or in solution. Explain why. (3 marks)

....

....

....

c Calculate the maximum mass of sodium oxide that could be formed in this reaction. (4 marks)

[Na = 23, O = 16]

....

....

....

....

3.1 Soluble salts can be formed by reacting dilute acids with bases. These are neutralisation reactions.

a Which of the following does not act as a base? Tick **one** box.
(1 mark)

Calcium carbonate	
Lithium sulfate	
Potassium oxide	
Ammonia	

b What is the pH of a neutral solution? Tick **one** box.
(1 mark)

7	
14	
1	
3	

3.2 **A student carries out an experiment to make magnesium chloride by reacting magnesium carbonate with hydrochloric acid. Carbon dioxide and water are also produced in the reaction.**

The equation for this reaction is: $MgCO_3(s) + 2HCl(aq) \rightarrow MgCl_2(aq) + CO_2(g) + H_2O(l)$

a **What is meant by the symbol (aq)?** (1 mark) ....

During this experiment, an excess of magnesium carbonate is added to 20 cm³ hydrochloric acid. The excess magnesium carbonate is removed by filtration, and the resulting solution is heated over a water bath to evaporate the water, leaving solid magnesium chloride.

b **State one observation the student would see in this reaction.** (1 mark)

....

c **How would the student know that he had added excess magnesium carbonate?** (1 mark)

....

....

4.1 **Electrolysis can be used to break down ionic compounds into their elements, and is often used to extract metals from their ores.**

a **Explain why potassium cannot be extracted from its ore using carbon.** (1 mark)

....

....

Molten potassium chloride (KCl) consists of potassium ions and chloride ions. It undergoes electrolysis to form potassium and chlorine.

b **What is the name of the electrolyte?** (1 mark) ....

c **State the formula of the potassium ion.** (1 mark) ....

The chloride ions are attracted to the positive electrode.

d **Complete and balance the half equation for the reaction that takes place at the positive electrode.** (1 mark)

............Cl^- $\rightarrow$ ....Cl_2^+ ....

e **What type of reaction is this?** (1 mark) ....

4.2 A student carried out the electrolysis of **aqueous** solutions of potassium chloride.

She was surprised to find that during the electrolysis of aqueous potassium chloride that bubbles of gas were produced at each electrode.

a Name the gas produced at the negative electrode and explain why this is formed rather than potassium. (2 marks)

....

....

b Write a half equation for this reaction. (2 marks)

....

c What is the name of the remaining solution? (1 mark)

....

5.1 A student investigated the reactivity of four different metals by measuring the temperature change when they were reacted with hydrochloric acid. The equipment they used is shown below.

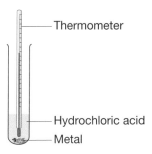

The student used the same amount of metal in each experiment.

a State **two** further variables that would need to be controlled. (2 marks)

....

....

b What is the **independent** variable in this reaction? (1 mark)

....

The table below shows the results of the experiment. The student concluded that the higher the temperature rise, the more reactive the metal.

Metal	Temperature change/°C
Zinc	5.5
Iron	0.5
Calcium	15.0
Magnesium	12.0

c **Place the metals in order of reactivity, from most reactive to least reactive.** (2 marks)

Most reactive	
Least reactive	

All of these reactions are **exothermic**.

d **Complete the word equation for the reaction between calcium and hydrochloric acid.**
(2 marks)

Calcium + hydrochloric acid → .... + ...

e **Draw a reaction profile diagram for this reaction on a separate piece of paper.** (3 marks)

5.2 **Ethanol is a very useful fuel as it can be produced from renewable sources. It has the formula C_2H_5OH.**

The equation below shows the complete combustion of ethanol.

$$H-\overset{\overset{H}{|}}{\underset{\underset{H}{|}}{C}}-\overset{\overset{H}{|}}{\underset{\underset{H}{|}}{C}}-O-H \ + \ \begin{matrix}O=O\\O=O\\O=O\end{matrix} \ \longrightarrow \ \begin{matrix}O=C=O\\O=C=O\end{matrix} \ + \ \begin{matrix}H\overset{O}{\diagup\diagdown}H\\H\overset{O}{\diagup\diagdown}H\\H\overset{O}{\diagup\diagdown}H\end{matrix}$$

The table below shows the bond energies of some common bonds.

Bond	Bond energy (kJ per mol)
C–C	350
C–H	415
O=O	500
C=O	800
O–H	465
C–O	360

a **Use this information to work out the energy change in this reaction.** (3 marks)

....

....

....

b **State, with a reason, if this reaction is exothermic or endothermic.** (2 marks)

....

....

For an additional practice paper, visit: www.scholastic.co.uk/gcse

1.1 a State the formula for calculating the kinetic energy of a moving object. (1 mark)

....

A dog is chasing a cat in a field. Both the dog and cat are running at a steady speed of 10 m/s. The cat has a mass of 3 kg and the dog has a mass of 8 kg.

b Calculate the energy in the kinetic store of the cat. (2 marks)

....

....

c Calculate the energy in the kinetic store of the dog. (2 marks)

....

....

d The dog accelerates to a new steady speed and increases the energy in its kinetic store to 576 J. Calculate the dog's new speed. (4 marks)

....

....

....

....

e The cat maintains the same speed of 10 m/s. The cat is 10 metres ahead of the dog. Calculate the time it takes for the dog to catch the cat. (2 marks)

....

....

1.2 Complete the following with the different energy stores. (6 marks)

a .... transferred from a torch.

b .... store of a stretched rubber band.

c .... from a singer performing.

d .... energy store of a battery.

e .... store of a moving bus.

f .... store of a boulder on the edge of a cliff.

1.3 Bradley has a breakfast of porridge followed by eggs.

Bradley then goes for a bike ride up and then down a hill.

At the bottom of the hill he has to use his brakes to stop.

Use ideas about energy stores and systems to describe his journey. (6 marks)

....

....

....

....

....

....

2.1 a **Explain with the use of diagrams the particle arrangements of solids, liquids and gases.** (6 marks)

....

....

....

....

....

....

Sometimes models are put forward to describe particle behaviour.

A student has a tray of marbles and wishes to explain ideas about matter and particles.

b **Explain what the marbles represent in the student's model.** (1 mark)

....

c **The student wishes to use the model to demonstrate a solid. Describe how he could he do this.** (1 mark)

....

d **The student wishes to use the model to demonstrate evaporation. Describe how he could do this.** (2 marks)

....

....

3.1   A student lights a fire lighter and uses it to heat up 0.25 kg of water.

When the fire lighter has all burnt away, the water temperature has increased by 10 °C.

All of the energy in the chemical store of the fire lighter is transferred to the thermal store of the water.

The specific heat capacity of water is: 4200 J/kg °C.

Calculate the (energy) increase in the thermal store of the water in joules. (4 marks)

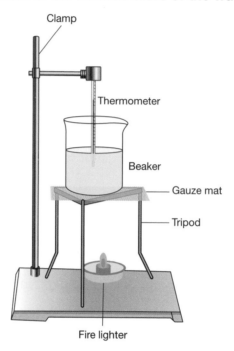

Clamp

Thermometer

Beaker

Gauze mat

Tripod

Fire lighter

....

....

....

....

3.2   Elena climbs up 3 flights of stairs. The total vertical distance she covers is 12 m.

The energy in her gravitational store increases by 6 kJ.

The Earth's gravitational field strength is 10 N/kg.

Calculate Elena's mass. (4 marks)

....

....

....

....

....

4.1 The current in a resistor and then in an unknown component X is measured for different voltages.

The table shows the results.

Voltage/V	Current/A	
	Resistor	Component X
1	0.10	0.20
2	0.20	0.40
3	0.30	0.60
4	0.40	0.75
5	0.50	0.80
6	0.60	0.84

a On the grid below and on the same axes, plot graphs of this data for the resistor and component X. Plot voltage on the *x*-axis and current on the *y*-axis. (5 marks)

b Draw lines of best fit for the resistor and component X. (2 marks)

c Determine what component X is and justify your choice. (2 marks)

d Use the graph to determine the resistance of the resistor. (2 marks)

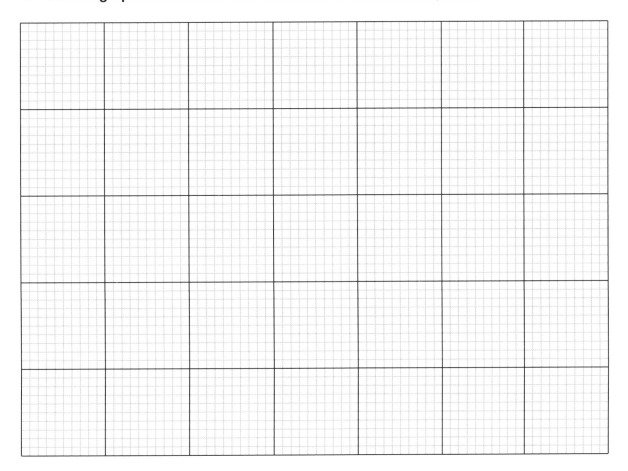

Resistance = _____

5.1 A carriage containing passengers on a roller coaster is raised through a vertical height of 90 m.

The combined mass of the carriage and the passengers is 2000 kg.

The Earth's gravitational field strength is 10 N/kg.

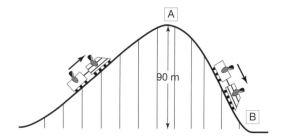

a The carriage is lifted 90 m vertically to point A on the diagram.

Calculate the energy increase in the gravitational potential store of the carriage in kJ.
(3 marks)

....

....

....

Increase in gravitational energy store = ... kJ

b During the ride the carriage drops from point A to point B as shown in the diagram.

Assume energy is conserved and friction or air resistance acting on the carriage are negligible and can be ignored.

Calculate the speed of the carriage at point B. (5 marks)

....

....

....

....

....

Speed of carriage at point B = ... m/s

6.1   The block in the image below is made of iron and has a mass of 192 g.

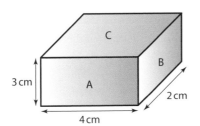

(Not drawn to scale)

a   **Calculate the volume of the block in cm³.** (1 mark)

....

b   **Calculate the block's density in g/cm³.** (2 marks)

....

....

c   **Convert the density value to kg/m³.** (2 marks)

....

....

d   **A student picks up the block and presses it down on the table first with face A and then with face B with the same force.**

Explain, without a calculation, which face (A or B) will exert the most pressure on the table. (2 marks)

....

....

e   **Calculate the pressure exerted on the table in kilopascals if face A is placed on the table.** (4 marks)

....

....

....

.... **kPa**

Answers

Cell biology

Eukaryotes and prokaryotes

1 a Nucleus – B; Cytoplasm – C.

 b *Any two from:* This cell has a nucleus, or prokaryotic cells do not have a nucleus; This cell has does not have a cell wall, or prokaryotic cells have a cell wall; This cell does not contain plasmids, or prokaryotic cells can contain plasmids; 'Prokaryotes can have flagella' is allowed.

 c 0.1 × 1000 = 100 µm

 d 0.6 mm

Animal and plant cells

1 Absorbs sunlight for photosynthesis – Chloroplasts; Provides strength to the cell – Cellulose cell wall; Filled with cell sap to keep the plant turgid – Permanent vacuole.

2 a A – cellulose cell wall; B – chloroplast; C – nucleus.

 b Cells near the top of a leaf have more chloroplasts to absorb more sunlight; for photosynthesis.

Cell specialisation and differentiation

1 a Many mitochondria

 b *Any two from:* Xylem cells; Phloem cells; Muscle cells.

 c To move mucus; out of the lungs OR To move an ovum; along the fallopian tube/oviduct.

2 a A cell that is undifferentiated and can become any type of cell.

 b Embryo

 c Take stem cells and grow them in a laboratory; Expose cells to chemicals/hormones to make them differentiate into a type of specialised cell; Grow the specialised cells on a Petri dish so that they form tissues; Use the tissues to form the new organ.

Microscopy

1 a The cells are not plant cells; There are no visible cellulose cell walls, permanent vacuole or chloroplasts.

 b Magnification = $\dfrac{5\,cm}{0.5\,\mu m} = \dfrac{50\,000\,\mu m}{0.5\,\mu m}$

   $= \times100\,000$

2 Higher magnification/resolution; Able to see sub-cellular structures clearly/in detail.

---

3 Size of image = magnification × size of real object;

   = 200 × 10;

   = 2000 µm or 2 mm.

Using a light microscope

1 a Move the lowest magnification objective lens over the specimen; Move the stage by moving the course focus, until the cells are in focus; Move the objective lens to a higher magnification, and focus using the fine focus.

 b To see the cells/tissues more clearly; different stains can be used to identify tissues/organelles.

 c ×400

2 a

	Number of cells after 12 hours			
	1	2	3	Mean
With mitotic inhibitor	12	10	**11**	11
Without mitotic inhibitor	108	110	106	**108**

 b *Any two from:* Type of cells; Starting number of cells; Temperature; Volume of nutrient broth/culture medium.

 c Use different concentrations of mitotic inhibitor.

Mitosis and the cell cycle

1 a G2 phase – Chromosomes are checked; S phase – Chromosomes are replicated; M phase – The cell divides into two daughter cells; Cytokinesis – Physical process of cell division.

 b So that when the cell divides during mitosis; each daughter cell has the correct number of sub-cellular structures.

2 i

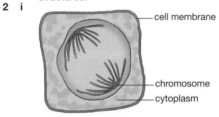

ii The replicated chromosomes are separating; to the opposite sides of the cell.

3 26 (lb)

Stem cells

1 B

2 *Any two from:* Replacing/repair of cells; Growth; Used in medical research/ treatments; Meristem used in plant cloning.

---

3 Meristem tissue; found in the shoots, roots and flowering parts of the plant.

4 Stem cells can be used to make organs for transplants, so there is no waiting time for organ donors; However, there is an ethical objection to using embryos, as they could potentially grow into humans/ animals; Using stem cells in medical treatments means that the body will not reject the cells; but there is a risk of transfer of viral infection from putting stem cells into the body.

Diffusion

1 a Diffusion is the spreading out of the particles of any substance in solution, or particles of a gas; resulting in a net movement from an area of higher concentration to an area of lower concentration.

 b *Any one from:* In the lungs for exchange of oxygen/carbon dioxide; In the small intestines for the movement of the products of digestion.

2 a 24:8 = 3:1;

   96:64 = 3:2

       = 1.5:1;

   Organism B has the smallest surface area to volume ratio.

 b They cannot get all the substances they need by diffusion alone; They need to increase the rate of diffusion; by increasing the surface area/ providing a short diffusion pathway.

3 Extract solution from outside the Visking tubing; at regular intervals/named time interval; test for the presence of glucose. Factors – surface area, concentration gradient and diffusion thickness.

Osmosis

1 Osmosis is the diffusion of water from a dilute solution to a concentrated solution; through a partially permeable membrane.

2 From inside the cell to outside the cell.

3 Percentage increase = $\dfrac{(14-10)}{10} \times 100\%$

   = 40%

4 a 3% sugar solution; because the plotted line crosses the *x*-axis at 3%.

 b The same volume of water left the cell as moved into the cell.

Investigating the effect of a range of concentrations of salt or sugar solutions on the mass of plant tissue

1 a In order, the percentage change is: 16.7; 0.0; –25.0; –34.1

b No units in third column; – should be (g). 4 in second column; should be given as 4.0

c

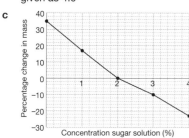

d −14%

e The cells would be plasmolysed/the cell membrane would be separated from the cell wall; because water has moved from inside to outside the cell; as the water potential inside the cell is higher than the water potential outside of the cell.

Active transport

1 The movement of substances from a more dilute solution to a more concentrated solution; It requires energy.

2 The movement of mineral ions into the root hair cells.

3 Osmosis – Involves the movement of water/Movement is from dilute solution to concentrated solution; Active transport – Involves the movement of particles/Movement is from dilute solution to concentrated solution.

4 The more mitochondria, the more respiration can be carried out; The cells in the wall of the small intestine need to carry out more respiration to provide energy; for the active transport of sugars across the wall of the small intestine.

5 **a** The carrot seedlings in the aerobic conditions take up more potassium ions than the seedlings in the anaerobic conditions.

b In the aerobic condition the cells can carry out aerobic respiration; and make energy for active transport to transport the potassium ions into the seedlings; In the anaerobic condition, only anaerobic respiration can be carried out which provides less energy for active transport.

c Repeat the investigation to make it more reliable; Keep named variable constant to make it more valid, e.g. temperature, surface area of seedlings, volume of water.

Tissues, organs and organ systems

The human digestive system and enzymes

1 **a** *Any two from:* Stomach; Small intestine; Large intestine; Pancreas; Liver; Gall bladder.

b Food mixes with saliva and travels down the oesophagus to the stomach; Food

is broken down with acid and enzymes in the stomach, before moving into the small intestine; Bile from the liver, and pancreatic juices from the pancreas are added to the food in the small intestine; Digested food/named small molecules of digested food (sugars, amino acids, etc.) move from the small intestine into the bloodstream; Any food that is not digested moves into the large intestine where water is removed and a solid mass known as faeces passes out of the body through the anus.

2 **a**

Enzymes	Substrate	Products
carbohydrase/ amylase	carbohydrates	sugars
proteases	**proteins**	amino acids
lipases	lipids	**fatty acids and glycerol**

b Bile breaks lipids into smaller droplets/emulsifies so that the lipase enzymes have a greater surface area to work on; Bile is alkaline and neutralises any hydrochloric acid that passes into the small intestine.

3 Food is burned inside a calorimeter; to work out the energy content in kilojoules/kJ.

4 **a** Proteins that can speed up chemical reactions.

b Amylase has an active site that is specific to starch; Lipids do not fit into amylase's active site.

c The rate of reaction of amylase would decrease; Amylase would denature; Starch will no longer fit in active site.

5 $24 \div 3 = 8$;

$= 8\,cm^3/min$

6

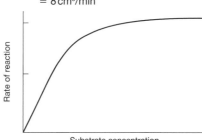

The rate of reaction of the enzyme increases as the substrate concentration increases; until all of the enzyme active sites are occupied and the rate of reaction remains constant.

Food tests

1 Starch – Iodine test; Protein – Biuret test; Lipid – Emulsion test.

2 Biuret test/Biuret reagent has been added; The sample contains/tested positive for protein.

3 Add Benedict's reagent to the sample; Heat the sample for several minutes; If the sample remains blue, there is no glucose

present; If the sample turns green, yellow, orange or brick red, then glucose is present.

4 Test the solution with Benedict's reagent; if the solution turns green/yellow/orange/brick red then maltose is present. Test the solution with biuret reagent; if the solution turns lilac then an enzyme/protein could be present.

The effect of pH on amylase

1 It is an enzyme; that breaks down starch into sugars.

2 **a** Amylase activity increases from pH1 to pH6; Amylase activity decreases from pH6 to pH9.

b pH6

c $10 \div 120 = 0.083\,cm^3/s$ or $5\,cm^3/min$

The heart

1 Vena cava; Pulmonary arteries; Pulmonary veins; Aorta.

2 **a** Blood flows from the vena cava into the right atrium which contracts; and squeezes the blood into the right ventricle; The right ventricle contracts and squeezes the blood into the pulmonary artery.

b The valves prevent the backflow of blood; between the atria and the ventricles and inside the aorta and pulmonary artery.

3 Pacemakers are a small electrical device; that can be used to regulate the contraction of the heart at rest; They can be used to correct an irregular heart rate.

The lungs

1 Air travels down the trachea; and into the bronchi; The air travels into the bronchioles; and then into the alveoli.

2 Many alveoli – Increase the surface area of the lungs; Alveolar wall is one cell thick – Gives short diffusion pathway for gases; Good supply of blood capillaries – Keeps the concentration gradient of gases high.

Blood vessels and blood

1 B and C only

2 Rate of blood flow = distance travelled by blood ÷ time

$= 2 \div 4$

$= 0.5\,mm/s$

3 Student A is correct; because arteries must have thick walls to withstand the high pressure; Arteries have narrow lumens to maintain the high pressure.

4 *Any two from:* Plasma; Platelets; Proteins; Hormones; Oxygen; Carbon dioxide.

5 A – white blood cell; B – red blood cell.

6 **a** Carry oxygen around the body.

b Protect the body from pathogens.

7 Phagocytes can change shape to engulf pathogens; Neutrophils have a lobed nucleus to squeeze through small spaces; Lymphocytes have a lot of rough endoplasmic reticulum to produce antibodies.

Coronary heart disease

1 A non-communicable disease that affects the heart and the coronary arteries.

2 Layers of fatty material and cholesterol build up inside the coronary arteries; and make the lumen inside the artery narrower, reducing the flow of blood to heart muscle.

3 Angina – Chest pains due to restricted blood flow to heart muscle; Heart failure – Muscle weakness in the heart muscle or a faulty valve; Heart attack – The blood supply to the heart is suddenly blocked.

4 *Any two treatments*, **with** name of treatment *and* one advantage *and* one disadvantage, from:

Stent - Advantage: holds the artery open; Disadvantage: only lasts for a few years;

Statins - Advantage: reduces blood cholesterol levels; Disadvantage: may have unwanted side effects;

Valve replacement - Advantage: heart functions properly; Disadvantage: people may object to animal valve being used;

Transplant - Advantage: heart functions properly; Disadvantage: long waiting lists for transplants/risks associated with surgery.

Health issues and effect of lifestyle

1 A disease caused by a pathogen; that can be transmitted from people or animals.

2 *Any two from:* Any viral disease; Any bacterial disease; Any fungal disease; Any protozoan disease. *Check which examples your exam board requires you to know.*

3 Immune system defects; make sufferers more likely to suffer infectious disease **OR** Viral infections; can be a trigger for cancer **OR** Physical ill health; could lead to mental health problems. *Use specific examples if they are included for your exam board.*

4 As the age of males and females increases, the number of deaths from CVD per 100 000 population increases; At each age range, the number of male deaths is greater than the number of female deaths from CVD per 100 000 population.

5 A medical condition that is not transmitted from people or animals.

6 *Any three from:* Smoking and not taking enough exercise could increase risk of cardiovascular disease; Drinking alcohol could affect liver and brain function; Smoking increases risk of lung disease and lung cancer; Smoking and alcohol could affect unborn babies.

7 *Any three from:* Person may have to change their diet; Person may have to change their level of exercise; Person may experience pain/discomfort; Person may have to pay for medicines; Person may have costs associated with hospital visits; Person may have to take time off work/be unable to work/lose income; Loss of social contact.

Cancer

1 *Any two from:* Smoking; Genetic risk factors; Drinking alcohol; Poor diet; Ionising radiation.

2 Substances in the environment/genetic factors cause mutations in DNA; that cause the cell to divide in an uncontrolled way; The cells form a mass, lying over the top of one another.

3 Benign and malignant tumours are both a growth of abnormal cells; Benign tumours are contained in one area, whereas malignant tumours can invade neighbouring tissues and spread through the blood to different parts of the body; Benign tumours do not invade other parts of the body, whereas malignant tumours form secondary tumours.

4 From 1971 to 2011, the number of cases of breast cancer in women increased; This could be because screening identified more women with breast cancer; From 1971 to 1987, the number of women dying from breast cancer remained the same, and from 1987 to 2011, the number decreased; This could be because screening identified more women as having breast cancer, and they were able to have treatment.

Plant tissues

1 Spongy mesophyll – Site of gas exchange in the leaf; Palisade tissues – The main site of photosynthesis in a leaf; Xylem – Transport of water to the leaf; Phloem – Transport of sugar sap around the plant.

2 Packed with chloroplasts to absorb light for photosynthesis; Tightly packed at the top of the leaf to absorb more light.

3

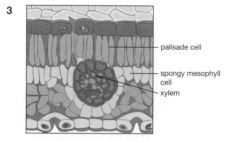

- palisade cell
- spongy mesophyll cell
- xylem

Transpiration and translocation

1 a Potometer

b Rate of transpiration = water lost ÷ time

= 20 cm³ ÷ 5 hours

= 4 cm³/hour

2 When there is plenty of water, the cells become turgid and change shape; the pairs of guard cells no longer touch in the middle, meaning the stomata (holes) are open; Water vapour can diffuse out of the stomata; there is little water, the guard cells become flaccid and touch, closing the stomata which means water vapour can no longer diffuse out.

3 Transpiration is the loss of water from the top part of the plant; Water moves up the xylem; Translocation is the movement of sugar sap around the plant; The sugar sap moves in the phloem, up and down the plant.

4 Curled leaves/sunken stomata/small hairs; to slow down the evaporation of water; store water in the stems; to have available water during the dry season.

Infection and response

Communicable (infectious) diseases

1 A microorganism that causes disease.

2 Bacterium – Tuberculosis; Fungus – Athlete's foot; Protist – Malaria.

3 In the lytic lifecycle pathway, the virus reproduces inside a host cell; then the viruses break out of the host cell; In the lysogenic lifecycle pathway, the DNA of the virus is incorporated into the DNA of the host cell.

4 From 1999 to 2011, the number of cases of HIV decreased from 65 to 5; This is because HIV is spread by contact with infected blood; Intravenous drug users who use the needle exchange scheme do not come into contact with infected blood and are not infected with HIV.

Viral and bacterial diseases

1 Red skin rash; fever.

2 a A plant virus that affects tobacco and tomato plants; It causes a black mosaic pattern to appear on leaves.

b Plants infected with TMV have a black mosaic pattern on their leaves. These areas of the leaf cannot carry out photosynthesis.

3 Influenza is spread through coughs and sneezes; The soldiers lived close together, so many caught influenza; When the soldiers went home, they came into contact with many people; Influenza can spread by direct contact with an infected person.

4 a *Any two from:* Fever; Abdominal cramps; Vomiting; Diarrhoea.

b Treated for dehydration; Antibiotics.

5 a The resistant strains of bacteria are not killed by most antibiotics; A mixture of antibiotics or an alternative treatment must be used.

b *Any one from:* Not practising safe sex; Not using condoms; Increase in people going for testing.

Fungal and protist diseases

1 a Fungal; Black/purple spots; Photosynthesis.

   b Fungicides; removing/destroying leaves.

2 a *Any three from:* Mosquito nets; Insect repellent; Wearing long-sleeved clothes; Taking antimalarial drugs as a preventative; Using pesticides to kill mosquitoes.

   b Mosquitoes breed in shallow pools of water; Get rid of shallow pools of water to prevent breeding.

3 Destroy infected trees; Cut down healthy ash trees between areas of diseased and healthy trees to prevent spread.

Human defence systems and vaccination

1 Skin – Physical barrier against pathogens; Nose – Small hairs and mucus trap airborne particles; Trachea – Cilia move mucus up to the throat; Stomach – Hydrochloric acid and proteases kill pathogens; Tears – Contain lysozymes which kill bacteria.

2 a Phagocytes; lymphocytes.

   b Lymphocytes produce antibodies; The antibodies attach to pathogens and prevent them from entering cells; The antibodies attach to pathogens and target them for phagocytosis; Macrophages engulf targeted pathogens; Antibodies act as antitoxins by attaching to toxins released by the pathogen.

3 Inactive; pathogen; white blood cells/lymphocytes.

4 Vaccines contain a dead or inactive pathogen which acts as an antigen; When this is injected into the body, it stimulates white blood cells/lymphocytes to produce antibodies; The antibodies bind specifically to the pathogen's antigens; If the vaccinated person is infected with the same pathogen, the antibodies bind to the pathogen to fight the disease.

5 Prevents/irradicates diseases; may have side effects.

Antibiotics, painkillers and new drugs

1 Any antibiotic, e.g. penicillin/erythromycin; Any painkiller, e.g. paracetamol/ibuprofen.

2 They kill bacteria that have infected the body; Some specific bacteria are killed by a specific type of antibiotic.

3 Antiviral drugs kill viruses while they are outside the body's cells; If a virus enters a cell, the antiviral drug cannot kill it.

4 Ibuprofen reduces pain more than glucosamine sulfate does; Glucosamine sulfate reduces pain for eight weeks, whereas ibuprofen reduces pain for two weeks.

5 Control prescriptions of antibiotics; make sure patients take the full course of antibiotics; discover new antibiotics.

6 Aspirin – Willow bark; Digitalis – Foxgloves; Penicillin – *Penicillium*.

7 During preclinical testing new drugs are tested on cells to test for toxicity/efficacy/correct dose; If the drug is safe it goes to clinical trial, where a low dose is given to healthy volunteers to check for toxicity; Then different doses are given to healthy volunteers and patients to find the optimum dose; Finally, the drug is given to patients and compared with another drug or placebo to test how effective it is.

Bioenergetics

Photosynthesis and the rate of photosynthesis

1 a Carbon dioxide + water $\xrightarrow{\text{light}}$ glucose + oxygen

   b Endothermic reaction (two stage reaction is allowed for OCR students).

   c Carbon dioxide is a reactant in photosynthesis; It supplies the carbon to make glucose.

   d *Any four from:* Place an aquatic plant in a funnel under water; Measure the volume of oxygen given off in a given time; Repeat the experiment at different given temperatures; Repeat investigation at least twice; Calculate the rate of reaction at each temperature.

2 *Any one from:* Increased light; increased temperature; Increased carbon dioxide concentration; Increased amount of chlorophyll.

3 a An environmental condition; that limits the rate of photosynthesis.

   b B

4 Rate of photosynthesis = $\dfrac{\text{oxygen given off}}{\text{time}}$
   $= 24 \div 4$
   $= 6\,\text{cm}^3/\text{min}$

Investigating the effect of light intensity on the rate of photosynthesis

1 a Independent variable: distance of the lamp from the plant; Dependent variable: volume of oxygen.

   b Make sure that the lamp is the only light source; Keep the room at the same temperature/stand tube with pond weed in a beaker of water; Use the same piece of pondweed.

   c In order from top to bottom: 39, 17, 8, 2.

   d Light energy is needed for photosynthesis to occur.

Uses of glucose

1 *Any two from:* Used in respiration, to release energy; Converted into starch for storage; Used to produce oil for storage; Used to produce amino acids for protein synthesis; Used to produce cellulose for cell walls.

2 Glucose has the chemical formula $C_6H_{12}O_6$.

3 By the process of photosynthesis.

Respiration and metabolism

1 a Glucose + oxygen $\rightarrow$ carbon dioxide + water

   b Exothermic

2 a Mitochondria

   b $C_6H_{12}O_6 + 6O_2 \rightarrow 6CO_2 + 6H_2O$

3 Respiration happens in the absence of oxygen for a short time; Glucose is converted to lactic acid. Lactic acid builds up in the muscles, causing muscle fatigue.

4 Place the yeast into a test tube, with sodium hydroxide/potassium hydroxide to absorb carbon dioxide; measure the volume of oxygen being given off by the yeast; using a respirometer/gas syringe/capillary tube.

5 Respiration; Breakdown of excess proteins to urea for excretion in urine.

6 Energy is needed to form new bonds when making new complex molecules; Energy is needed to break bonds when breaking complex molecules into simpler ones.

Response to exercise

1 a Find pulse in wrist/radial artery or neck/carotid artery; Count the number of pulses in 15 seconds; and multiply the number by four.

   b 18 x 4 = 72 beats per minute.

2 a *Any two statements with reasons:* Increase in heart rate; so that blood flows to the cells more quickly; Increase in breathing rate; to oxygenate the blood more quickly/remove carbon dioxide quickly; Increase in breath volume; to take in more oxygen with each breath; Increased rate of respiration in muscle cells/increased production of energy.

   b 80 x 60; 4800 cm³ per minute/4.8 dm³ per minute.

3 He still needs to remove extra carbon dioxide; He will have carried out some anaerobic respiration; and lactic acid would have been made; The lactic acid needs to be broken down by oxygen.

Answers

Homeostasis and response

Homeostasis

1. Homeostasis keeps all the **internal** conditions of the body **constant/the same**, whatever the **outside** conditions might be.

2. a. Controlling the internal temperature of the body; Controlling the water levels in the body.

   b. When the blood glucose concentration is too high, insulin is released by the pancreas; Insulin causes cells to take up glucose, so the blood glucose concentration returns to normal; In the liver, excess glucose is converted to glycogen for storage; When the blood glucose concentration is too low, glucagon is released by the pancreas; Glycogen is broken down into glucose and more glucose is released, so the blood glucose concentration returns to normal.

3. The brain is the coordinator in homeostasis; It receives and processes information from receptors; It sends nerve impulses to effectors to restore optimum conditions.

The human nervous system and reflexes

1. C

2. a. Stimulus → receptor → coordinator → effector → response (mark for each)

   b. To receive nerve impulses from the receptor; and send nerve impulses to the effectors.

3. The light stimulus is detected by the receptor; A nerve impulse is sent to the coordinator; The coordinator sends nerve impulses to the effectors; The response is for the hand to press the button.

4. *Any two from:* Sensory neurones; Motor neurones; Relay neurones.

5. Sensory neurones have their cell body near the centre of the axon, but motor and relay neurones have their cell body at the end of the axon; Sensory neurones carry nerve impulses to the central nervous system, motor neurones carry nerve impulses from the central nervous system and relay neurones carry nerve impulses from sensory neurones to motor neurones; Relay neurones are only used in reflex arcs, but sensory and motor neurones are used in reflex arcs and voluntary reactions.

6. a. Reflexes are automatic, but voluntary reactions are under conscious control; Reflexes are quicker than voluntary reactions.

   b. Protection from harm; Voluntary reaction times are too slow.

Investigating the effect of a factor on human reaction time

1. a. Repeat investigation three times; Measure out same volume of coffee each time; Repeat investigation at the same time of day each time; Leave the same time interval between drinking coffee and measuring reaction times.

   b and c

Condition	Reaction time 1 (s)	Reaction time 2 (s)	Reaction time 3 (s)	Mean reaction time (s)
Before caffeine	0.55	0.45	0.50	0.50 (1)
After caffeine	0.40	0.35	0.30	0.35 (1)

Human endocrine system

1. Pituitary gland—Growth hormone, FSH and LH; Pancreas—Insulin and glucagon; Thyroid—Thyroxine; Ovary—Progesterone and oestrogen.

2. The pituitary gland in the brain controls many of the other glands in the body; by releasing hormones that affect them.

3. The nervous system targets effectors more quickly than the endocrine system; The nervous system uses nerves/neurones and the endocrine system uses hormones; The effects of the nervous system last for a short time whereas the effects of the endocrine system last for a long time; The nervous system is controlled by the brain, and the endocrine system is controlled by the pituitary gland.

Control of blood glucose concentration

1. Pancreas

2. Cells take up glucose; Glucose is converted into glycogen; in the liver and muscle cells.

3. Glucagon converts glycogen into glucose; in the liver and muscle cells; This increases the concentration of blood glucose in the blood.

4. *Any two from:* The cells in the body would not take in glucose; The cells would have less glucose for respiration; The person would feel tired.

Diabetes

1. Disease where no insulin is produced; or the body stops responding to insulin.

2. When the blood sugar level is too high.

3. In type 1 diabetes, the body does not release insulin, but in type 2 diabetes the body stops responding to insulin; Type 1 diabetes has a genetic cause, but type 2 diabetes is caused by lifestyle factors; such as obesity and poor diet; Type 1 diabetes is treated by injecting insulin but type 2 diabetes is treated with a carbohydrate-controlled diet and exercise.

4. The blood sugar levels rise after a meal; and remain high for several hours.

Hormones in human reproduction

1. Testosterone – Testes; Oestrogen – Ovaries; Follicle – stimulating hormone – Pituitary gland.

2. a. Causes eggs in the ovaries to mature.

   b. Oestrogen

3. a. LH stimulates the ovaries to release an egg/ovulation.

   b. Progesterone maintains the lining of the uterus; If the egg released on day 14 is fertilised, then it will implant into this lining.

Contraception

1. Condoms – Trap sperm; Intrauterine device (IUD) – Prevents implantation of an embryo; Spermicidal agents – Kill sperm.

2. a. *Any two from:* Oral contraceptives; Hormone injection; Hormone skin patch; Hormone implant.

   b. Oral contraceptives contain oestrogen and progesterone; so that FSH is inhibited, and no eggs mature; Other hormonal contraceptives contain progesterone to inhibit the maturation and release of eggs.

3. *Any four from:* Oral contraceptives/ intrauterine devices are effective at preventing pregnancy, but have some side effects on the female body; Condoms/ diaphragms/spermicidal agents do not have any side effects, but are not 100% effective at preventing pregnancy; Surgical methods are very effective at preventing pregnancy but are difficult to reverse; Condoms and oral contraceptives allow couples to choose the time to start a family; Abstaining from intercourse around the time that an egg may be in the oviducts does not have any side effects on the body, but is difficult to use to prevent pregnancy as menstruation cycles and ovulation dates can fluctuate.

Using hormones to treat infertility

1. **iii** A and C only

2. FSH and LH are given to the woman in order to produce enough eggs for IVF; Eggs are surgically removed from the woman and fertilised by the man's sperm in a laboratory; The fertilised eggs develop into embryos and then placed surgically into the woman's uterus.

3. IVF allows the mother to give birth to her own baby; The baby will be the genetic offspring of the mother and father;

However, the success rates are not high; and it can lead to multiple births.

Negative feedback

1 A mechanism that keeps the body functioning at set levels; If something goes above or below the set level, negative feedback brings it back again.

2 **a** Adrenal glands.

b **iii** A, B and D only

3 When the level of thyroxine in the blood is low, the hypothalamus releases TRH, which stimulates the anterior pituitary to release TSH, which stimulates the thyroid gland to release thyroxine; TSH inhibits the hypothalamus producing TRH; When the level of thyroxine is high, it inhibits both the hypothalamus producing TRH and the anterior pituitary producing TSH.

Inheritance, variation and evolution

Sexual and asexual reproduction

1 **a** Female – Egg/ovum; Male – Sperm.

b Meiosis

2 Bacteria – Binary fission; Yeast – Budding; Strawberry plants – Runners; Potatoes – Tubers.

3 Sexual reproduction produces variation in the offspring, which gives a selective advantage in natural selection; However, you need to find two parents in order to have sexual reproduction; Asexual reproduction produces many identical offspring quickly; However, genetically identical offspring are vulnerable to changes in the environment.

Meiosis

1 Mitosis: 2, Full, Yes; Meiosis: 4, Half, No.

2 Meiosis goes through two rounds of cell division to produce four daughter cells; Each daughter cell has half of the number of chromosomes as the original body cell; The chromosomes are randomly assorted into the four daughter cells so that they are genetically different from each other.

3 A male and a female gamete join together and the two nuclei fuse; When this happens, the new cell/zygote has a full set of chromosomes; The zygote divides many times by mitosis to form an embryo.

DNA and the genome

1 **iii** A, B and D only

2 **a** 46 chromosomes

b 19 chromosomes

3 To find out which genes are linked to diseases; To learn how to treat inherited diseases; To trace human migration patterns from the past.

4 The soap is needed to break down the cell membrane and nuclear envelope/ membrane; the DNA will form a precipitate in the ethanol and become visible; ice-cold ethanol will prevent enzymes in the solution digesting the DNA.

Genetic inheritance

1 Homozygous – When two copies of the same allele are present; Heterozygous – When two different alleles are present; Genotype – The alleles that are present in the genome; Phenotype – The characteristics that are expressed by those alleles.

2 **a**

	B	b
b	Bb	bb
b	Bb	bb

b Black or brown

c 1:1

3 The allele for colour blindness is carried on the X chromosome; The daughter has inherited one X chromosome from her father, but the two sons have inherited a Y chromosome from their father.

Inherited disorders

1 **a**

	C	c
C	CC	Cc
c	Cc	cc

b 1/4 or 0.25

c They will discuss the chances of having a child with cystic fibrosis; They may decide not to have children/ use embryo screening.

2 **a** When there are three or more alleles; Blood groups have the alleles, A, B and O.

b When two alleles are both expressed; Alleles A and B are both expressed in the genotype, AB.

Variation

1 Genetic; Environmental

2 **a** A change in the base sequence of the DNA; Can be a base change/ substitution, deletion or addition of bases.

b A change in the base sequence changes the three base code that decides the sequence of amino acids; The amino acid sequence of the polypeptide changes; The shape of the protein changes.

c If the new variation has little influence on the phenotype, then there will be no advantage to the organism; If the new variation changes the phenotype but is not advantageous to the organism, then the organism is less likely to have offspring and the new variation will not spread through the population; If the new variation changes the phenotype and it is advantageous to the organism, those with the advantageous phenotype are more likely to survive and reproduce passing the new allele to their offspring; Over many generations the numbers with the mutation will increase.

3 The sequencing of the entire human genome; used to find out which gene codes for each protein; allows research into inheritable diseases/new drug targets for medicine.

Evolution

1 C B E A D

2 The process by which complex living organisms; gradually evolved from simpler organisms by natural selection.

3 **a** The brown snails are less easy for the predators to spot against the brown background; They are more likely to survive; and produce offspring; Over time, more of the snail population will have brown shells.

b They are the same species if they can interbreed; and produce fertile offspring.

Selective breeding and genetic engineering

1 **ii** A and D only

2 **a** Breed together a male and a female cat that do not cause allergies; Select any offspring that also do not cause allergies; Breed these offspring with other cats that do not cause allergies; Keep breeding until all of the offspring do not cause allergies.

b *Any two from:* Long/short fur; Temperament; Short claws; Coat/eye colour; *Any sensible answer.*

c More likely to have two copies of a recessive allele; More likely to become ill/have disorders.

3 **a** The addition of a gene from another organism; into an organism's genome.

b *Any from:* Disease-resistant plants; Plants that produce bigger fruits; Bacteria that produce human insulin; Gene therapy; *Any sensible answer.*

4 **a** Rice plants do not contain the genes that control beta carotene production; Selective breeding takes many generations, genetic engineering takes one generation.

b Advantage - Makes the rice more nutritious/prevents vitamin A deficiency; Disadvantage - Could potentially cause harm/difficult to get genes into the right place.

Answers

Classification

1

Group	Example
Kingdom	Animal
Phylum	Vertebrate
Class	**Mammal**
Order	Carnivore
Family	Felidae
Genus	Panthera
Species	tigris

2 According to: anatomy: physiology: and behaviour.

3 a Binomial system

   b Humans and chimpanzees; because the branches on the evolutionary tree branched off from each other the most recently.

Ecology

Communities

1 Population—A group of organisms of the same species living in the same area at the same time;

Habitat—The environment in which a species normally lives;

Community—A group of populations living and interacting with each other in the same area;

Ecosystem—A community and its abiotic environment.

2 a *Any two from:* Food; Water; Territory/space; Light; Mineral ions.

   b Interspecific competition

3 a When species depend on each other for survival; They depend on each other to provide food/shelter/pollination/seed dispersal; If one species is removed from a habitat, it can affect the whole community.

   b The number of aphids will decrease, as their food source decreases; The number of ladybirds will also decrease, as their food source decreases.

Abiotic and biotic factors

1 ii B and D only

2 a 10, 21

   b The cliff edge is very windy; and removes a lot of moisture from the soil, making it more difficult for the sea campion plants to grow.

3 a The birds eat the insects that have been killed by DDT.

   b The hawks are further up the food chain/top predators; DDT accumulates in the organisms as it moves up the food chain.

4 Just after the prey/snowshoe hare population increases, the predator lynx population increases; This is because the snowshoe hares are a food source for the lynx, and provide energy for the lynx to reproduce; Just after the prey/snowshoe hare population decreases, the predator/lynx population decreases; This is because the lynx do not have as much food and some will die of starvation.

Adaptations

1 Structural adaptations; are adaptations to the body of the organism; Behavioural adaptations; are changes to a species' behaviour to help their survival; A functional adaptation; is one that has occurred through natural selection over many generations in order to overcome a functional problem.

2 Cactus has needles; to reduce water loss/prevent evaporation from the plant; Water storage in the stem of the cactus; ensures the cactus has a supply of water when there is no rain/no water available.

Food chains

1 a Phytoplankton

   b Seal

   c From sunlight; through photosynthesis.

   d The amount of phytoplankton would increase because the primary consumers would not be eating them; The number of chinstrap penguins would decrease because there would be fewer krill for them to eat; The number of seals would decrease because there would be fewer chinstrap penguins for them to eat.

Measuring species

1 a B

   b Removes bias; and makes sure that the sample is representative.

   c i 2.4

      ii Area of the field = 50 m
                 = 1000 m^2

        2.4 x 1000 m^2; = 2400 buttercups.

2 a Pitfall traps; because the snails move along the ground.

   b Using a non-toxic paint/marker pen/sticker on the shell.

   c If the paint/pen is toxic it could kill the snail; If the paint/pen/sticker is bright it may attract predators to eat the snail.

   d (10 x 16)/2 = 80 snails

   e Snails had time to mingle with the rest of the population; No snails migrated; No snails died or were born.

The carbon cycle, nitrogen cycle and water cycle

1 Water in the oceans evaporates into the atmosphere; The water droplets condense to form clouds and are transported inland by the wind; As the clouds rise, the water droplets are released as precipitation; The water moves into streams and rivers, and back to the oceans.

2 a Photosynthesis

   b Aerobic respiration; Combustion

   c Dead and decaying organisms are decomposed by bacteria and fungi/the decomposers; which release carbon dioxide through aerobic respiration.

3 The number of people has increased; and the amount of deforestation has increased as we make room for housing and fields to grow food; so less carbon dioxide is removed from the atmosphere by photosynthesis; More fossil fuels are being burned by combustion as we increase the use of cars/power plants; An increase in industrial processes has increased the amount of carbon dioxide released into the atmosphere.

4 a Adding fertiliser/nitrates/manure; growing leguminous plants/peas/clover.

   b Plants are consumed by animals; Fertilisers leach off the fields during rainfall; Nitrates in the soil are converted into atmospheric nitrogen by bacteria in the soil.

Biodiversity

1 The variety of living species of organisms on the Earth, or within an ecosystem.

2 Land pollution—Decomposition of landfill and from chemicals; Water pollution - Sewage, fertiliser leeching off the fields, chemicals; Air pollution - Smoke, acidic gases from vehicle exhausts or power stations.

3 As humans increase in number, there is an increase in deforestation, to provide land for houses and farming; Farming large areas with the removal of hedgerows and the planting of one crop (monoculture) decreases biodiversity; Humans use more resources which creates more pollution destroying habitats for other organisms; Humans burn fossil fuels which leads to increased carbon dioxide in the atmosphere and leads to global warming; This leads to climate change that decreases biodiversity.

4 Decrease pollution; Decrease deforestation; Decrease global warming.

Global warming

1 Increase in global temperature; caused by an increase in greenhouse gases in the atmosphere.

2 Radiation from the Sun warms the earth, and this heat is reflected from the Earth's surface; The greenhouses gases in the atmosphere absorb the heat; increasing the temperature of the atmosphere.

3 Global weather patterns will change causing flooding in some areas and drought in other areas; This will decrease available habitats, and food and water availability; Sea levels will rise; decreasing available habitats; Increased migration of organisms as species will move to more suitable habitats with enough available water and food; There will be an increased extinction of species, as some species will not be able to migrate or adapt quickly enough to the changing climate.

4 *Any two from:* Conservation areas; Using renewable energy; Recycling waste; Reducing waste and pollution; Fish farming; Sustainable farming methods.

5 Protects endangered species from being hunted; Keeps species in their original habitat; Protects rare habitats; Reduces deforestation; the more habitats which are maintained, the greater the variety of food, so a wider variety of species can be supported.

Atomic structure and the periodic table

Atoms, elements and compounds

1 a Atom – The smallest part of an element that can exist; Element – A substance made of only one type of atom; Compound – A substance that contains two or more elements chemically combined; Mixture – A substance that contains two or more elements not chemically combined.

   b Br_2; Ar   c B   d 9   e 3

2 a *Any two from:* fluorine, chlorine, bromine, iodine or astatine (must be the name, not the symbol).

   b *Any two from:* Li, Na, K, Rb, Cs or Fr (not H as not in group 1 of the periodic table).

Mixtures and compounds

1 Element: hydrogen, oxygen; Compound: sodium hydroxide, water; Mixture: air, salty water.

2 Heat the solution; Allow water to evaporate/leave to form crystals.

3 a Condenser

   b Water boils and turns into a gas/vapour; The vapour is then cooled in the condenser and turns back into water; The salt remains in the flask as it has a higher melting/boiling point than water.

4 *Any four from:* Crush rock salt; Add rock salt to water; Heat/stir until NaCl dissolves; Filter to remove sand; Heat remaining solution; Leave to crystallise/allow water to evaporate.

Pure substances and formulations

1 Pure substances are either single elements or single compounds.

2 a Although milk doesn't contain additives; it is a mixture of compounds.

   b You could heat the mixture and using a thermometer; observe a range of boiling points; pure substances have a specific boiling/melting point. (No mark for 'separate the mixture'.)

3 It is not pure – it contains other elements or compounds.

4 a A formulation is a mixture that is designed to be an improvement on the activate substance on its own – the lubricant stops the paracetamol sticking/makes it easier to swallow.

   b $0.5g + 0.25g + 1.25g = 2g$
      $0.5g/2g = 0.25 \times 100 = 25\%$

   c i Paracetamol $= 151 \rightarrow 0.5/151$
         $= 0.003$ moles or 3×10^{-3} moles

      ii Starch $= 162 \rightarrow 1.25/162$
         $= 0.008$ moles or 8×10^{-3} moles

      iii Magnesium stearate $= 591 \rightarrow 0.25/591 = 0.0004$ moles or 4×10^{-4} moles

   d $0.003 + 0.008 + 0.004 = 0.0114$.
      $0.003/0.0114 \times 100 = 26.3\%$

Chromatography

1 Chromatography is a technique that can be used to separate mixtures into their components; Chromatography works because different compounds have different levels of attraction for the paper and the solvent.

2 a Water line is above the base line; which will cause the inks to disperse in the water rather than up the paper; The base line is drawn in ink; which may contain colours that could contaminate the chromatogram/which could interfere with the experiment.

   b $R_f =$ distance travelled/solvent front $= 22/25 = 0.88$. C is yellow.

Scientific models of the atom

1 Before the discovery of the electron, atoms were thought to be tiny spheres that could not be divided.

2 Ball/sphere of positive charge; electrons embedded in the sphere.

3 a Positive

   b Most of the atom is empty space.

   c Only part of the atom has a positive charge.

   d Mass of the atom is concentrated in the middle/nucleus; this positive charge is found in the middle of the atom/nucleus.

   e Neutrons

Atomic structure, isotopes and relative atomic mass

1

Sub-atomic particle	Relative charge	Relative mass
Proton	+1	1
Electron	−1	Very small
Neutron	0	1

2 There are equal numbers of protons and electrons/6 protons and electrons; The positive and negative charges cancel each other out.

3 a 74 protons and 74 electrons; 110 neutrons.

   b Gold (not Au)

4 Atomic; mass; protons; neutrons; 6; 6; 7

5 Both isotopes have 35 protons; and 35 electrons; Br-79 has 44 neutrons and Br-81 has 46 neutrons or Br-81 has 2 more neutrons than Br-79.

6 The other isotope makes up 25%;
   $(35 \times 75) + (Cl \times 25)/100 = 35.5$;
   $Cl = 37$.

The development of the periodic table and the noble gases

1 a 4   b 4

   c Same number of electrons/5 electrons in outer shell

   d Same number of electron shells

2 a Periods

   b For missing/undiscovered elements

   c By increasing atomic/proton number

   d They are unreactive.

3 a Increase down the group.

   b Any number between −185 and −109

Electronic structure

1 a Nucleus

   b Protons; and neutrons

   c Aluminium or Al   d 14

2 a C   b A   c B, E

   d B, F   e D   f A

Answers

Metals and non-metals

1 Malleable – Can be hammered into shape; Ductile – Can be drawn into wires; Sonorous – Makes a ringing sound when hit.

2 **a** Na **d** Ar **g** Ca

   b Au **e** B **h** N

   c Si **f** Br

3 **a** Non-metal **b** 2

   c Good electrical conductor; shiny.

Group 1 – the alkali metals

1 They all have 1 electron in their outer shell.

2 Potassium

3 Francium

4 Na

5 *Any three from*: Fizzing/bubbling/effervescence, not gas given off; Lithium floats; Lithium moves on the surface; Lithium dissolves/gets smaller/disappears.

6 *Any two from*: Potassium melts/forms a ball; Potassium catches fire; Lilac/purple; Reaction is faster/more vigorous.

Group 7 – the halogens

1 F **2** Fluorine

3 Br_2 **4** Chlorine

5 **a** Lithium and chlorine, as chlorine is more reactive.

   b Lithium + chlorine → lithium chloride

   c $2Li + I_2 \rightarrow 2LiI$ (correct; balanced)

6 **a**

	Chlorine	Bromine	Iodine
Potassium chloride	x	No reaction	**No reaction**
Potassium bromide	Orange solution formed	x	No reaction
Potassium iodide	Brown solution formed	**Brown solution formed**	x

   b Chlorine + potassium bromide → bromine + potassium chloride

   c Add iodine to potassium astatide (or any astatide salt); Brown colour of iodine disappears/solution turns darker.

   $I_2 + 2At^- \rightarrow 2I^- + At_2$

Bonding, structure and the properties of matter

Bonding and structure

1

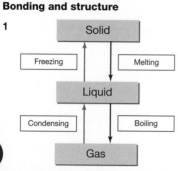

---

2 **a** 0°C **b** 100°C

3 **a** Gas **b** Solid

   c Liquid

4 **a** Oxygen **b** Nitrogen

   c Oxygen **d** Oxygen

Ions and ionic bonding

1 Magnesium is a metal which is found in group **2** of the periodic table. This means it has **2** electrons in its outer shell. When it reacts, it loses **2** electrons and forms an ion with a **2⁺** charge. Fluorine is a non-metal which is found in group **7** of the periodic table. When it reacts, it **gains** 1 electron to form an ion with a **1⁻** charge. When magnesium reacts with fluorine, it forms magnesium fluoride which has the formula **MgF_2**.

2 Potassium chloride, KCl; Magnesium oxide, MgO_2; Magnesium chloride, $MgCl_2$; Aluminium fluoride, AlF_3.

3 **a** Formula = LiCl

   (correct ion; correct formula)

   b Formula = $BaBr_2$

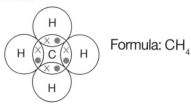

   (correct ion; correct formula)

The structure and properties of ionic compounds

1 High melting points; Conduct electricity when molten or in solution; Made of ions.

2 **a** B **b** A **c** C

3 Ionic bonds are formed when **metals** react with **non-metals**. Atoms either lose or gain **electrons** to become positive or negative particles called ions. The ions are held together in a giant ionic **lattice** by strong **electrostatic** forces of attraction acting in all **directions**.

4 Level 1 (marks 1–2)

KI is ionic/made of ions/consists of a giant ionic lattice.

KI will have a high melting point *or* will conduct electricity when molten or in solution.

Level 2 (marks 3–4)

KI will have a high melting point because the ions are strongly attracted together/lots of energy is needed to break the strong ionic bonds *or*

KI will conduct electricity when molten or in solution/dissolved because the ions are free to move.

Level 3 (marks 5–6)

KI will have a high melting point because the ions are strongly attracted together/lots of energy is needed to break the strong ionic bonds *and*

KI will conduct electricity when molten or in solution/dissolved because the ions are free to move *and*

KI will not conduct electricity when solid as the ions do not move/are in fixed positions.

Covalent bonds and simple molecules

1 NH_3; Water.

2 **a and b**

Hydrogen

Formula: H_2

Methane

Formula: CH_4

3 **a**

   b Covalent bond – triple bond

4 **a**

   (each single bond; correct double bond)

   b Covalent bonds – 4 × single and 1 × double

Diamond, graphite and graphene

1 **a** A **b** C

2 **a** Strong covalent bonds; large amounts of energy needed to overcome/break covalent bonds.

   b Each carbon is bonded to 4 other carbon atoms; covalent bonds are very strong.

   c Both have delocalised electrons; both conduct electricity.

3 **a** Does not have delocalised electrons. (do not allow free/mobile ions).

   b High melting/boiling points hard. (due to no delocalised electrons).

Fullerenes and polymers

1 **a** D **b** C

   c A **d** B

2 **a** Hollow/spherical

   b Large surface area

3 **a** Covalent

b Polyethene is a bigger molecule so has larger intermolecular forces; More energy needed to overcome these intermolecular forces; Increases the melting point; Allow reverse argument.

Giant metallic structures and alloys

1 Metals are **giant** structures. The atoms are arranged in **layers**.

The outer shell electrons become detached from the rest of the atom and are said to be **delocalised**. This means they are free to move throughout the whole metal.

Metallic bonding is strong because of the **electrostatic** attraction between the positive metal ions and the electrons.

2 **free electrons** from outer shells of metal atoms

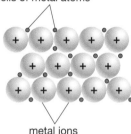

metal ions

Giant structure; Positive metal ions drawn and labelled; Delocalised electrons drawn and labelled; Electrons can carry charge throughout the metal.

3 a Strong electrostatic attraction between positive metal ions and delocalised electrons; Lots of energy needed to overcome the strong attraction.

b Carbon/different sized atoms distort the regular lattice; Layers cannot slide over each other.

Quantitative chemistry

Conservation of mass and balancing equations

1 a Magnesium + oxygen → magnesium oxide

b Reactants: Magnesium, oxygen; Products: Magnesium oxide.

c 12 + 8 = 20 g

2 a Nitrogen + hydrogen → ammonia

b

	Reactants	Products
N	2	1
H	2	3

c $N_2(g) + 3H_2(g) \rightarrow 2NH_3(g)$

3 $Fe_2O_3 + 2CO \rightarrow 2Fe + 2CO_2$

Relative formula masses

1 The relative atomic mass (symbol = A_r) of an element is the weighted average mass of its naturally occurring isotopes;

You calculate the relative formula mass (symbol = M_r) of a compound by adding up all the relative atomic masses of all the atoms present in the formula of the compound;

The elements hydrogen, oxygen, nitrogen, chlorine, bromine, iodine and fluorine exist as diatomic molecules- in equations their relative formula masses are twice their relative atomic masses;

The law of mass conservation means that in a chemical reaction the sum of the relative formula masses of the reactants is equal to the sum of the relative formula mass of the products.

2 Carbon − 12; Oxygen − 16; Chlorine 35.5; Iron − 55.8

3 a NaOH − 40; H_2SO_4 − 98; Na_2SO_4 − 142; H_2O − 18

b 10 g/98 = 0.010 → 0.010 × 18 = 1.84 g

c 5 g/142 = 0.35 → 0.035 × 40 × 2 = 2.82 g

d So they know how much product will be made OR to avoid waste.

The mole and reacting masses

1 a 0.1 moles **b** 0.1 moles

c 0.003 (or 3.125×10^{-3}) moles

d 0.5 moles

2 a 36.5 g **b** 60 g
c 31.8 g **d** 171 g

3 a

Substance	A_r or M_r	Mass/g	Moles
sodium	23.0	2.30	0.1
sulfur	32	0.32	0.01
CH_4	16	1.60	0.1

b 1.37 moles

4 a 152 **b** 38 g
c 19 g **d** 7.5×10^{22}

5 a 14 g

b 1 136 364 (or 1.13664×10^6) g

6 a 0.003 moles **b** 0.02 moles

c 2.29×10^{23}

Limiting reactants

1 a Hydrochloric acid

b Magnesium

2 How many moles of water can be produced by 1 mole of H_2? 1

How many moles of water can be produced by 1 mole of O_2? 2

Which is the limiting reactant? H_2

How much H_2O is produced in the reaction? 1

Which reactant is in excess? O_2

How many moles of O_2 is used in the reaction? 1

3 a $4Cu + O_2 \rightarrow 2Cu_2O$

b Cu → 1.26 moles; O_2 → 1.56 moles

c Copper; because in the equation, the ratio of moles is Cu:O_2 4:1, however in the experiment there was only 1.26:1.56 moles.

4 a $C_3H_8 + 5O_2 \rightarrow 3CO_2 + 4H_2O$

b 5.68 g

c The limiting reactant is oxygen; because in the balanced equation the ratio is 1:5 (0.3:1.5), but the engine only has 0.3:0.1; they could make the engine more efficient by increasing the amount of oxygen.

Concentrations in solutions

1 a 1 **b** 2

2 a Test 1 − 250 g/dm³

Test 2 − 400 g/dm³

Test 3 − 571 g/dm³

b Test 1 − 0.09 moles

Test 2 − 0.17 moles

Test 3 − 0.34 moles

3 a 143

b 0.01 moles/143 g/mol = 1.43 g/mol

c 3 575 000 g; = 3.575×10^6 g

Chemical changes

Metal oxides and the reactivity series

1 a Magnesium + oxygen → magnesium oxide

b $2Mg(s) + O_2(g) \rightarrow 2MgO(s)$ (correct; balanced)

c Oxygen is gained/electrons are lost.

2 a Aluminium + lead chloride → aluminium chloride + lead

b Silver + copper oxide → no reaction

c Calcium + zinc nitrate → calcium nitrate + zinc

d Iron chloride + copper → no reaction

3 a 1-Sodium, 2-X, 3-Magnesium, 4-Copper.

b Copper

Extraction of metals and reduction

1 Carbon is less reactive than magnesium ore.

2 It's unreactive/doesn't easily form compounds.

3 a Tin(IV) oxide + carbon → carbon oxide/dioxide + tin

b Carbon

4 a $2CuO (s) + C (s) \rightarrow CO_2 (g) + 2Cu (s)$ or (l)

b Any metal above iron in the reactivity series; Too expensive/metals above carbon extracted by electrolysis so require more energy.

Answers

c   Iron is a liquid.

d   Carbon is more reactive than iron.

e   Any metal above iron in the reactivity series; Too expensive/metals above carbon extracted by electrolysis so require more energy.

The blast furnace

1 a   Carbon + oxygen → carbon dioxide

b $C(s) + CO_2(g) → 2CO(g)$ — 1 mark for correct formulae and balancing, 1 mark for state symbols

c   Reduction/redox

d $2Fe_2O_3(s) + 3C(s) → 4Fe(l) + 3CO_2(g)$

e   Iron is a liquid

f $CaSiO_3$

g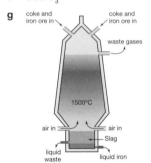

The reactions of acids

1   Both neutralise acid; Bases are insoluble/alkalis are soluble bases/alkalis form hydroxide/OH^- ions ins solution.

2 a   Sodium chloride – sodium hydroxide and hydrochloric acid.

b   Potassium nitrate – potassium carbonate and nitric acid.

c   Copper sulfate – copper oxide and sulfuric acid.

3 a   Solid dissolves/colourless solution forms.

b   Fizzing occurs with magnesium carbonate.

c   Magnesium oxide + hydrochloric acid → magnesium chloride + water

d $MgCO_3$

4 a $Mg(s) + 2HCl(aq) → MgCl_2(aq) + H_2(g)$

b $Li_2O(s) + H_2SO_4(aq) → Li_2SO_4(aq) + H_2O(l)$

c $CuO(s) + 2HCl(aq) → CuCl_2(aq) + H_2O(l)$

5 a $Ca(s) + 2H^+(aq) → Ca^{2+}(aq) + H_2(g)$ (reactants; products; state symbols)

b   Ca oxidised; H^+/hydrogen reduced.

The preparation of soluble salts

1 a   Copper carbonate + sulfuric acid → copper sulfate + water + carbon dioxide

b   Any two from: Copper carbonate dissolves; Fizzing/bubbles/effervescence; Blue/green solution forms.

c   To ensure all the acid reacts

d   Filtration

e   Copper oxide/copper hydroxide

f   Any one from: Salt lost from spitting during evaporation; Solution left in container; Not all the solution crystallises.

2 a $Ca(s) + 2HNO_3(aq) → Ca(NO_3)_2(aq) + H_2(g)$ (reactants; products; state symbols)

b   % yield = 2.6/3.0 x 100; 87.7%

3   **Possible steps to include:** Reactants (zinc/zinc hydroxide/zinc oxide/zinc carbonate) and hydrochloric acid; Correct equation for chosen reactants; Heat acid; Add base until no more reacts/dissolves so the base is in <u>excess</u>; Filter unreacted base; Heat solution on a steam bath until half the water has evaporated; Leave remaining solution to cool so crystals form.

Equipment list: Bunsen burner; Heatproof mat; Tripod; Gauze; Beaker; Evaporating dish; Funnel; Filter paper; Conical flask; Spatula; Measuring cylinder; Safety glasses.

Oxidation and reduction in terms of electrons

1 a $Mg(s) + Cu^{2+}(aq) → Mg^{2+}(aq) + Cu(s)$

b   Mg is oxidised and Cu is reduced.

2 a $Mg(s) + Zn^{2+}(aq) → Mg^{2+}(aq) + Zn(s)$; Mg oxidised, Zn reduced.

b $2Na(s) + Zn^{2+}(aq) → 2Na^+(aq) + Zn(s)$; Na oxidised, Zn reduced.

c $Cu(s) + 2Ag^+(aq) → Cu^{2+}(aq) + 2Ag(s)$; Cu oxidised, Zn reduced.

d $3Ca(s) + 2Fe^{3+}(aq) → 3Ca^{2+}(aq) + 2Fe(s)$; Ca oxidised, Fe reduced.

pH scale and neutralisation

1   Strong acid — pH2 — Red, Weak acid — pH5 — Yellow, Strong alkali — pH13 — Purple, Weak alkali - pH9 — Blue, Neutral — pH7 — Green.

2   Hydroxide ion

3   H^+

4   pH1

5   pH12

6 a   Potassium hydroxide

b $2KOH + H_2SO_4 → K_2SO_4 + 2H_2O$

c $H^+ + OH^- → H_2O$ **or** $2H^+ + 2OH^- → 2H_2O$

7   OH^- and NH_4^+

Strong and weak acids

1 a $HNO_3(aq) → H^+(aq) + NO_3^-(aq)$

b $HCOOH(aq) → H^+(aq) + COO^-(aq)$

c $H_2SO_4(aq) → 2H^+(aq) + SO_4^{2-}(aq)$ **or** $H_2SO_4(aq) → H^+(aq) + HSO_4^-(aq)$

2   Weak acid only partially ionises in solution; Dilute acid has fewer moles of solute dissolved.

3 a 1×10^{-3}

b   Answer is 100 times greater as if pH decreases by 1, H^+ concentration increases by 10; 0.1 (overrides previous mark); 1×10^{-1}

Electrolysis

1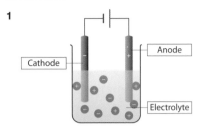

2   Ions are free to move when molten/aqueous; Ions in fixed positions/ions can't move in solid lattice.

3 a   Zinc and chlorine

b   Silver and iodine

c   Copper and oxygen.

4 a $Pb^{2+} + \mathbf{2e^-} → Pb$; $2Br^- → Br_2 + \mathbf{2e^-}$

b   Lead/lead ions reduced and bromine/bromide ions oxidised.

Electrolysis of copper(II) sulfate and electroplating

1 a   Unreactive

b   Copper(II) sulfate

c   Relights a glowing splint

d   Copper

$Cu^{2+} + 2e^- → Cu$

e   Fades, Copper ions form copper

f   Any 2 from: Solution does not fade; No oxygen given off; Anode gets smaller; Cathode gets bigger.

2 a   In this reaction:

i   Pure chromium

ii   Should be the tap

b   Any chromium compound

c $Cr^{3+} + 3e^- → Cr$

The extraction of metals using electrolysis

1 a   Strong ionic bonds/strong electrostatic attraction between oppositely charged ions; Requires lots of energy to overcome.

b   So the ions are free to move.

c   Reduce the operating temperature; Saves energy/reduces energy costs.

d   Electrons are lost.

e $Al^{3+} + 3e^- → Al$ (correct; balanced electrons)

f   They react with the oxygen produced; Carbon + oxygen → carbon dioxide/$C + O_2 → CO_2$

g   Electricity wasn't discovered/electricity not needed to extract iron.

Practical investigation into the electrolysis of aqueous solutions

1 a Independent – Metal/metal ion in salt; Dependent variable – Product formed at cathode; Control variables – Volume of solution, Concentration of solution, Negative ion in salt, Voltages.

b Only 1 variable is changed.

2 Place a lighted splint into the gas; Positive test – burns with a squeaky pop.

3 a $CuCl_2$ – Copper; all others – Hydrogen.

b Solutions containing metals above hydrogen in the reactivity series produce hydrogen on electrolysis; Solutions containing metals below hydrogen in the reactivity series produce the metal on electrolysis.

4 Chlorine; Bleaches blue litmus paper **or** bleaches UI in solution.

Energy changes

Exothermic and endothermic reactions

1 a Endothermic – surrounding temperatures decrease as heat energy is needed by the reaction.

b Exothermic – surrounding temperatures increase as heat energy is released by the reaction.

2 a $15.4°C − 23.7°C = −8.3$. The reaction is endothermic as the temperature decrease.

b i $37°C − 25°C = +12$

ii Exothermic

Practical investigation into the variables that affect temperature changes in chemical reactions

1 a

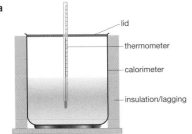

lid
thermometer
calorimeter
insulation/lagging

b To reduce heat loss; to give a more accurate result.

c *Any two from:* The reaction of iron and oxygen is exothermic; The temperature increase is greatest with iron filings; Iron filings are more reactive.

d To make the results valid; oxygen may be controlling the rate of reaction.

2 Possible steps to include: Use an insulated calorimeter; to reduce heat loss; use a thermometer to record temperature; use same equipment throughout; use hydrochloric acid at different concentrations; use same volume of hydrochloric acid; same volume of calcium carbonate; same particle size of calcium carbonate; to ensure the results are valid; temperature increase will increase with concentration; because the rate of reaction will increase; record data on a table

	Concen-tration 1	Concen-tration 2	Concen-tration 3
Initial temperature / °C			
Final temperature / °C			

Reaction profiles

1 A **reaction profile** shows how the energy changes from reactants to products

In a reaction profile for an **exothermic** reaction the products are lower in energy than the reactants because **energy** is released to the surroundings during the reaction.

In a reaction profile for an **endothermic** reaction the **products** are higher in energy than the **reactants** because energy is taken in from the **surroundings** during the reaction.

Chemical reactions occur when reacting particles collide with enough energy to react. This energy is called the **activated energy** (Ea).

2 a Products are higher in energy that reactants; the student is incorrect; the reaction is endothermic.

b i A – Activation energy.

ii B – Energy absorbed from surroundings.

c Catalyst reduces the activation energy:

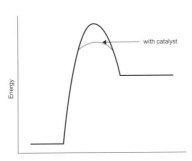

with catalyst

Energy

The energy changes of reactions

1 a H–H = 436 kJ

Cl-Cl = 243

Sum (bond breaking): 436+243 = 679 kJ

b 2 × 432 = 864 kJ

c Exothermic

d 864 − 679 = 185

2 a 2x (H-Br) → H-H + Br-Br

b Reactants = 366 × 2 = -732 kJ (breaking).
Products = 432 + 193 = + 625 (making).
625–732 = –107kJ = Endothermic.

Rates of reaction and equilibrium

Ways to follow a chemical reaction

1 a Size of marble chips

b Time

c Volume of carbon dioxide given off (if collected); OR change in mass (if carbon dioxide allowed to escape); OR time for marble chips to disappear (if excess hydrochloric acid).

d *Any two from:* Mass of marble chips; volume of acid; Concentration of acid; Amount of stirring; Temperature.

2 a Production of sulfur, S, which makes the solution opaque.

b Concentration of sodium thiosulfate.

c *Any two from:* Volume of sodium thiosulfate; Volume of acid; Concentration of acid; Amount of stirring; Temperature; Same person doing the timing.

d Could use a light meter and a lamp; to reduce uncertainty about whether the x is visible or not.

3 Possible steps to include: Measure a fixed volume of (e.g. 50 cm³) of hydrochloric acid; using one of the measuring cylinders and pour it into the conical flask; Put a bung in the conical flask with a delivery tube which goes into an upturned measuring cylinder which is full of water and in a water trough; this allows me to measure the amount of hydrogen gas given off; Cut the magnesium into pieces the same size; put one piece into the conical flask; start the timer; record the amount of hydrogen gas at regular intervals on a table; Repeat for different concentrations of hydrochloric acid.

Calculating the rate of reaction

1 Rate of reaction = Amount of product formed/Time taken

Answers

2 a The rate of reaction is constant

b The rate of reaction is constant

c The rate of reaction decreases with time

d The rate of reaction increases with time

3 a $Mg + 2HCl \rightarrow MgCl_2 + H_2$

b $99/120 = 0.825$ cm^3/second

c

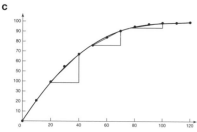

d See above

e 30s = 1.8 cm^3/s (Allow +/− 0.2)

60s = 0.75 cm^3/s (Allow +/− 0.2)

90s = 0.15 cm^3/s (Allow +/− 0.2)

f 30s – from graph: 1.8 cm^3/s;
110/24 = 0.75 moles/s

60s – from graph: 0.75 cm^3/s; 168/24 = 0.03125 moles/s

The effect of concentration and on reaction rate and the effect of pressure on the rate of gaseous reactions

1 For a reaction to happen, particles must **collide** with sufficient **energy**. The minimum amount of **energy** that particles must have for a specific reaction is known as the **activation energy**. The rate of a reaction can be increased by increasing the **energy** of collisions and increasing the **frequency** of collisions.

2 There are more particles; The frequency of successful collisions increases.

3 a C   **b** A

4 a

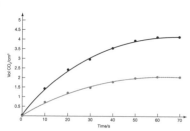

b Rate of reaction starts off fast; slows down as the reaction progresses.

c One (or more) of the reactants has been used up.

d See above (light grey line)

e There are half as many hydrochloric acid particles; reducing the frequency of successful collisions; reducing the rate of reaction.

Rates of reaction – the effect of surface area

1 a B   **b** B

c More particles exposed to the other reactant; increasing the frequency of collisions.

d Sugar is used to make marshmallows; sugar has a larger surface area; the rate of reaction with oxygen under heat would be much higher.

2 a Cut tablets; grind into powder using a pestle and mortar.

b

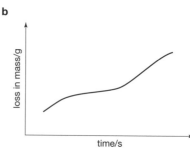

c Collect carbon dioxide bubbles in upturned measuring cylinder; allow carbon dioxide to escape and measure mass change.

The effects of changing the temperature and adding a catalyst

1 a The particles have more energy so they collide more frequently; and with more energy

b 10°C increase ~doubles rate. So at 30°C= 20 s. 40°C = 10 s.

2 a It is a catalyst.

b It provides an alternative route for the reaction; reducing the activation energy.

c

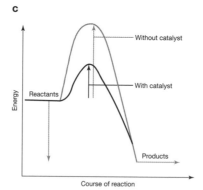

3 a Collect oxygen given off in an upturned measuring cylinder.

b Possible steps to include: Put hydrogen peroxide in a test tube; Use the same volume and concentration for both tests; Put a bung at the top of the test tube with a delivery tube to an upturned measuring cylinder; Add a quantity of liver to the hydrogen

peroxide; Record the volume of oxygen produced at intervals; Repeat with the same mass of manganese oxide.

An investigation into how changing the concentration affects the rate of reaction

1 a $2HCl(aq) + Na_2S_2O_3(aq) \rightarrow 2NaCl(aq) + SO_2(g) + S(s) + H_2O(l)$

b As the concentration increases, the rate of reaction will increase.

c The hypothesis will be confirmed/ as the concentration increases the rate of reaction will increase; there will be more particles; more frequent collisions.

d **Possible steps to include:** Measure out the same volume of different concentrations of sodium thiosulfate / hydrochloric acid into conical flasks; Measure out a volume of hydrochloric acid/sodium thiosulfate; Using the same volume and concentration throughout; To ensure the results are valid; Mark a cross on a sheet of white paper; Put conical flask on cross; Mix reactants; Record the time it takes for the cross to disappear; Repeat for other concentrations.

e Temperature would increase the frequency and energy of collisions; increasing the rate of reaction.

f Cross to disappear – easy and convenient/requires no special equipment; but can be subjective (it is down to an individual's opinion).

Lamp and light sensor – more accurate; because it is not dependent on an individual's opinion; requires additional equipment.

Reversible reactions

1 a $\rightleftharpoons$

b Reversible reactions can go both forwards and backwards in certain conditions.

c A dynamic equilibrium is when the rate of the forward reaction is equal to the rate of the backward reaction; the concentration of the reactants and products remains constant.

2 a A reversible reaction is one which can go both ways. This means that as well as reactants forming products, the products can also react to give the reactants.

b Exothermic; the forward reaction requires heat so is endothermic; the backwards reaction is always the opposite of the forwards reaction.

c The reversible reaction has reached dynamic equilibrium; both reactions are occurring at the same rate; there is no net change in the volume of carbon dioxide.

The effect of changing conditions on equilibrium

1 At dynamic equilibrium, the rate of the forward reaction is the same as the backward reaction.

2 Temperature; pressure; concentration.

3 If a chemical system is at equilibrium and one or more of the three conditions is changed; then the position of equilibrium will shift so as to cancel out the change; and we get either more reactants or more products.

4 a The reaction would shift to the left; because the forward reaction is exothermic as it gives out heat; producing more nitrogen and hydrogen gas.

b The forward reaction needs enough energy to overcome the activation energy or the rate of reaction will be too slow.

c It provides an alternative route for the reaction – reducing the activation energy; and increasing the rate of reaction; meaning the reaction can be run at the lowest possible temperature which reduces the backward reaction (a compromise temperature).

d There are fewer moles of gas in the products; increasing pressure therefore increases the forwards reaction.

Organic chemistry

Alkanes

1 a They are molecules that contain *only* hydrogen and carbon.

b They only contain C-C single bonds.

c *Any two from:* They have similar chemical properties; They have the same general formula; Each member differs by CH_2; Same trend in physical properties.

2 a $C_{20}H_{42}$

b C_8H_{18}

3

(Correct C-H bonds; Correct C-C bond)

4 a

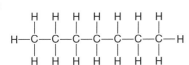

b C_7H_{16}

5 CH_4

6 Pentane

7 C_4H_{10}

Fractional distillation

1 *Any four from:* Crude oil heated; Crude oil evaporates; Vapour rises up fractionating column; Fractions with lower boiling points rise further up column/Temperature gradient in column (hotter at the bottom, cooler at the top); When vapour cools to boiling point of fractions molecules condense into a liquid; Statement relating to bigger molecules having higher boiling points.

2 a Fuel for aeroplanes

b $C_{12}H_{26}$

c Bigger molecules so greater intermolecular forces; More energy is needed to overcome these forces.

3 a $C_2H_6 + 3\frac{1}{2}O_2 \rightarrow 2CO_2 + 3H_2O$

b $C_3H_8 + 5O_2 \rightarrow 3CO_2 + 4H_2O$

c $C_5H_{12} + 8O_2 \rightarrow 5CO_2 + 6H_2O$ (correct; balanced)

Cracking and alkenes

1 Contain a C=C bond; Molecules made of only carbon and hydrogen.

2 a i

Pentene + Hydrogen

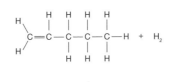

ii

Butene + Steam

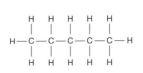

iii

Propene + Chlorine

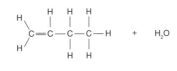

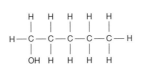

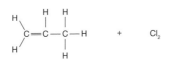

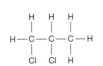

b Only one product/no waste products.

3 a $C_8H_{18} \rightarrow C_5H_{12} + \mathbf{C_3H_6}$

b $C_{18}H_{38} \rightarrow C_3H_6 + \mathbf{C_{15}H_{32}}$

c $\mathbf{C_{13}H_{28}} \rightarrow C_4H_8 + C_9H_{20}$

d $C_{14}H_{30} \rightarrow C_4H_{10} + C_6H_{12} + \mathbf{C_4H_8}$

e $C_{14}H_{30} \rightarrow C_8H_{18} + \mathbf{2C_3H_6}$

4 a $C_{10}H_{22}$ **b** Fuel/petrol

c It's an alkene.

d Polymers

e $C_{10}H_{22} \rightarrow C_6H_{14} + C_4H_8$

Chemical analysis

Testing for gases

1 Hydrogen – a lighted splint put into a test tube of the gas – is extinguished with a 'pop';
Oxygen – a glowing splint put into a test tube of the gas – Relights;
Carbon dioxide – bubble the gas through a solution of limewater – produces solid calcium carbonate, turning the limewater cloudy.

2 a The gas turns limewater turns cloudy **Carbon dioxide**

b The gas bleaches litmus paper **Chlorine**

c The gas extinguishes a lighted splint with a pop **Hydrogen**

d The gas relights a glowing splint **Oxygen**

3 a $CH_4 + 2O_2 \rightarrow CO_2 + 2H_2O$ Bubble through limewater – would turn cloudy.

b $Mg + H_2SO_4 \rightarrow MgSO_4 + H_2$ A lighted splint put into the gas – extinguishes with a pop.

c $CO_2 + H_2O \rightarrow C_6H_{12}O_6 + O_2$ A glowing splint put into the gas – will reignite.

d $HCl + MnO_2 \rightarrow MnCl_2 + 2H_2O + Cl_2$ Litmus paper when exposed to the gas – will bleach.

4 Carbon dioxide gas produced so the limewater will turn cloudy; because it is a combustion reaction involving a fuel and oxygen.
Description of different tests for each gas: hydrogen – lit splint in flame/ oxygen – glowing splint will reignite/ chlorine – bleaches litmus paper; these tests will be negative.

Chemistry of the atmosphere

The composition and evolution of the Earth's atmosphere

1 a Carbonate rock formation; Fossil fuel formation.

b Condensation/formation of oceans OR used in photosynthesis by plants.

c It reduced; carbon dioxide dissolved in the oceans.

d $6CO_2 + 6H_2O \rightarrow C_6H_{12}O_6 + 6O_2$ (correct; balanced)

2 a $2Cu + O_2 \rightarrow 2CuO$

b 21.5%

c To make sure no other variables were affecting the results; to reduce error.

Climate change

1 a Climate is complex **or** models are simplifications.

b Results of experiments are checked by other scientists.

c Carbon dioxide; methane; water vapour.

d *Any four from:* Carbon dioxide – burning fossil fuels in our homes/industry/cars; deforestation;

Methane – cattle farming; rice crops; landfill; Water – small increases from farming and burning fossil fuels, most is due to natural evaporation; higher global temperatures increases the rate of evaporation.

2 a Temperature increases at the same time as CO_2 increases; There is a big increase in temperatures more recently.

b The graph shows a correlation between CO_2 and temperature; it is known that human activity has increase atmospheric CO_2; it is known that CO_2 is a greenhouse gas; recent temperatures are much higher than in the past.

The carbon footprint and its reduction

1 Alternative energy – Renewable energy sources such as solar cells, wind power and wave power do not rely on the burning of fossil fuels;

Energy conservation – Reducing the amount of energy used by using energy-saving measures such as house insulation, using devices that use less energy, reduces the demand for energy;

Carbon Capture and Storage (CCS) – Removing the carbon dioxide given out by power stations by reacting it with other chemicals. The product of this reaction can then be stored deep under the sea in porous sedimentary rocks;

Carbon taxes – Penalising companies and individuals who use too much energy by increasing their taxes reduces the demand for energy;

Carbon offsetting – Removing carbon dioxide from the air using natural biological processes such as photosynthesis. This is achieved by planting trees and increasing marine algae by adding chemicals to the oceans.;

Using plants as biofuels – Plants take in carbon dioxide as they grow, when they are burned they only release the same amount of carbon dioxide. This makes them carbon neutral.

2 a *Any two from:* High use of cars/preference for large cars; developed countries use more energy; high level of industrialisation in USA and Qatar; China and India and developing countries.

b It has **reduced** from 10 tonnes per person to 7.1 tonnes per person.

c Increase in population; increase in industry; increased development has resulted in greater energy use.

Atmospheric pollutants

1

Soot	Global dimming and lung damage	Ensure complete combustion of fossil fuels
Carbon monoxide	A toxic gas which binds to haemoglobin in the blood, preventing the transport of oxygen around the body	Ensure complete combustion of fossil fuels
Sulfur dioxide	Dissolves in clouds to cause acid rain and causes respiratory problems	Desulfurisation of petrochemicals before combustion
Oxides of nitrogen	Dissolves in clouds to cause acid rain and causes respiratory problems	Catalytic converters used after combustion

2 a Petrol emits more carbon dioxide/diesel emits less carbon dioxide; diesel emits four times more sulfur dioxide; diesel emits particulate matter, petrol does not; diesel emits slightly more oxides of nitrogen.

b *Any two from:* Energy and materials are used in construction and transport of vehicles; energy is required to power the vehicles; this energy comes from electricity; which may be produced by burning fossil fuels.

3 a Complete combustion = $CH_4 + 2O_2 \rightarrow CO_2 + 2H_2O$, therefore:

i $CH_4 + 1\frac{1}{2} O_2 \rightarrow CO + 2H_2O$

ii $CH_4 + O_2 \rightarrow C + 2H_2O$

b When 4 moles of coal are burned, 960 moles of carbon dioxide are produced; therefore, 960/4 = 240 moles of carbon dioxide per mole of coal. 240 × 8 = 1920 moles of carbon dioxide.

c Burning coal produces nitric acid (HNO_3) and sulfuric acid (H_2SO_4); causing acid rain which is corrosive/reacts with limestone.

Using resources

Finite and renewable resources, sustainable development

1 The **natural resources** used by chemists to make new materials can be divided into two categories – **finite** and **renewable**. **Finite** resources will run out. Examples are fossil fuels and various metals. **Renewable** resources are ones that can be replaced at the same rate as they are used up. They are derived from plant materials.

Sustainable development meets the needs of present development without depleting natural resources for future generations.

2 Have reactions with high atom economy with as few waste products as possible; Use renewable resources from plant sources; Have as few steps as possible to eliminate waste and increase the yield; Use catalysts to save energy.

3 They reduce the activation energy required for reactions; reducing the use of heat which typically comes from fossil fuels.

4 a Company A = 22/25 × 100 = 88%; Company B = 17.5/19 × 100 = 92%.

b Company B has a higher percentage yield so is more sustainable.

Life cycle assessments (LCAs)

1 A life cycle assessment is an assessment of the environmental impact of the manufacture and use of different materials and products.

2 Resources used, production, use and disposal.

3 a

Stage of LCA	Plastic bag	Paper bag
Source of raw materials	From ethene, which is produced during cracking of petrochemicals	Come from trees
Production	Simple process involving no chemical change	Consumes water and produces acidic gases and greenhouse gases
Use	Reusable	Damaged by water and more difficult to reuse
End of life	Decompose slowly but produce less **solid waste**	Decompose quickly but generate more **solid waste**

b Any two from: Paper bags come from a renewable source whereas plastic comes from a finite resource; Plastic bags are reusable but decompose slowly at the end of their life whereas paper bags can't be reused easily but decompose quickly at the end of their life; Paper bags produce more pollution and consume more water.

4 The supermarket has conducted a selective/shortened/abbreviated LCA, ignoring negative points, e.g. slow decomposition/source materials are finite.

Alternative methods of copper extraction

1 a

b It is not pure copper.

2 Smelting and electrolysis use a lot of energy; Copper-rich ores are scarce.

3 a Bioleaching using bacteria; Phytomining using plants; Displacement using iron.

   b i Bioleaching: produces pure copper so needs little further processing; but is slow.

     ii Phytomining: environmentally friendly; but is slow/requires further processing.

     iii Displacement using iron: can use scrap metal; may increase demand for iron.

Making potable water and waste water treatment

1 Water that is safe to drink – harmful chemicals and microbes have been removed.

2 A pure substance is one element or compound; potable water contains other substances like salts and minerals.

3 a

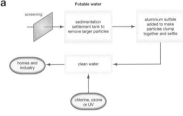

b To sterilise the water.

4 a Reverse osmosis.

   b Distillation separates the water from the salt by heating the salt water until the boiling point of water; this requires energy.

5 a

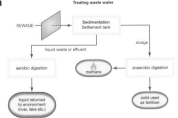

b Removal of harmful chemicals.

Ways of reducing the use of resources

1 a Reduces use of glass bottles; Reduces use of limited raw materials to make other glass products.

   b Separation; Reforming; Melting.

2 a It is magnetic.

   b Steel is made with iron, carbon and other metals; recycling iron in steel

uses the amount of iron needed by extraction from its ore.

   c Aluminium extraction uses a lot of energy; which comes from burning fossil fuels – releasing carbon dioxide; recycling aluminium uses less energy.

The Haber process

1 Ammonia

2 $N_2 + 3H_2 \rightarrow 2NH_3$

3 The reaction is reversible and the forward reaction is exothermic. This means that the backward reaction is endothermic.

4 The conditions used are a temperature of 450°C; a pressure of 200–250 atmospheres; and an iron catalyst.

5 As the forward reaction is exothermic, it would be favoured by lowering the temperature; the problem is that a low temperature would make the reaction slow; compromise is arrived 450°C; forward reaction reduces number of moles of gas; increasing pressure favours forward reaction; an iron catalyst is used to speed up the reaction.

6 a Few molecules of gas in forward reaction; higher pressure favours fewer molecules of gas.

   b Higher temperatures reduce percentage yield of ammonia; but lower temperatures make the reaction too slow.

   c i 300 atmospheres and 400°C = 50%

     ii 200 atmospheres and 350°C = 54% (accept ± 2 percentage points)

Energy

Energy stores and systems

1 A system is an object, or group of objects. The **energy** in a system is a numerical **value** that tells us whether certain **changes** in the system could, or could not, happen. The total **amount** of energy in a system is always the **same** no matter what changes happen in the system, but the energy available can be **redistributed** in different parts of this system.

2 3–d; 4–g; 5–e; 6–c; 7– f; 8–a

3 1 – Chemical; 2 – Heating; 3 – Heating; 4 – Thermal; 5 – Thermal.

Changes in energy stores: kinetic energy

1 a Kinetic energy = 0.5 × mass × speed²
Or $\frac{1}{2}mv^2$

   b J or joules

2 Kinetic energy = 0.5 × mass × speed²
Kinetic energy = 0.5 × 1 000 × 10²
50 000 J or 50 kJ

3 Kinetic energy = 0.5 × mass × speed²
rearrange to:
mass $= \dfrac{\text{kinetic energy}}{0.5 \times \text{speed}^2}$
mass = 800 000/0.5 × 10²

16 000 kg or 16 tonnes

Changes in energy stores: elastic potential energy

1 $E_e = 0.5 \times$ spring constant $\times$ extension²
or $E_e = \frac{1}{2}ke^2$.

2 $E_e = 0.5 \times$ spring constant $\times$ extension²
Extension = 25 − 5 = 20 cm;
Extension = 0.2 m
$E_e = 0.5 \times 10 \times 0.2^2$
$E_e = 0.2$ J

3 $F = ke, k = \dfrac{F}{e} = \dfrac{2.5}{0.1} = 25$ N/m

4 $E_e = 0.5 \times$ spring constant $\times$ extension² :
rearrange to
Extension $= \sqrt{\dfrac{E_e}{0.5 \times \text{spring constant}}}$
Extension $= \sqrt{\dfrac{20\,\text{J}}{0.5 \times 10\,000}}$
Extension = 0.063 m
convert to cm = 6.3 cm

Changes in energy stores: gravitational potential energy

1 $E_p = mgh$ or gravitational potential energy = mass × gravitational field strength × height.

2 $E_p = mgh$
$E_p = 4 \times 10 \times 4$
$E_p = 160$ J or joules

3 $E_p = mgh$
$E_p = 40 \times 10 \times 5$
$E_p = 2000$ J or joules

4 $E_p = mgh$ rearrange to:
$h = \dfrac{E_p}{m \times g}; m = 300\,\text{g} = 0.3\,\text{kg}$
$h = \dfrac{90}{0.3 \times 10}$
$h = 30$ m

Energy changes in systems: specific heat capacity

1 a Specific heat capacity is the amount of energy required to increase the temperature of 1 kg of a substance by 1 °C

   b Change in thermal energy = mass × specific heat capacity × temp change or $\Delta E = m \times c \times \Delta\theta$

   c J/kg °C.

2 Copper has a lower specific heat capacity than iron; The same amount of energy is delivered to each block;

Copper will require less energy to raise its temperature.

3   $\Delta E = m \times c \times \Delta\theta$ rearrange to:

$m = \dfrac{\Delta E}{c \times \Delta\theta}$;

Temp change

$= 35 - 25 = 10\,°C$

$m = \dfrac{1500}{2400 \times 10}$

$m = 0.063\,kg$

Power

1   a   Bill: $\dfrac{7500}{60} = 125\,W$;

$\dfrac{17\,800}{60} = 297\,W$; $\dfrac{7200}{60} = 120\,W$

Ted: $\dfrac{6300}{60} = 105\,W$;

$\dfrac{20\,000}{60} = 333\,W$; $\dfrac{8040}{60} = 134\,W$

   b   Ted; average power =

$\dfrac{105 + 333 + 134}{3} = 191\,W$,

Bill average power =

$\dfrac{125 + 297 + 120}{3} = 181\,W$

Therefore Ted is the most powerful.

2   Energy = power × time
time = $7.5 \times 60 \times 60 = 27\,000\,s$

Energy = $50 \times 27\,000$

Energy = $1.35\,MJ$ or $1\,350\,000\,J$

3   Time = $\dfrac{energy}{power}$

Time = $\dfrac{2\,200\,000}{100\,000}$

Time = $22\,s$

Energy transfers in a system

1   Energy stores can neither be created nor destroyed; but can be redistributed to other parts of the system via transfer or dissipation.

2   *Any sensible suggestion*. Battery-powered helicopter; MP3 player; electric fire.

3   a   Gravitational potential to kinetic

   b   Chemical to thermal

   c   Elastic potential to kinetic (and thermal and vibrational)

   d   Chemical to thermal and kinetic (and vibrational)

Efficiency

1   a   Efficiency =

$\dfrac{\text{useful output energy transfer}}{\text{total input energy transfer}}$

   b   Ratio or percentage

2   Answers in order: initial; final. Gravitational; kinetic, thermal and vibrational. Chemical; kinetic, gravitational potential, thermal and

vibrational. Chemical; Chemical, kinetic and vibrational.

3   Efficiency = $\dfrac{360}{500} = 0.72$ or 72%

4   Efficiency = $\dfrac{900}{5000} = 0.18$ or 18%

National and global energy resources

1   a   Renewable: Wave; Solar; Wind; Hydroelectric [Remove 1 mark per incorrect response]

   b   Requires burning: Oil and coal (both required)

2   Only renewable if extensive replanting takes place.

3   a   15 m/s

   b $\dfrac{\text{Total power output}}{\text{Max turbine power output}} =$

$\dfrac{10\,000\,000}{1\,000\,000} = 10$ turbines

   c   Wind supply fluctuates, is weather dependent.

4   Advantages: wind is renewable, doesn't emit greenhouse gases.

Disadvantages: wind is unreliable, requires a huge amount of land, is considered an eyesore.

Electricity

Standard circuit diagram symbols

1   Correct drawings of the following:

2 LDR	
3 Diode	
4 Variable resistor	
5 Fuse	

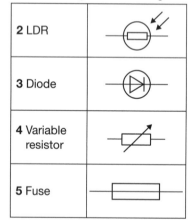

2   a   Diagram includes a battery (or cell), variable resistor, ammeter and bulb connected in series; Voltmeter must be connected in parallel with the bulb.

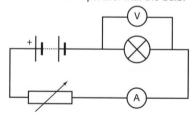

   b   Connect bulb, ammeter, variable resistor and battery in series; Connect voltmeter in parallel to bulb; Vary current using variable resistor; Use the

voltmeter and ammeter to measure potential difference and current, respectively; Record at least 5 values of potential difference and current. (If possible repeat results.); Plot graph with potential difference on the x-axis and current on the y-axis.

Electrical charge and current

1   Charge flow = current × time;
or $Q = I \times t$

2   **Current** is the name given to the flow of negatively **charged** particles around a closed circuit. These particles are called **electrons**. Because of their charge they are attracted to the **positive** terminal of a cell or **battery**. In books we refer to the opposite direction and call this **conventional** current flow.

3   Time = $\dfrac{\text{charge flow}}{\text{current}} = \dfrac{40}{2} = 20\,s$;

time = $\dfrac{\text{charge flow}}{\text{current}} = \dfrac{10}{2} = 5\,s$;

current = $\dfrac{\text{charge flow}}{\text{time}} = \dfrac{100}{500} = 0.2\,A$;

charge flow = current × time = $6 \times 150 = 900\,C$

4   Time = $\dfrac{\text{charge flow}}{\text{current}}$; $= \dfrac{1800}{6} = 300\,s$,

$300\,s$; or 5 minutes

Current, resistance and potential difference and resistors

1   a   Potential difference = current × resistance or $V = I \times R$

   b   Ohm's law

   c   Constant temperature

2   Series circuit; with resistor and variable resistor; and ammeter; Voltmeter connected in parallel with fixed resistor.

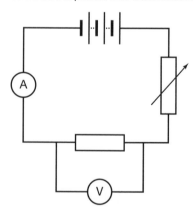

3   Vary current using variable resistor; Use the voltmeter and ammeter to measure potential difference and current respectively; Record at least 5 values of potential difference and current (If possible repeat results.); Plot graph with current on the x-axis and potential

difference on the *y*-axis; Draw line of best fit; Calculate gradient of line to get resistance value.

4 a Thermistor

b Series circuit; with thermistor and variable resistor; and ammeter; Voltmeter connected in parallel with thermistor.

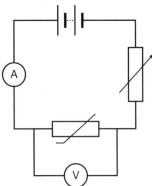

c i Thermometer; and kettle or Bunsen burner

ii $19\,k\Omega$

iii Temperature sensor or thermostat to control central heating system

5 $R_{total} = R_1 + R_2$; $= 10 + 5 = 15\,\Omega$

6 $A_2 = 0.5\,A$, $A_3 = 1\,A$, $V_2 = 5\,V$, $V_3 = 5\,V$

Series and parallel circuits

1 In a series circuit, current is the **same** throughout the circuit and potential difference **splits** across the components. In a parallel circuit, **potential difference** is the same across each branch of the circuit and current splits through the parallel branches. An ammeter must be connected in **series** to work correctly. A voltmeter must be connected in **parallel** to work correctly.

2 a Cell in series with bulb and switch.

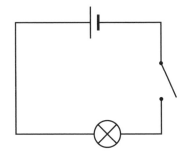

b Three bulbs in series with a battery/two cells and an ammeter connected in series.

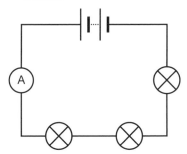

c Battery is series with bulb and thermistor. Voltmeter in parallel with thermistor.

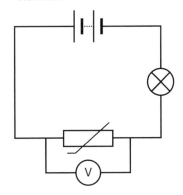

3 a Battery with two bulbs in parallel, switch correctly placed.

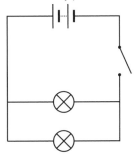

b Battery with three bulbs in parallel, switch correctly placed.

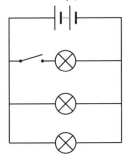

c Battery, bulb and thermistor in series bulb connected in parallel with thermistor.

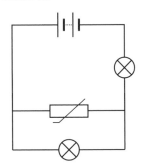

4 Idea of ring main; and parallel circuit.

Mains electricity: direct and alternating potential difference (ac/dc)

1 a dc: direct current; and ac: alternating current

b Alternating current continually changes direction and can flow in two directions; Direct current flows in one direction.

2 Transformers needed to change voltage; Transformers only work with ac; Transmission requires large potential differences to minimise current; and reduce power losses.

3 dc, 5V (± 0.5V)

4 10V

Mains electricity

1 The **electricity** supplied to our homes is called **mains** electricity and it is an **alternating** current supply. This type of current **changes** direction many times per second. In fact the current goes forwards and back **fifty** times per second. This means it has a **frequency** of 50 Hz.

2 a fuse; **b** live wire; **c** neutral wire; **d** earth wire.

3 a Earth wire has zero potential difference/current unless there is a fault and ensures that any metal casing is safe to touch by also being at zero pd.

b Live wire is at 230V and provides the potential difference which makes the current flow through the appliance.

c The neutral is at 0V this causes a potential difference between the neutral and the live wire; This causes a current to flow through the appliance.

4 a The live wire is still connected to the live terminal at 230V and if touched the person will provide a path for charge to move to Earth; closing the circuit; A surge of current will flow through the person until the fuse melts.

b Device is double insulated; and the (plastic) casing is not a conductor.

Electric Power (with electrical devices)

1 $P = I^2 R$ or $P = IV$ or $P = \dfrac{V^2}{R}$ or $P = Et$ or other correct answer

2 $P = VI = 20 \times 2$; $= 40$; W

3 $P = I^2 R = 0.1^2 \times 100$; $= 1\,W$

4 $P = \dfrac{\text{energy transferred}}{\text{time taken}}$ rearrange to:

$t = \dfrac{E}{P} = \dfrac{36\,000\,000}{10\,000} = 3600\,s$;

or 1 hour

Energy transfers in appliances

1 $E = Pt$; or $E = VIt$ (or other correct answer)

2 Everyday electrical **appliances** are designed to bring about **energy** transfers. The **amount** of energy an appliance **transfers** depends on how **long** the appliance is switched on for and the **power** of the appliance.

3 a $E = QV = 500 \times 20$; $= 10\,000\,J$ or 10 kJ

b $t = \dfrac{Q}{I} = \dfrac{500}{2}; = 250\,\text{s}$ or

4 minutes 10 seconds

4 a $V = IR$ rearrange to :
$$R = \frac{V}{I} = \frac{12}{2} = 6;\ \Omega$$

b $t = 120\,\text{s};\ Q = It = 2 \times 120 = 240;\ \text{C}$

c $P = V \times I = 12 \times 2 = 24\,\text{W}$

2 minutes = 120 s

$E = P \times t = 24 \times 120 = 2880\,\text{J}\ 2880\,\text{J}$

The National Grid

1 a 2.3 kV; **b** step-up transformer; **c** 675 kV;
d pylon; **e** step-down transformer; **f** 230 V

2 Power is constant so if V goes up I goes down ($P = VI$); Power losses are proportional to the square of current ($P = I^2R$); Reducing the current reduces the power losses.

3 a Power losses due to comparatively high resistance of long power lines, so a lot of power is wasted on the power lines and relatively little is used to light the bulb. ($P = I^2R$).

b Student uses a step-up transformer for transmission; This increases the potential difference; and decreases the current and reduces the power losses; He uses a step-down transformer to reduce the potential difference and increase the current supplied to the bulb.

Static charge and electric fields (1)

1 a Negatively charged particles/electrons transferred by friction from the hair to the balloon; balloon becomes negatively charged.

b Hair becomes positively charged as it has lost electrons; Positively charged hair is attracted by and moves towards the negatively charged balloon; Unlike charges attract.

c Negative charges on the surface of the balloon repel negative charges in the wall; Force of attraction exists between remaining positive charges in the wall and negatively charged electrons; Unlike charges attract.

d (Water molecules are polarised so they attract charged particles.) The effect is that water is a better conductor than air and charge is able to escape the balloon.

Static charge and electric fields (2)

1 Charged, electric, friction, transferring, air, positive.

2 a Radial lines growing further apart; arrows pointing away from proton:

b Radial lines growing further apart; arrows pointing away from protons; lines showing repulsion effect:

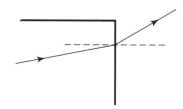

3 A lightning rod is made of a conductive material such as copper; The lightning rod is grounded or earthed; This provides a low resistance path to earth in the event of a lightning strike; The strong field around the lightning rod ensures that a lightning strike would pass through the low resistance copper generating less heat so it will not be as destructive.

Particle model

Particle model of matter and density of materials

1 The formula for density is **mass** divided by **volume** and the standard SI unit is **kg/m³**. Sometimes the values are very large so **g/cm³** are used instead. A density of **1000** kg/m³ is equal to the density of **1** g/cm³. This is also the density of water.

2 a Density $= \dfrac{\text{mass}}{\text{volume}} = \dfrac{56.5}{0.005}$;

$= 11\,300,\ \text{kg/m}^3$

b $\text{kg/m}^3 \rightarrow \text{g/cm}^3 = \div 1000$
$$\frac{11\,300}{1000} = 11.3\ \text{g/cm}^3$$

3 Mass = density × volume

$\text{cm}^3 \rightarrow \text{m}^3 = 1\,000\,000 : 1$ so $8000\,\text{cm}^3 = 0.008\,\text{m}^3$

mass $= 600 \times 0.008 = 4.8\,\text{kg}$

4 Volume of stone = 27.5 ml − 20.0 ml = 7.5 ml; and 7.5 ml = 7.5 cm³

Density $= \dfrac{\text{mass}}{\text{volume}} = \dfrac{18}{7.5} = 2.4\ \text{g/cm}^3$

Changes of state and internal energy

1 A – solid; B – gas; C – liquid.

Solids: ordered, regular pattern, close together, vibration around a fixed point;

Liquids: Close together, disordered, multidirectional weaker bonds;

Gases: far apart, high speed, random motion.

2 Molecules in gases have higher average E_k than molecules in liquids; Change of state from gas (steam) to liquid (water) leads to drop in E_k of molecules; Condensation leads to steam transferring energy to glass as steam changes to water.

3 Physical

Changes of temperature and specific latent heat

1 Thermal energy change of state = mass × specific latent heat
or E = mL

2 From −40°C to 0°C energy is supplied to the atoms by heating and it increases the energy in the kinetic store of the atoms, increasing temperature; During the melting stage energy continues to be supplied but there is no temperature change as the energy is being used to break the bonds as the substance changes state into a liquid; The energy store is called the latent heat of fusion; From 0°C to 100°C the energy in the kinetic store of the molecules increases; At 100°C the energy is used to break the bonds and change the water from liquid into steam; This energy store is called the latent heat of vaporisation.

3 Thermal energy change of state = mass × specific latent heat = 33.4 kJ

Thermal energy change of state = 0.1; × 334 000 J; 33 400 J = 33.4 kJ

Particle motion in gases (1)

1 The molecules of gas are in constant **random** motion. The average **kinetic** energy of the **particles** is proportional to temperature on the **kelvin** scale. Changing the temperature of a gas in a container of fixed volume will change the **pressure** exerted on the sides of the **container**.

2 Random; with a range of speeds (or kinetic energies).

3 Total energy in the kinetic and potential stores; of all the particles that make up a system.

Particle motion in gases (2)

1 Pressure × volume = constant or pV = constant

2 a Initial temp in kelvin = K = °C + 273 = −23°C + 273 = 250 K

Final temp = 477°C + 273 = 750 K

Temp change =
final temp − initial temp =
750 − 250 = 500 K

b Change in kinetic energy of the particles is proportional to increase in temperature on the kelvin scale; Increase from 250 to 750 is × 3 so E_k store triples

3 $p_1V_1 = p_2V_2$ so $V_2 = \dfrac{p_1V_1}{p_2}$;

$= \dfrac{120 \times 75}{225}$; $= 40 \text{ cm}^3$

(kilo prefix ignored as cancels out)

4 The work done on the gas leads to an increase in the internal energy store of the gas molecules; increasing their potential and kinetic energy stores; Subsequent increases take place in the thermal energy store of the tyre due to transfer in thermal energy stores.

Atoms

The structure of the atom (1)

1 **a** Protons; neutrons; and electrons. (in any order)

b Nucleus; protons, neutrons (protons and neutrons any order).

c Protons; electrons; neutral (protons and electrons any order).

2 Outer circle – electron; Inner circle with positive symbol – proton; Inner blank circle – neutron.

3 Row 1: 1; row 2: 0; row 3: 0, −1

4 Atoms are very small having a radius of about 1×10^{-10} m; The basic atomic structure is a positively charged nucleus; composed of both neutrons and protons orbited by negatively charged electrons; The majority of the mass of an atom is contained within the nucleus; The nucleus is very small with a nucleus less than 1/10 000 of the radius of the atom; Protons and neutrons have considerably larger masses than electrons; or The electrons are arranged at specific distances from the nucleus.

The structure of the atom (2)

1 Order p, n, e: Li = 3, 4, 3;
Be = 5, 4, 5; Cu = 29, 34, 29;
Na = 11,12,11;
K = 19, 20,19; Eu = 63, 89, 63

2 An **isotope** is an atom with the same number of **protons** and a different number of **neutrons**. **Isotopes** have the same chemical properties as the atom. If the **atomic** number is altered, the **element** changes.

3 **a** F

b T

c T

d F

Developing a model of the atom

1 Plum pudding is solid thereby atom is solid; Positive charge is thinly spread throughout atom (the dough); Negatively charged electrons are dotted throughout the pudding like currants.

2 Path A: A very small deflection confirms that the atom could be composed of thinly spread positive charge; This was predicted by and could be explained by the plum pudding model.

Path B: Results indicated that particularly in the case of the larger deflections that there could be a concentration of positive charge repelling positive alpha particle; This would not be predicted by the plum pudding model.

Path C: The deflections through large angles demonstrate that the atom has a concentration of positive charge and mass in a very small place; This was the first conclusive evidence for a nucleus, which was not included in the plum pudding model.

Radioactive decay and nuclear radiation

1 Some atomic nuclei are **unstable**. The nucleus emits **radiation** as it changes to become more stable. This is a **random** process called radioactive **decay**. Activity is the rate at which a source of **radioactive** nuclei decays. Activity is measured in **becquerel** (Bq).

2 Row 1: helium nuclei, mm of paper or a few cm of air; row 2: high speed electrons, medium ionising effect; row 3: a few cm of lead or metres of concrete, low ionisation effect.

3 **a** Alpha not penetrative enough; gamma too penetrative.

b Signal indicates thickness of paper; Feedback controls whether rollers go closer or further apart to control paper thickness.

Nuclear equations

1 $^{214}_{82}\text{Pb} \rightarrow {}^{214}_{83}\text{Bi} + {}^{0}_{-1}\text{e}$

2 $^{214}_{84}\text{Po} \rightarrow {}^{210}_{82}\text{Pb} + {}^{4}_{2}\text{He}$

3 $^{230}_{90}\text{Th} \rightarrow {}^{226}_{88}\text{Ra} + {}^{4}_{2}\text{He}$

Half-life of radioactive elements

1 The half-life of a radioactive isotope is the time it takes for the number of radioactive nuclei in a sample to halve; or the time it takes for the count rate (or activity) from a radioactive sample to fall to half its initial level.

2 **a** $1 \rightarrow \dfrac{1}{2} \rightarrow \dfrac{1}{4} = 2$ half-lives;

$2 \times 5700 = 11\,400$ years

b $1 \rightarrow \dfrac{1}{2} \rightarrow \dfrac{1}{4} \rightarrow \dfrac{1}{8} \rightarrow \dfrac{1}{16} =$

4 half-lives; $4 \times 5700 = 22\,800$ years.

c x-axis and y-axis correctly labelled; with correct units;

First point 4000 cpm at time zero;

Plotting of 2nd, 3rd and 4th points showing 2000, 1000, 500 as count rates;

Points being plotted at times (approximately): 5700 years, 11 400 years, 17 100 and 22 800 years;

Smooth curve through plotted points.

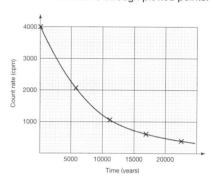

Hazards and uses of radioactive emissions (1)

1 Exposure can take place by contamination; Contamination is when the radioactive material is breathed in or ingested; Once inside the body the radiation can do damage by causing ionisation; Or irradiation; Irradiation is exposure to radiation directly; The radiation emitted can cause ionisation; Both forms can cause damage to DNA, cells and cause mutations that lead to cancer.

2 **a** Wearing film badges that monitor exposure; Limit exposure to as short a time as possible; Keep as far away from radioactive source as practical; This could be achieved by handling radioactive sources at arm's length (or by using tongs); Wearing protective clothing or working behind screens; Washing stations to ensure that any traces of radioactive material are removed from clothing or body to prevent later ingestion (or direct irradiation).

b It is important for the findings to be shared with other scientists; Then the findings can be checked by peer review.

3 **a** Radiation that is ever present emitted by man-made and natural sources.

Answers

b Atmosphere shields humans from cosmic rays; Astronauts travel above the atmosphere.

Hazards and uses of radioactive emissions (2)

1 Bismuth-214 has half-life of 20 minutes; 1 hour = 60 minutes.

Number of half-lives =

$$\frac{\text{total time}}{\text{time per half-life}} = \frac{60}{20}$$

= 3 (half-lives)

For 3 half-lives half 4000 3 times,

$4000 \rightarrow 2000 \rightarrow 1000 \rightarrow 500$

Count-rate 1 hour later is 500 counts/minute.

2 **a** To have $\frac{1}{8}$th of the original sample the sample must have undergone 3 half-lives

because $1 \rightarrow \frac{1}{2} \rightarrow \frac{1}{4} \rightarrow \frac{1}{8}$; is 3 half-lives.

b Radium-226 has a half-life of 1600 years; and $3 \times 1600 = 4800$ years.

3 **a** 1 lead-210 for every 7 bismuth-210 means $\frac{1}{8}$th lead remains in sample $1 \rightarrow \frac{1}{2} \rightarrow \frac{1}{4} \rightarrow \frac{1}{8}$ means 3 half-lives have elapsed

b $3 \times 22 = 66$ years

Hazards and uses of radioactive emissions (3)

1 Technetium-99; It emits gamma radiation that can be detected outside body; The half-life is short so as not to cause unnecessary irradiation but long enough to trace blood flow to liver.

2 **a** Xenon-133; Gamma radiation can be used in a gamma knife set-up; Individual rays do little damage due to the low ionisation of gamma, but their combined effect can destroy cells in a tumour; Gamma radiation is penetrative enough to reach the tumour.

b Cobalt-60 can be reused several times; (As its half-life is much longer than that of xenon-133).

3 Risk of irradiation; and contamination; Chemotherapy and radiotherapy are aggressive treatments that also kill healthy cells, and can cause mutation that can also lead to cancer.

Forces

Forces and their interactions

1 Velocity

2 1– c; 2 – d; 3 – a; 4 – b

3 Direction; and magnitude/size/value.

4 **a** A contact force requires two surfaces to be touching for force to act; A non-contact force does not require surfaces to be touching for force to act.

b Gravitational; magnetic; electrostatic, etc.

Gravity

1 Weight = mass × gravitational field strength or $W = m \times g$ and units: N or newtons.

2 Karen is correct; Mass is a measure of how much material (or how many atoms) something contains; Mass cannot be changed unless some of the material is removed; Weight is a force; A force due to an object's position in a gravitational field; Mass is measured in kg and weight is measured in N.

3 $W = mg$

$W = 75 \times 1.6; = 120\,\text{N}$

Resultant forces

1 1 a; 3 b; 4 c; 5 e

2 **a** 3 N →

b 0 N

c 6 N ←

Work done and energy transfer

1 Work done = force × distance or $W = F \times s$

2 N m

3 **a** Work done = force × distance

Work done = 30×4; = 120; N;

b Work done = force × distance rearrange to

distance = $\frac{\text{work done}}{\text{force}}$

distance = $\frac{240}{30} = 8\,\text{m}$

c Yes; friction between the go-kart and surface would increase the temperature of the wheels.

Forces and elasticity

1 Extension is proportional to force; provided the spring is not stretched beyond elastic limit.

2 **a** Straight line through the origin; Axes are force and extension.

b Label force on y-axis and extension on the x-axis; then calculate gradient or reverse axes and reciprocal of gradient.

3 Inelastic deformation means the material has been permanently; stretched or squashed and will not return to its original length or shape.

Distance, displacement, speed and velocity

1 **a** Distance

b Displacement

2 **a** Steady speed

b Acceleration

c Deceleration

3 **a** 45 m

b Distance travelled = speed × time, rearrange to

speed = $\frac{\text{distance travelled}}{\text{time}}$;

= $\frac{10}{6}$;

= 1.67 m/s

c B → C has steeper gradient/slope than A → B

4 1 – c; 2 – d; 3 – b; 4 – a

Acceleration

1 **a** Acceleration

b Constant speed

c Deceleration

2 **a** Acceleration = $\frac{\text{change in velocity}}{\text{time taken}}$

= $\frac{10}{10} = 1$; m/s²

b Acceleration = $\frac{\text{change in velocity}}{\text{time taken}}$

Acceleration = $\frac{15 - 10}{30 - 10}$

= 0.25 m/s²

c Steady or constant speed

3 Triangle area = $0.5 \times b \times h$ rectangle area = $b \times h$

triangles: $0.5 \times 10 \times 10 = 50$ m and $0.5 \times 5 \times 20 = 50$ m

rectangle: $10 \times 20 = 200$

Total distance = 50 + 50 + 200

= 300 m

Equations of motion

1 **a** 7.1 m/s²

b 11 m/s²

c The cheetah's acceleration is significantly (about 60%) higher than that of the sports car. This is surprising because the car is a sports car, designed for high acceleration, and the cheetah is an animal.

2 **a** 60 s

3 **a** 3.75 m/s²

b 4 s

Newton's laws of motion

1 The **velocity** of an object will only change if there is a **resultant** force acting on it. When a car is at a **steady** speed the driving force and **resistive** forces of friction and **drag** are equal and act in **opposite** directions.